Innovative Reward Systems for the Changing Workplace

Innovative Reward Systems for the Changing Workplace

Second Edition

THOMAS B. WILSON

McGraw-Hill

New York   Chicago   San Francisco   Lisbon   London   Madrid
Mexico City   Milan   New Delhi   San Juan   Seoul
Singapore   Sydney   Toronto

Copyright ©2003 by Thomas B. Wilson. All rights reserved. Printed in the United States of America. Except as permitted under the United States Copyright Act of 1976, no part of this publication may be reproduced or distributed in any form or by any means, or stored in a data base or retrieval system, without the prior written permission of the publisher.

1 2 3 4 5 6 7 8 9 0   DOC/DOC   0 9 8 7 6 5 4 3 2

ISBN 0-07-140294-2

This publication is designed to provide accurate and authoritative information in regard to the subject matter covered. It is sold with the understanding that neither the author nor the publisher is engaged in rendering legal, accounting, or other professional service. If legal advice or other expert assistance is required, the services of a competent professional person should be sought.

—From a Declaration of Principles jointly adopted by a Committee
of the American Bar Association and a Committee of Publishers

McGraw-Hill books are available at special quantity discounts to use as premiums and sales promotions, or for use in corporate training programs. For more information, please write to the Director of Special Sales, Professional Publishing, McGraw-Hill, Two Penn Plaza, New York, NY 10121-2298. Or contact your local bookstore.

Library of Congress Cataloging-in-Publication Data
Wilson, Thomas B.
   Innovative reward systems for the changing workplace / Tom Wilson.

   p. cm.
Includes bibliographical references and index.
 ISBN 0-07-140294-2 (hardcover : alk. paper)
 1. Incentives in industry—United States. 2. Compensation
management—United States. 3. Organizational change—United States. I.
Title.
 HF5549.5.I5 W45 2002
 658.3'142—dc21   2002013888

 This book is printed on recycled, acid-free paper containing a minimum of 50% recycled de-inked fiber.

Contents

PART III

Putting Rewards into Practice   273

List of Figures

Foreword to the First Edition

TOM WILSON'S BOOK is timely, insightful, comprehensive, informed by first-hand experience, and above all, useful. Wilson crystallizes the experience of the best companies, showing how these leaders link their reward systems to effective business strategies. He presents a comprehensive array of innovative incentives and shows managers how to choose and implement them. He goes behind the system to the people, showing what actually drives human behavior. He provides nuts-and-bolts, top-to-bottom, start-to-finish advice on performance management for organizations in the midst of change.

And as if all that were not enough, Wilson does one more thing: He issues a wake-up call to companies everywhere *to change their assumptions about the design of effective organizations.* The revitalization of American business rests increasingly on the delegation of more responsibility to more responsible people. It requires workforce professionalism to use the disciplines of total quality management or to permit the empowerment of frontline service workers to better care for customers. It means encouraging entrepreneurial initiative—managers and workers behaving like owners. To get there, we have to undo almost a century of management theory and practice.

Traditional reward systems were defined by hierarchy. Rewards were tied to level or position, not to performance. Positions were evaluated in terms of staff or assets controlled, not in terms of strategic contributions to building the future. Behavior was controlled by procedure manuals and supervisors who watched closely, monitoring activities rather than measuring results. People were evaluated by their immediate boss and were thought to be motivated by the hope of a promotion. In fact, as befit hierarchical structures, rewards were largely linked to promotion. Without promotion to a higher rank, people soon reached ceilings in terms of salary or wages, influence, and responsibility. While such systems controlled performance, they also encouraged behaviors that could constrain the achievement of high levels: building organizational empires, focusing on getting promoted rather than achieving results, doing the least to meet minimum standards, following internal rules rather than producing excellent results for customers.

Today, the fault lines in this costly, slow-moving, bureaucratic system have been exposed from inside and outside: from inside, by the declining performance of aging, giant U.S. industrial corporations; and from outside, by the explosive growth of newer, high-technology firms that work integratively to produce rapid innovation. In the 1980s, America's small-business job-creation engine, led by high-technology companies, created new models, less hierarchical and more flexible. Increased global competition, which threatened rigid and parochial large corporations in once-secure industries such as autos and steel, made companies more receptive to new models. Large American companies began to emulate the innovative and team spirit of smaller ones as well as to look beyond their organizational boundaries for ideas about how to be competitive. The process of change, seeded in the 1980s and accelerated in the 1990s, is loosening structures and breaching boundaries, tearing down the walls between levels, functions, departments, divisions, suppliers, and customers.

The most successful organizations today are characterized by what I call the "4 F's" of strategy and management.[1] They are more *focused* on fewer lines of business and fewer activities that they perform with greater depth and skill; they are *faster*, quick to innovate and speedier in their ongoing operations; they are *more flexible*, crossing traditional boundaries of departments, functions, and levels to put teams together to get results; they are *friendlier*, engaged in alliances and partnerships with customers, suppliers, and external collaborators.

These four strategic "F's" imply important shifts in the emphasis for workplaces and people:[2]

• From fat to lean: the new staffing principle. Empowerment assumptions have moved away from "bigger is better" to "smaller is beautiful"—and more flexible. Increasingly, the desire for "fat" organizations that relied on redundancy, encouraged overstaffing, and could afford to waste people on nonessential tasks, has been replaced by a preference for "lean" organizations with focused efforts. Such organizations are willing to try outsourcing and external suppliers for internal services; they expect existing staff to do more before they add others.

• *From vertical to horizontal: the new organization.* The hierarchical emphasis of classic American corporations inhibits their ability to act like entrepreneurs, create change, or produce innovation. Because companies need to encourage higher performance by making rewards more contingent on actual contributions, compensation is more likely to fluctuate rather than rise steadily year by year as individual or team performance changes and company fortunes ebb and flow. In short, *companies need creative new reward systems because the old ones cannot work in today's competitive business environment.*

To compete effectively in the global economy, businesses must attract, retain, motivate, and utilize effectively the most talented people they can find. But people do not want to invest their talents without feeling that they are getting something in return. In the 1990s, it is harder to get the balance right using assumptions from the hierarchical, bureaucratic model of the 1970s. As Wilson shows, companies today must use a wide variety of innovative rewards linked closely to business strategy and supported by multiple, frequent measures of performance.

The rhetoric about valuing human capital is increasingly in place; leaders speak of "core competence" and "competing on capabilities," or say "our most important assets walk in and out the door every day." But accounting systems have not caught up with the shift that is needed from measuring only the use of financial capital to measuring the building of human capital. And reward systems have not yet fully translated strategic goals into concrete performance incentives and measures that give people and their managers the tools to take effective action in a demanding competitive environment.

So Tom Wilson's book is a wake-up call to American business. It is also a wake-up call to America's human resource managers and professionals—those who design and implement performance management and reward systems. For all the talk of the last decade and more about a "strategic" role for the HR departments, HR managers have been laggards, not leaders. It was not human resource executives but engineering and statisticians advocating total quality management who led the redefining of performance management and reward systems. (The expert whom Wilson quotes frequently in this book is the quality guru W. Edwards Deming.) It was not compensation professionals but corporate raiders, institutional investors, economists, and other shareholder rights activists who led the rethinking of managerial pay levels, incentives, and stock options. It was not HR departments but market pressure to better respond to customers that raised the need for redefinition of performance measures.

But this book gives human resource managers another chance. With the comprehensive approach outlined here, the dream of marrying business strategy to human resource policies and practices can become a reality. I hope managers throughout American industry and the world read this wise book, absorb its messages, and use its helpful tools.

Rosabeth Moss Kanter, Ph.D.
Class of 1960 Professor of Business Administration
Harvard Business School

What This Book Will Do for You

Problems can't be solved by thinking within the same framework in which the problems were created.

Albert Einstein

LEADERSHIP, STRATEGY, CULTURE, AND TALENT are becoming the characteristics that define the truly successful company. Technology can be replicated, capital can be acquired, and distribution channels can be created through new alliances, but the actions of people (what they do or fail to do) have become the critical factor in achieving enduring success.

How does an organization determine who is the "best"? What makes an organization able to attract and retain talent better than its competitors? If a very good person is put into a bad system, the system will win every time. It is only a matter of time. To change the system, the organization can turn to training and developing people to do the "right thing." Right? But what usually happens when a person participates in a training program (whether in a classroom setting or through an electronic learning experience)? How often is he or she encouraged to put new skills and ideas to work? How long does it take to develop a superior business unit leader, sales professional, or technical wizard? Training is critical to developing talent, but it is part of a long-term strategy to increase the capabilities of the organization.

The purpose of this book is to provide readers with new ideas for performance management and total reward systems. The innovations described in this book are not achieved by using totally unique techniques, technologies, or programs but by using traditional approaches in new ways so that the outcomes are better than in the past.

What is the purpose of rewards? Fundamentally, a reward system should encourage and reinforce the actions necessary for the organization to succeed. A reward system should contain a variety of programs that are designed to fit the unique needs and characteristics of the organization and operate in an interdependent manner. It is a system in which each element is focused on what it does well.

This is the only book that fully integrates all programs involved in rewards—formal and informal, short and long term, cash and symbolic, performance- and culture-driven. We start from the premise that rewards are much more than just compensation, stock options, or recognition programs. The concepts and principles used to develop effective rewards come from research and practices in strategic management, leadership, group and individual psychology, and systems theory, as well as tax, legal, and accounting conventions. Finally, various principles found in organizational change theory, political science, and spiritual movements have been integrated into the principles discussed in this book. On the surface, this book will emphasize pragmatic applications of programs and practices, but these programs and practices are based on well-researched and established principles. The reader who seeks to learn the determinants of these principles should find the Bibliography an excellent resource.

This second edition was written because much has changed in what makes the workplace successful in today's markets. While the fundamental principles of human behavior, reward systems, and organizational cultures have remained constant, the context and the tools have changed greatly. Since the first edition, more people participate in variable compensation plans, receive stock options in their organizations, and participate in creative recognition programs. Organizations have become more global, complex, and competitive. So, it became important to bring the concepts of human performance and reward systems into this new reality. As organizations and the environment in which they operate continue to change, leaders will face increasing challenges for bringing forth the talents and commitment of their people. Hopefully, this new edition will provide additional insights and guidance to make this possible.

This book is divided into three sections. Part I provides the background, context, and strategic principles needed to develop rewards that work. Part II explains each of the key elements of total rewards—salaries, performance assessments, variable pay or bonus programs, stock options and equity programs, recognition practices, and so on. These chapters examine in depth how traditional practices work, why they fail to meet today's requirements, and what to do to fix them. Each chapter presents issues, solutions, and illustrative case studies. Part III includes chapters that provide guidance on the application of these principles and programs to specific situations. This enables readers to understand what needs to be done to move their organizations to the next level.

You do not need to read this book from beginning to end. Instead, become familiar with the key concepts and principles at the heart of all reward systems (Part I), and then select the practice areas (salaries, variable pay, etc.) that are of most immediate importance to you and your situation (Part II). Then move to the next related chapter and so forth until you have a plan of action. As a personal plan develops, see how these programs can be put into practice (Part III). This book should become a valuable resource to you for ongoing situations, providing the ability to educate and communicate with others within your organization about what needs to change.

A primary objective of this book is to enable readers to more quickly and effectively create an organization that has an enduring competitive advantage based on its rewards systems. This requires an effective strategy, strong leaders, a compelling culture, and the talent and capabilities to do what needs to be done. Reward systems, in concert with recruitment and selection, training and development, and leadership and communication, create the capabilities to achieve greatness.

This book is the product a collaborative effort. Susan Malanowski outlined the issues and provided alternatives on how to make the performance management process and variable compensation programs enhance relationships and commitments (Chapters 8, 9, and 10). Sue Murray provided clarity and insights on how to make recognition and celebrations succeed (Chapter 11). Ralph Nelson provided definitions and strategies to make stock options and other equity-type incentives create long-term value (Chapter 12). Kym Pierce took the responsibility for managing the development of this book and, along with Kelly DiMauro, enabled the content to be well-organized and understood. Jo-Anne Bourassa and Lynne Kondracki provided frequent support, feedback, and encouragement to meet our commitments. As a team, we tried to create a roadmap for executives, managers, advisers, and members of organizations on how to create an environment where strategic vision becomes reality.

We hope that you both enjoy and gain a great deal from working with this book. We further hope that you use it to guide the decisions of your organization to make it a leader in its markets. We also hope that your people share in the benefits that are created by this success.

We like to hear from our readers about their best practices in reward systems. To share your story with us, please contact us at *www.wilsongroup. com*. Let us know what you are doing, what is working, and what is not working. We can discuss why—by knowing the "why," you can expand the practices that work and avoid those which do not. We would enjoy hearing about whatever you are willing to share—what has worked, what has not, what you have tired, and what you are pursuing.

Innovative Reward Systems for the Changing Workplace

The Fundamentals of Effective Reward Systems

Knowing Why Reward Systems Work (or Don't Work) Is as Important as Knowing How

IN ORGANIZATIONS that are pressed for time and resources, executives often have a strong action orientation. This is a common success characteristic. However, action without an understanding of why something works often leads to unrealistic expectations about the time it takes to produce results. Many executives do not realize the time and expense involved in the constant changing of programs and approaches. Without applying the principles that make systems effective, organizations often jump from one program to another and repeat mistake after mistake. It is no wonder that many executives frequently are characterized as chasing after fads or gimmicks to achieve quick results.

The purpose of the chapters in Part I is to provide you with an understanding of the underlying principles that make reward systems effective. There are those who believe that rewards do more harm than good and that organizations would be better off if they focused on communicating strategies and involving people in decision making. Research frequently shows how compensation is of secondary importance to people behind factors such as working for a strong leader, having challenging and meaningful work, and seeing their work make a difference.

We support these beliefs and demonstrate how reward systems can reinforce an individual's commitment to performance. We present a new definition of rewards and a broader perspective of what they include. Rewards provide great support to strategic business initiatives and indeed may be a greater influence than most executives realize.

As you read these chapters and consider your own situation, look for the reasons why your organization has the programs it does and whether they are enhancing or limiting the organization's ability to succeed. The principles presented in Part I will enrich your understanding of the application chapters in Part II. This in turn will increase your ability to create reward systems that are truly successful.

Why You Should Be Concerned about Reward Systems

An invasion of armies can be resisted, but not an idea whose time has come.

Victor Hugo, *Historie d'un Crime*, 1852

GEORGE AND MARTHA have been sales professionals for an established durable goods manufacturer for more than 12 years. They have separate territories and sell many of the same products. They receive salary and commissions paid quarterly based on their individual total sales. They are eligible for a variety of sales contests, including the President's Club, an annual recognition program for top performers. Both are regarded as successful, but Martha is seen as a superior performer.

George and Martha enjoy discussing many of the challenges of selling their products and the lack of support they receive from marketing and customer service. They seek each other's advice about how to handle difficult situations, but both are guarded in their responses. They are cautious about revealing the "tricks of the trade" because it may cause one to significantly exceed the performance of others. Then managers may increase the quotas for all salespeople.

Martha consistently exceeds her sales quota and regularly attends the President's Club. George periodically exceeds his sales quota, but he believes that his territory is more challenging than those of his peers. George has more competition for his customers, and he frequently has to overcome entrenched customer-vendor relationships. Most of Martha's customers are new, and she seems to get to key decision makers more easily than George does. George feels that Martha gets better leads from sales management.

The company periodically conducts special sales contests, especially when the company is not achieving its quarterly goals. Since the awards are limited to the top salesperson in each region, Martha always seems to walk away with the prize. George pays little attention to these "games" because he sees little possibility of beating Martha. This situation frequently frustrates George, so he has no discomfort with occasionally pursuing other job opportunities. He keeps his eyes open for a better job.

The company promotes the President's Club as a big recognition event for sales professionals. The top salespeople from each region are invited to attend a 3-day company meeting in some exotic location. Most of the company's top executives attend, and the work meetings are limited so as to give ample time for golf and other recreational activities. Martha always attends these meetings and is known by the company's senior managers. George attended one several years ago. He enjoyed the session but felt that it was more political than meaningful to the business.

The sales commission plan is quite simple. Each salesperson is paid a percent of his or her sales up to a quota. For sales above quota, the commission increases. If a region exceeds its goals significantly, the quotas usually are raised the next year.

Martha always exceeds her quota, but if possible, she pushes some sales into the next quarter to get a jump-start on the next period. She makes sure to time her sales and order processing to correspond with the quota period. George and the other salespeople in their region work in a manner similar to Martha's, and they appreciate the "teamwork" attitude they share. Everything seems to be working normally.

The regional sales manager is paid an override commission on the total sales of his or her sales staff. This permits the managers to spend most of their time with other managers in the company or with key customers. When there is a problem with sales, a customer, or an order, the sales manager gets involved. When there are no apparent problems, the manager focuses on other activities of the company.

The company frequently needs to make a major push at the end of a quarter and at the end of the fiscal year to meet its revenue goals. This push always puts a strain on everyone, but it creates an opportunity for the salespeople to earn extra money.

The company's executives focus on setting business strategies, creating new strategic alliances, and making resource-allocation decisions. Managers focus on initiating new marketing campaigns, introducing new products, and lowering manufacturing costs. The salespeople seldom concern themselves with these issues because their job is to generate sales.

The competitiveness of the company is slowly eroding. Each year the company's sales and profit objectives are getting more difficult to achieve. Driven by the poor stock performance of the company, the executives are increasing the pressures to achieve these extremely high goals. In the past, profitability growth was attributed to acquisitions and major cost-reduction measures and not to revenue growth. As the pressure increases, there is a growing frustration that things are not getting any better.

Understanding the Problem

The preceding story illustrates a situation that is common to many organizations worldwide. In fact, many who read this story will not perceive anything as unusual. For them, this is the natural order of things. George and Martha and millions like them are responding normally to the conditions they face. Supervisors and managers have resigned themselves to believing that this is business as usual and that solutions need to come from new products, lower costs, better services, and visionary leadership.

Executives often watch the macro numbers of the organization and are frustrated by the lack of dramatic improvements. They turn to restructuring the organization, conducting special studies, or acquiring new companies. For this company and many in similar situations, market position is eroding, and standard solutions are no longer effective.

So what is the real problem? There are more opportunities with existing customers, and there are capabilities within the organization that are not being used. This is neither new nor surprising. What is important is that the solutions to these issues frequently exist within the organization. The company can increase its competitiveness substantially by finding and changing the way it influences how people within the company take action.

In the preceding story and in millions of similar organizations, there are some basic conditions that limit each company's ability to compete in the changing marketplace. Here is a summary of some of these conditions:

1. Each person often has a part of the solution, but because he or she is discouraged from sharing ideas, no solution is found. People have techniques that may be effective in acquiring new sales or in performing their jobs, but they resist sharing their innovations. The company becomes less competitive because ideas that work to improve its competitiveness are never incorporated into the processes of the organization.

2. The company does not realize revenue or profitability when it can. Revenue is managed at the customer contact point based on what enables the salesperson to achieve personal objectives.

3. Many special contests are defined more by who is excluded than by what is achieved. By selecting only the top performer, internal competition is used to spur desired performance. It is interesting to note that this creates situations where the meaning of rewards is enhanced by their exclusivity, not by the value of the achievement. Consequently, there are clear and compelling reasons for individuals *not* to share ideas, customer opportunities, or other actions that may benefit the company.

4. An individual who feels that objectives cannot be achieved will either disregard their importance or view associated awards as "childish games." This perspective exists regardless of whether the conditions are caused by internal or external barriers. Consequently, the organization realizes little value from its business planning, performance tracking, or incentive programs.

5. When managers see their role as planners and problem solvers, people often do not receive the support they need to succeed. Everyday problems get left unattended, and people create "work-arounds" to deal with internal process barriers. Top performers receive little encouragement, and individuals who have performance problems become defensive for weaknesses that must be fixed. Thus, seeking assistance from those with more experience, broader perspectives, or access to information or resources may be viewed as a sign of weakness. The company once again fails to capitalize on its internal resources and capabilities to improve performance.

6. When leaders set bold and dramatic goals for the organization, they either expand or diminish their credibility. People are often inspired by dramatic visions of leaders. However, if there are no clear indications on how to achieve these ends, people regard these pronouncements as more of a sermon than a strategy. If strategies fail to become personalized, then people fail to see the link between the vision and their actions. Thus what often starts as an impressive strategy becomes rhetoric or just another fad for the executives. People then conclude that they can ignore new initiatives.

7. When individuals have limited involvement in improving the organization or feel that there is little to gain from their contributions, their commitment to the organization diminishes. This means that they do their jobs as required and may be open to new job opportunities. In the recruiting industry, these people are regarded as *passive job seekers.* There is little to hold these individuals to the organization, except the risk or effort required to make a job change.

8. When there is little clarity about performance expectations, little feedback on progress, and little connection between results and rewards, people regard their rewards as entitlements. This is a normal response because the only connection between the action and the reward is the person's continued employment. A mentality of entitlement causes people to expect similar rewards in the future. If, for some reason, such rewards are not provided, the response is anger and frustration, not a desire to improve performance.

9. When performance criteria are vague, people often will create their own standards or ignore the criteria altogether. This performance-management process creates an adversarial situation between individuals and their managers. Once again, this weakens the organization's ability to move in new directions, hold people accountable for actions, or improve performance.

10. When individuals and executives see that performance-management and reward programs are unreliable, create more conflict, and take more time and effort than the value they produce, they conclude that the programs are inherently ineffective. It is no wonder that the popular literature and executive leaders have little confidence in the ability of these programs to create competitive advantage or encourage desired performance.

Perhaps the greatest issue that the story of George and Martha illustrates is the disconnect between the leaders of the organization and the people involved in implementing the firm's strategy. Consequently, the company is at a competitive disadvantage, and, as the marketplace continues to change, its future prospects grow dimmer. The solution lies within the organization, but because the executives are unwilling to examine what it has created, they will never know how to build a winning organization.

Searching for the Answer

Many organizations exist with conditions that limit their ability to compete. In these situations, employees focus on what they can control and what will protect their personal interests. Executives implement changes that are bold and dramatic and achieve short-term results with tools and processes that they believe are driving the desired change. There are great opportunities for more revenues with the current customer relationships and for reducing costs and time to market from internal processes, but there are few real incentives to take advantage of them. Organizations exist in a state of mutual equilibrium in which self-interests are in conflict with the organization's interests, where only the obvious improvements are achieved and maintained for only the short term. Executives develop strategies and structures, invest in new technologies and systems, and seek external alliances to strengthen their ability to achieve market leadership. Employees frequently support one another when appropriate—but not to the point where they will be placed at a personal disadvantage. As with George and Martha, organizations get into this situation by responding normally to increasingly abnormal situations.

If there is a desire to change this situation, the answers can be found within the organization and in changing the way it encourages, uses, and rewards the talents of its people. True high-performing companies have used this simple principle. It makes common sense, but it is not common practice.

Rewards Are More Than Just Pay

All organizations have reward systems. Without them, people would not join, come to work, or perform in any manner consistent with the mission or strategy of the organization. Executives and managers often think of rewards only as compensation, but in the context of this book, we will see that rewards go well beyond pay. They include systems, programs, and practices that influence the actions of people. Further, the intent or objectives of most formal programs often become distorted when one examines the impact they actually have on people. Let's review the key elements of reward systems and what they have become in most of today's organizations.

Base Salaries

Salaries are the most obvious form of reward. They are the regular income received for being employed by an organization. Some people refer to it as "show-up pay," meaning that one receives a salary for coming to work. Traditionally, the amount received reflects different levels of responsibilities within the organization as well as the skills, capabilities, or reputation the person brings to the organization. Different industries pay people in similar roles differently because of their ability to afford the costs and their requirements for talent. For example, companies in the oil and gas and pharmaceutical industries pay their people 20 to 50 percent more than individuals with comparable responsibilities in the manufacturing, retail, and social service industries. Pay also differs based on the cost of living in different geographic locations.

However, pay is not always consistent with living costs. The rates of pay are determined by the demand and supply of people who want to and are capable of fulfilling responsibilities for an organization. The cost of living often sets minimum and maximum parameters for pay.

Traditionally, many companies offered salaries that were higher than others in the market with the belief they could attract and retain top talent. However, given the changes in the marketplace, few companies that pay above market average for salaries see this as a virtue.

Performance Ratings and Increases to Pay

Organizations and people within most developed countries have come to expect that salaries will increase on an annual basis. The basis may be performance or cost of living. The concept of merit pay is simple—those who perform better should receive higher pay increases than those who function at average or below-average levels. The problem today is that merit increases over the past 10 to 12 years in the United States have averaged around 4 percent. Studies and opinion samples demonstrate that high performers should receive at least two or three times the standard pay increase in order to be appropriately rewarded. Thus, as companies seek to control increases in salary costs (because they cannot often pay for these additional costs through price increases), managers need to provide one person with 0 percent increase for every other person they wish to reward with an 8 percent or more increase. Simply put, merit pay is often made into a zero-sum game.

To compound this further, people have come to expect regular salary increases and also be evaluated as "above average" on the performance-rating scales. Further, a top performer who receives several pay increases that are well above the norm begins to expect this as regular treatment. Since decisions concerning pay increases are made usually only once a year, on an individual's anniversary date (of being hired or promoted) or on a common date for all company employees, merit pay increases have little influence in motivating people for most of the year. However, those who felt punished by the process will remember the decision for a long time. It is no wonder that the merit review process frustrates managers and employees. While it is a desirable concept, merit pay is filled with dilemmas.

Promotions, Career Development, and Performance Coaching

A promotion is the most common form of formal recognition. A person who excels in his or her job is promoted by the organization to broader responsibilities and challenges and to higher pay. People naturally seek to climb the ladder of success because it provides greater job satisfaction, higher income, and more stature. In many firms, people who remain in their current roles for more than 3 years are seen as being stuck, and their potential is questioned. Traditional organizations create levels just so people can have a sense of progress in their careers. The problem today is that many firms are delayering their organizations, expanding control, and reducing opportunities for promotion. Furthermore, an increasing number of firms are reducing the number of job levels through the use of broader salary ranges or by setting individual pay targets based on the external market. Finally, as the baby boomers of the 1950s and 1960s progress up the organization, there are fewer opportunities for promotion. The only opportunities appear to be in small companies that are growing and thus expanding their need for specialized and managerial talent. While this gives a competitive advantage to small companies, these firms cannot afford to pay people as much as they may have received in a larger company.

An increasing number of companies are investing in the development of their leaders and their key technical talent. This is highly important in providing the capabilities needed for enduring success. However, when financial resources become tight, training and development are seen as discretionary spending. Although e-learning training programs have become more prevalent, they are seldom integrated into how the individual performs a job. Further, some companies employ external "coaches" to work with selected executives on improving their leadership capabilities. This may increase the performance of an individual, but is too expensive to apply more broadly. If these efforts are regarded as a reward as well as an investment, then executives can see the impact of these programs in multiple dimensions. While training can be applied generally, top performers may receive special, personalized investment as a reward for their achievements and as a statement of commitment to them by the organization. Few organizations use this framework to view training, coaching, and career development.

Bonus and Incentive Programs

These programs provide executives, managers, and employees with payment based on their performance for a designated time period. The dollars do not get added to one's salary but are regarded as part of the total annual compensation. The amount of the payout is often determined by the performance of the company or business unit and by the individual. The program may be based on performance against objectives or a share of a profit pool. Salespeople often receive commissions for selling products or services and bonuses for accomplishing other specific sales objectives.

While the purpose of these programs is to reward people directly for their performance, these programs have become distorted in many companies. Those who have received bonuses over several years have adjusted their lifestyle to include these dollars. If performance is not achieved, there are tremendous pressures for the company to find some way to make bonus payouts regardless. Since bonuses are often tied to personal objectives and these are seldom written or made public, such programs soon become another entitlement, a measure of loyalty and compliance, or an 11-month deferred compensation program (i.e., a portion of pay is withheld until the end of the year).

Special Recognition

Programs to recognize individual top performers have gone in and out of favor in American industry. Employee-of-the-month and spot tangible awards (e.g., movie passes, dinners for two, points for merchandise, and so on) abound as ways to reward individuals who perform above and beyond their current job. These programs are also used to recognize individuals who achieve a certain length of service (e.g., 25 years) or are part of a company's celebration of a milestone event.

The problems with these programs are more in how they are practiced than in their objective. Some companies use them to reward the nonmanagerial, nonprofessional staff, and so major segments of the population (the leaders) are excluded. Some companies use them in very limited ways, providing large rewards to the few people who executives believe made major differences. If employees do not understand the award or selection criteria or feel that the award is not achievable or worth the effort, these programs have little impact on behavior. Some managers use these programs to reinforce their stature and perceived power within their unit; others use them to reinforce both results and desired actions in sincere, meaningful ways. The same program can create vastly different environments. In fact, it has been observed that greater value accrues to the people who distribute the awards than to those who receive them.

Stock Options and Other Equity-Related Programs

The dot-com businesses of the 1990s expanded the awareness and use of stock-related programs in many companies. Where they were once the purview of top executives, stock options or the ability to buy the company's shares at a discount through an employee stock purchase program (ESPP) are important parts of compensation for many of today's organizations. In short, these programs provide the individual the opportunity to earn additional income through the rise in their company's value in the marketplace.

These programs are intended to accomplish several objectives. First, executives want their employees to feel that they have a personal stake in the company, expecting that this will influence their actions to control costs or better serve customers. Second, such programs are designed to retain employees, because a person who leaves the company forfeits any appreciated value of nonvested shares. Finally, these programs provide a benefit by increasing the personal wealth of individuals, usually with little or no cost to the company. The wealth is created by what the marketplace pays for the stock, not the financial resources of the company.

As we have seen in other reward programs, stock option and similar programs have caused significant problems for organizations and employees alike. The boom-bust phenomena of the 1990s have caused people to see dramatic reductions of their personal wealth. Several very large and apparently successful companies have collapsed, taking the value of stock-based incentives and retirement accounts of employees with them. Companies that used stock options as a primary tool to attract, retain, and reward people have lost a low-cost, meaningful tool. Finally, people have lost significant confidence in these programs and perhaps are disillusioned about them currently because they had expectations for their creating personal wealth in the 1990s.

Employee Benefits and Services

Employee benefits have always been an element of the total compensation package for organizations. These benefits usually include insurance programs for health care, life, or disability; retirement or investment programs; and policies related to vacation, holidays, and personal leave. As companies become larger, the number and provisions of these programs expand and become standard practice. Companies differentiate themselves by the services they offer employees, such as child care, exercise programs, financial counseling, and dry-cleaning and concierge services.

Such programs are highly important to employees, and when they work well, they reflect a culture that executives want to establish in the organization—fun, exciting, personal support, and so on. However, the individual determines the value of these programs based on his or her particular needs. Individuals want different things at different stages of their lives. However, many of these programs are designed with little consideration of what is truly meaningful to employees. Designers and decision makers mostly look at what other companies do, what laws require, what such programs will cost, and how they will be administered. When these programs backfire, they are seen as wasteful, and they undermine the credibility of executive leadership. This is especially true when the company uses limited resources to support aggressive programs for a limited few.

What Is the Organization to Do?

While conditions vary by organization, the compelling conclusion of this brief overview is that current reward programs often fail to live up to their purpose. They have become ineffective in achieving the desired impact, or their practice has had an undesirable impact on the organization or its people. Each of these programs will be examined in greater detail in subsequent chapters, and alternative solutions will be proposed.

The organization is left with a few alternatives. These are as follows:

Ignore All Formal Reward Systems

This approach says that if you can just pay people a fair salary, you should forget about trying to do anything else. This alternative is based on the belief that reward systems are inherently ineffective and cause more problems than they solve. Organizations adhering to this approach are concerned about programs that focus on individual performance and seek to differentiate the contributions. This means that companies would

- Minimize the pay differentials among people.
- Eliminate all bonus or incentive pay.
- Recognize people only as a total group.
- Eliminate performance appraisals and merit pay increases.
- Set and keep pay levels based only on the market rates.

This is perhaps the easiest alternative to implement. However, it likely will result in many unintended negative consequences. How would those who make special efforts or take initiatives that create real value be treated? Would people continue to seek innovations and implement new ideas when they receive little personal reinforcement for these actions? Why should an employee perform in any manner that the organization demands or requires? Many individuals are inherently committed to their organization's success, but will this attitude continue if they realize few personal benefits from the results achieved by the organization? Also, if the organization is successful and is able to achieve a leading role in the marketplace, the shareholders and perhaps executives will benefit. How will people benefit except through keeping their jobs, possibly a higher salary, and more benefits? While the approach sounds appealing on the surface, it likely will have a seriously damping effect on morale and performance. It gives the organization few tools to reward performance.

Make Incremental Improvements

This approach focuses on "fixing" specific programs or developing new programs as independent tasks. For example, an organization develops a new team incentive plan, expands a special recognition program, or adjusts its stock option awards to address specific problems. This programmatic approach may solve an immediate issue but fails to address underlying requirements of the company. This approach can become a never-ending series of "fixes." Such efforts address the symptoms or structures but often fail to develop the core capabilities the organization needs to implement its strategy effectively.

Develop and Implement a Strategic Reward Framework

This approach involves rethinking the total rewards—formal and informal, short and long term, cash and symbolic—and developing a framework that reflects the fundamental requirements of the organization. The process entails viewing rewards from the perspective of the strategy of the organization—what it needs to do to be successful and by what values it needs to function. It goes beyond looking at how people are paid and looks at how they are treated. This goes beyond benchmarking practices with the market and looks at how to establish competitive advantage. This means that programs and practices should be grounded on proven principles of the behavioral sciences. Finally, the process builds programs and services into an integrated system in which the weaknesses of one program are offset by the strengths of another. This creates a system of rewards that directly support the strategy and build the desired culture of the enterprise.

The outcome of this approach is an organization that is more capable and more effective at competing in today's marketplace. This creates competitive advantage and enables the organization to implement its strategy and realize its vision, generating shareholder value that exceeds expectations. The task of developing a strategic rewards framework is challenging but necessary to survive in the changing marketplace. The process cannot be copied from another company; it needs to be designed, developed, and "grown" within the unique environment of the organization. Nor can the process be accomplished in a short time frame. Programs can be developed rather rapidly, but learning, integration of practices, and making the systems work take time. Similar to the time required to develop a new product or service or to implement a new management information system, the time to develop integrated reward systems is critically important.

The process is simple to understand, but it requires commitment and attention (Figure 1-1). First, understand the strategy and culture that the organization needs in order to succeed and endure. Then determine what various groups of people (executives, salespeople, managers, operations people, and so on) need to do to realize these ends. Some groups will have the same things to do, and some will be uniquely defined by their role or function. Next, assess current reward systems and practices for their alignment and effectiveness. Examine what exists

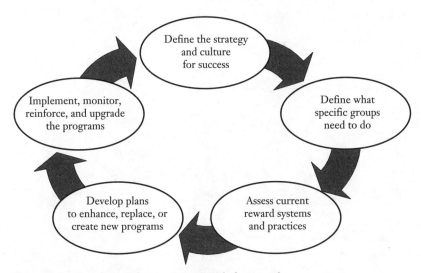

Figure 1-1   Developing the strategic rewards framework.

and what does not exist, what works and what does not work. Identify where the greatest value is created for the key elements of the strategy. The gaps that are uncovered then form the focus for investment and change. Build a plan to enhance, replace, or develop systems that create real value for the organization. Finally, implement, monitor, reinforce, and continue to upgrade programs to reflect changes in the strategy of the business, its people, and the marketplace.

Why is this important? This is answered by knowing that the results will be achieved by the successful implementation of a firm's strategy. These are the systems that encourage, influence, and reinforce people for taking desired actions. They give the organization a competitive advantage in translating its strategy from paper to results.

How Rewards Work and Why They Sometimes Fail

Stupidity got us into this mess—
Why can't it get us out?

Will Rogers

THIS CHAPTER FOCUSES on understanding the fundamental forces that influence human behavior within organizations and the role reward systems play in this dynamic. The reason is simple: An organization's success depends primarily on what people do.

Organizations often cannot afford the time and investment to dramatically change the character and nature of their employees. Effective recruitment and selection practices should screen out individuals who are not suited to the organization. Once individuals are employed, the challenge to the organization is to bring out their best talents and use their skills to benefit the organization.

This chapter provides a foundation for understanding how reward systems work. By knowing the factors that determine success, we are better situated to develop programs to address specific needs. In a sense, we will examine the "operating system" that determines the efficiency and capabilities of the "application programs," such as base salaries, incentives, special recognition, and so on. As programs are developed in specific areas, they can be designed to do what they do best. Then the challenge will be to integrate such programs into everyday practice. This creates an integrated, holistic system that increases the capability and probability that an organization's strategy will be implemented.

The Importance of Understanding the Reasons Why

During World War II, there was an island in the Pacific Ocean that became a major hub for supplies and support of the U.S. war effort. U.S. forces saw that the island was barely inhabited, so they proceeded to set up an air base for operations. They built a runway, complete with lights and towers and with sheds in which to store supplies.

The few people who inhabited the island saw what was happening and observed with great interest what the foreigners were doing. When the native people began to see the results, they proceeded to build an exact replica of the landing strip on another part of the island. They did not have the same equipment, but they crafted their "landing strip" as close to what the American's had created as possible. Then they sat and waited for the "great birds" to provide them with food and supplies.

This story demonstrates a simple, important principle: Understanding the principles and underlying practices of what we are attempting to do can enable us to achieve what we want. Without this understanding, we are destined to imitate what others do and hope that success will be realized. If it isn't, then we blame the system; and if it is, we celebrate our effectiveness. Neither is the truth—success or failure is purely due to the circumstances of the situation.

We see this frequently when an organization implements a specialized reward program copied from another company, such as in executive compensation or special recognition. Then the company expects to see similar results. It is essential to understand what is possible as well as what is required before moving forward. It is also essential to understand how a program affects the actions of people in order to adjust the design to make it as effective as possible. Then the organization is more able to achieve its objectives. This does not determine success, but it does give one a competitive advantage.

Business Success Depends on Systems That Influence Behavior

The success of an organization depends on many factors, such as its markets, products and services, capital, technology, distribution channels, and locations, as well as government regulations. The degree to which any of these factors provides competitive advantage depends on what people do about them. If it were as simple as telling people what to do or retaining people who inherently know what to do, the tasks of management would be quite simple.

However, people are more complex than that, and so are the cultures and business conditions in which they operate. What is needed is a framework for understanding what influences the things that people do. There is a framework in marketing for understanding customer preferences, in operations for understanding how to produce products, and in finance for understanding the uses and returns on capital. Thus, in creating and implementing a strategy, we need a framework for understanding what is necessary to align the actions of people with the requirements of the organization's mission, values, and strategy.

Richard Herrnstein, the Edgar Pierce professor at Harvard University, says that the business of business is behavior.[1] Gary Hamel of the London Business School writes that the key to global conquests is the ability of organizations to create an environment that merges knowledge, skills, and abilities with the needs of customers.[2] David Ulrich, a professor at the University of Michigan and author of many books on human resources and organizational performance, clearly demonstrates that much of the market value of organizations is achieved by what people do within the organization.[3] Organizations that are able to maximize human performance are always at a significant competitive advantage. Organizations that do not appreciate this fact are destined to struggle for survival.

The key term *behavior* is defined simply as "something that somebody does or says." Many of the quality management and organizational change models indicate that success is based on work process. If you get this right, people will respond appropriately. This assumes that if you simply "get out of their way," people will become highly productive, and the organization's performance will excel. Oh how we all wish success were this simple to achieve!

When people do not respond as expected, we tend to blame it on the systems, work process, work culture, or lack of leadership. Organizations try more training, do more communicating, restructure business units and jobs, or invest in new information and technology systems. As the chief executive of a major technology company said at his company's strategic retreat, "For us to implement this strategy, we need to either change the people or change the people!"

As many organizational experts conclude, if you put a good person into a poor system, the system will win every time. This implies that we need to develop and influence the processes that encourage and reinforce desired actions. By understanding what influences human behavior, we can increase the likelihood of success. This requires going beyond just how people are rewarded to examine what factors influence people.

Using Sciences to Understand Behavior

To develop a process that works, we need to base our work on sound research evidence. There is a long-standing controversy in the behavioral sciences between those who believe that desired behaviors are best reinforced by the work itself—*intrinsic reinforcement*—and those who believe that rewards and recognition are necessary factors in achieving desired behaviors—*extrinsic reinforcement*. Much of the research based on intrinsic motivation demonstrates that it is more effective than extrinsically motivated rewards, which result in lowering self-esteem and creativity and do not serve to improve organizational performance.[4] According to this research, extrinsic rewards condition people to do only what is needed to get the reward, creating temporary compliance that blossoms into resentment when the rewards ultimately are withdrawn. This carrot-and-stick or reward-and-punishment approach to management causes people to feel dehumanized, in dependent relationships, and manipulated. This philosophy considers the role of genetics and the inherent capabilities of individuals to perform certain tasks.

However, the degree of influence genetics has on behavior is often in dispute.

The solution to improving organizations is to create jobs and work cultures that fulfill the needs of people or inspire them to action. Maslow's hierarchy of needs is the foundation concept for this point of view.[5] According to this well-established theory, people advance to the next level of needs once the preceding need has been fulfilled. These levels include the following:

1. *Basics*—hunger, thirst, sex, and other core needs for survival
2. *Safety*—security, preservation, order, and stability
3. *Belongingness*—affection, friendship, and peer group approval
4. *Self-esteem*—self-respect, pride, and confidence
5. *Self-actualization*—personal fulfillment, achievement, and growth

Many of these concepts have been translated into more contemporary terms by authors and lecturers such as Steve Covey, Warren Bennis, John Kotter,[6] and others.

The strategy employed to improve organizational performance is to create meaning in the work itself and place little emphasis on external recognition and rewards. According to this model, the workplace should give individuals room for self-determination and personal fulfillment. If people do not perform as expected, proponents argue, workplace systems should be examined and changed to create better structures, processes, or communication.

This perspective has some very appealing aspects. First, it recognizes that people have an inherent interest in bettering themselves and the organizations for which they work. Second, it eliminates the need to fix blame on or find fault with people and instead focuses on the work systems. Third, it places emphasis on creating a strong vision and mission for the organization and encourages executives to communication business strategies and build organizational structures and work processes that use the inherent capabilities of people. Finally, the messages of such an approach are often personally meaningful and appeal to an individual's ideals. It is fulfilling and meaningful to embrace these principles.

There is also compelling evidence that when reward systems are too task-specific, people exhibit the characteristics of tunnel vision and resentment of authority. One only needs to examine piece-rate incentive systems, sales commission plans, and discretionary bonus programs to see this. Such programs demonstrate how the organization manipulates people and people manipulate the organization to achieve personal gain.

On the other hand, there is significant research that supports the idea that behavior is a function of its consequences.[7] Extrinsic rewards proponents argue that if an individual is rewarded for taking certain actions, he or she likely will continue to demonstrate that behavior. As a simple illustration, watch someone waiting for an elevator and count the number of times he or she presses the call button even though the signal has already been transmitted to the elevator's control system, or observe a gambling casino or lottery system to see the lengths people will go to realize personal gain.

Further, habits are developed when the same behaviors are reinforced over time. Success (defined as someone receiving something that he or she wants) then leads the individual to conclude that his or her actions are effective and should be continued. The behavior will continue as long as the external rewards confirm its value or the actions themselves become internally fulfilling to the individual. Then intrinsic reinforcement replaces external reinforcement, and the individual responds in a similar fashion (i.e., habit) when faced with a similar situation. There is both wisdom and caution in understanding this simple principle.

Finally, some of those who support consequence behavior theories cite research showing that behaviors are based on what the individual "expects" to receive from taking certain actions. In other words, based on one's personal history of consequences (or those learned by observing others), an individual will gauge the likelihood that he or she will experience a similar outcome (whether positive or negative, whether intrinsic or extrinsic) before taking certain actions. The conclusion is that behavior is a function of both immediate and anticipated consequences.[8]

The controversy about extrinsic rewards is not about whether reinforcement impacts behavior—there is a common agreement that it does. Both intrinsic and extrinsic theories agree that behavior is influenced and shaped by a pattern of consequences, but they disagree on which method is more desirable. People with a variety of competencies, habits, preconceived assumptions, expectations, and needs present a complex challenge to an organization attempting to bring out their best qualities. The challenge to today's organizations is to determine what is the best approach to encouraging actions that will lead to success.

A Model for Understanding the Factors That Influence Human Behavior

We can conclude that consequences have a significant influence on the actions of people. We also can conclude that consequences influence the ways in which people approach their work, their responsibilities, and the cultures of their organizations. However, if we focus only on managing the consequences, we limit our ability to strategically and effectively influence behaviors. People have inherent attributes, beliefs, and habits that are far easier to screen for during the hiring or promotion processes than to teach or change once people are on the job. Therefore, we need to use an integrated framework for developing high-performance organizations.

Figure 2-1 illustrates four primary forces that influence what people do. It is important to remember that no organization can control people's actions; the best strategy is to establish conditions under which people make the desired choices to realize the results needed by the organization—that is, create a win-win situation.

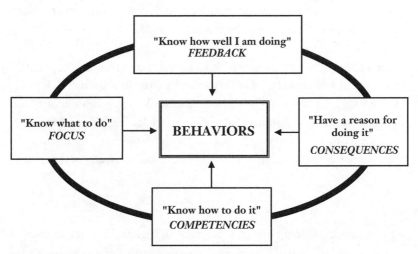

Figure 2-1   The forces that drive human behavior.

Focus

Focus consists of the strategies, directions, accountabilities, and tasks that an individual should undertake to support the organization. In essence, focus answers the question: "What should I do?" In the behavioral sciences, these actions are known as *antecedents* because they precede an action or behavior and are used to start a given set of behaviors.

There are many avenues through which people achieve focus:

1. When an organization states its vision, mission, and values, it frequently indicates the types of actions people should take as members of the organization.
2. When an organization establishes business plans and defines strategies, people can begin to determine what is important and what they should do to support the implementation of such plans.
3. When an organization develops a job description or clarifies accountabilities, individuals know what they are responsible for.
4. When a team defines its charter, roles, tasks, and norms, team members know what is needed to make it a high-performing group.
5. When an organization provides training to people on specific tasks or skills, the people know how to complete certain functions at a higher level of performance.
6. When an organization sets goals and standards of performance, people know what they should be doing and against what criteria their effectiveness will be evaluated.

Focus is essential for people to operate to their maximum potential, whether they are leaders of an organization, those responsible for certain units or departments of the organization's business, or individuals who provide direct or indirect services. A key leadership task therefore is to find the right balance between giving people sufficient focus to take desired actions and the flexibility to create, innovate, and perform.

Feedback

Feedback is the information people need to receive in order to know if they are performing in a manner consistent with what is required for success. Feedback can be as simple as monitoring tasks according to a schedule or seeing whether certain tasks comply with quality standards. It can be as complex as analyzing financial or operating reports that reflect a broad array of actions by many people inside and outside the organization. Finally, feedback can come informally through comments by one's manager or peers about actions taken or a formal report and presentation. When it is based on information or facts (not a criticism or compliment), then it is feedback. Feedback is made effective by its timing, reliability, and the awareness it creates about performance.

Competencies

Competencies are the knowledge, skills, and abilities that enable a person to perform certain tasks. Competencies are not behaviors; they are the ability to translate an antecedent into an action. For many organizations, competencies are the basis of selection, training, and assessment feedback programs. These competencies can develop and change as a person has other experiences; this is called *learning and development*. They are considered part of the forces of human behavior because they provide the abilities of an individual to take desired actions and shape expectations and decisions.

Consequences

Consequences are the things that happen to an individual when he or she takes certain actions or performs certain behaviors. They always occur after a behavior, but they may or may not be noticed. The impact of consequences is influenced by many factors. Consequences may

1. Be positive or negative, based on what the individual wants or needs
2. Have minor or major importance to the individual
3. Have a low or high likelihood of being experienced
4. Be experienced internally (based on internal feelings or responses) or provided externally (by someone or something)
5. Be based on the degree to which the person understands what he or she did to experience the consequence

Behavioral research clearly demonstrates that positive consequences that are important, sufficiently frequent, and experienced from both internal and external sources have the most significant influence on sustaining high performance.

How Consequences Affect People

While a great deal of research has been done on the types, frequencies, and patterns of consequences, as well as in responses to them, they can be summarized as having one of three possible impacts on an individual.

Negative consequences create an adverse reaction in an individual. In the work context, this could be public or private criticism, a freeze in pay, reassignment, demotion, or termination. The setting, timing, and degree of severity can all affect how an individual experiences the negative consequences. A manager or one's peers usually deliver negative consequences. These consequences are very appropriate when an individual does something that is unsafe, illegal, against policy or corporate values, or inappropriate for the workplace or its customers. When provided in a clear, direct, and sincere manner, negative consequences work to stop or rapidly diminish the behaviors. People understand that they cannot engage in such activities in the future. In essence, such consequences create a "compliance" type of environment.

A second form is a *positive consequence*. Traditionally, this is known as *positive reinforcement* because the recipient experiences something good, pleasurable, satisfying, or fulfilling associated with an action or outcome. The individual may receive a special letter from an executive, a recognition award, a promotion, a spot bonus, a large merit pay increase, above-target bonus payouts, or special stock option awards for his or her performance. This may be done in public or private, but the consequence is clearly associated with what the person did or contributed to. Once again, the relationship between the positive consequence and the action and the timing and importance of the consequence will influence the individual's future actions. While positive consequences can be applied to teams, units, or departments, individuals experience such consequences in their own way.

A third form of consequence is basically the absence of anticipated consequences, and this is known as *extinction*. Extinction occurs when an individual feels that he or she is entitled to something and does not receive it. If the desired action or result is known and achieved and yet no positive consequence is received, the response may be some degree of confusion or the conclusion that more is needed or that the action is no longer valued. If this continues, the individual may either develop internal (or personal) criteria for judging success or decrease the actions over time.

If an individual receives a positive consequence when it is not associated with an action or result, there will be some degree of appreciation. If this continues, then the individual will disassociate the positive consequence from the desired performance. Classic examples include the annual cost-of-living pay raise, the receipt of a company-wide profit-sharing bonus, and service awards that are provided to all employees. Initially, the individual will appreciate the reward, and then, over time, he or she will become accustomed to receiving the award and will regard it as standard and normal. If after some time the award or pay raise is reduced or eliminated, the response is likely to be anger, frustration, and loss of security. The award becomes disassociated with performance and is seen as an entitlement. If, on the other hand, individuals know the current reality of the business and can anticipate the loss of some reward before it becomes a final decision, then the response is most often disappointment but not loss of commitment.

As stated earlier, different factors determine the impact of consequence on current and future actions, but positive consequences have the greatest impact on achieving and sustaining high performance. However, an organization cannot devote resources to developing and managing consequences fitted to each individual in every situation. The organization needs systems and processes that provide programs to create an environment of motivation, engagement, and commitment.

The Purpose of Reward Systems

As we have seen, many factors influence what, when, and how people do things. In this context we can see that the ultimate purpose of a reward system is *to provide a systematic way to deliver positive consequences*. There are several key elements to this simple definition. First, a *systematic* process means that there are several elements directed at accomplishing specific outcomes. Their purpose, structure, and delivery are integrated to accomplish common goals. Further, while there are some immediate impacts, these consequences are delivered consistently over time—that is what an effective system does.

Second, there is a direct alignment between the success of the organization and actions that are encouraged and rewarded. The rewards are based on these actions and/or the results they produce. Third, the delivery of the consequences can be accomplished in many ways—informal or formal; by a manager, by peers, or by the work itself; and immediately or over time. While the organization may create specific programs to deliver certain consequences (e.g., sales commission plan), the programs all influence the practices or culture of the organization. Fourth, the consequences are perceived as positive to the individual. Remember, the person defines their value, not the organization, and ideally, the person is left with the desire to do more.

Finally, effective consequences have the desired impact on the individual. They leave the person feeling good and valued for something he or she has accomplished. By not receiving a particular consequence, an individual may feel a loss, a missed opportunity, or the desire to adjust his or her actions to achieve the desired consequences. While the feelings may appear negative, they underscore the importance of the contingency nature of rewards. When rewards ultimately lose their link with performance or action, they rightly become an expected part of employment (e.g., an entitlement).

Types of External Consequences

As indicated earlier, there are many ways consequences are delivered to an individual. For our purposes, we will focus the materials in this book on external consequences, but readers should be highly aware of intrinsic or internally experienced consequences. In fact, the easiest form of consequences (from the organization's perspective) occurs when an individual experiences strong satisfaction or a sence of importance from the work itself. Then the organization can use external systems to enhance or multiply the intrinsic reinforcement experienced by the individual.

Further, the meaning of many external consequences is determined by the individual's frame of reference and personal situation. Reward systems, for our purposes, will address externalconsequences that have the potential of being positive and meaningful to an individual.

External consequences can be categorized into the following four types (Figure 2-2):

1. *Verbal/social.* These are the things that are said, expressed, displayed, or communicated about the actions or results. These are the most common and immediate forms of consequences because they are delivered at the time the behavior or result occurs. These include direct comments by one's manager or a person of importance, letters or other expressions of appreciation, or special events or activities that are based on the achievement. They produce the highest returns on investment. What does it cost for a senior executive to provide an individual or team with a clear, meaningful statement of appreciation? What is the likely impact?

2. *Tangible/symbolic.* These are the trophies or awards that are given to people for special achievements. These are the types of

VERBAL/SOCIAL
Specific compliments
Recognition
Commendation letters
Award dinners
Celebration lunches/activities
Taking an interest in one's work/ideas

TANGIBLE/SYMBOLIC
Trophies/plaques
Special achievement clubs
Trips, tickets, and dinners
$$$ Spot awards
Personal items of interest

WORK-RELATED
Promotions
Special development programs/projects
Increased decision authority
Increased control over resources
More challenging assignments

MONEY-RELATED
Salary and salary increases
Overtime or special assignment pay
Promotion or relocation pay
Variable or incentive payouts
Stock options/equity participation
Deferred compensation

Figure 2-2 The four types of external consequences.

rewards that most people associate with recognition and rewards programs. They may include dinners, tickets, or trips, as well points that can be transferred into merchandise. Spot awards ($50 to $1000) are included in this category because of how they are presented and what they symbolize.

3. *Work-related.* These are the awards that involve the person's role within the organization as well as the authority exercised or involvement in decisions. This is a reward because it is frequently based on performance. An individual may be hired to do a particular job with a specific set of responsibilities and resources and specific authority, but to succeed the individual needs to perform well. Promotions are the most frequently applied rewards, but many organizations use involvement in key projects and increasing control over resources as additional rewards for the high performer.

4. *Mone-related.* These rewards most commonly are associated with total compensation programs. They are the compensation one receives as well as payouts from variable-pay programs. They also include stock option awards or other equity- or ownership-related awards provided to individuals. If the organization makes special contributions to the individual's deferred compensation account, such as a 401(k) plan or special retirement program based on the organization's performance, these take on the characteristics of rewards.

In summary, rewards can take many forms. Theie fundamental purpose, however, is to provide a positive consequence for contributions to desired performance. This performance is defined by the focus on key areas and is supported by the feedback and competencies employed in the process. Consequently, the organization is well served to consider both "how much" and "how" one receives rewards.

Making Rewards an Effective Positive Consequence

Because an organization has a specific program to encourage certain behaviors or results does not mean that the program is effective. In fact, the problem with most reward programs is not the purpose but how they function within the organization. Further, programs and practices that are regarded as a standard part of an organization's culture may in fact be the most important systems that enable the organization to succeed or that limit its competitiveness. Therefore, the key to successful reward systems is their design, effective use, and ongoing management (Figure 2-3).

To this end, research and experience indicate that there are several overriding determinants of effective reward systems, including the following:

Strategy. An effective program to reward individuals must be linked directly to what makes the organization effective in attracting, retaining, and motivating its primary resource—people. Further, we will see in later chapters that different programs, such as salaries, variable pay, recognition, and so on, have inherent strengths and weaknesses and how they can be interwoven to build on their strengths to create a winning organization.

Translation. For any program to deliver rewards effectively, the individual needs to know what to do. This means that he or she must be able to translate the desired vision, goals, results, or values into actions that he or she can take. There are some aspects that are common to all members of the organization and some aspects that are unique to roles and capabilities. Reward systems depend on people knowing how they are doing during the performance period. They have little effect if people are not able to make adjustments or take critical actions before the end of the performance period.

Relationships. The interactions of people create relationships within and outside an organization, and these relationships often deter-

- **S**trategy
- **T**ranslation
- **R**elationships
- **I**ntegrity
- **V**alue
- **E**ngagement

Figure 2-3 What makes rewards an effective consequence?

mine the success of the organization. Whether this involves a customer service representative who handles a difficult customer effectively, an executive who addresses the concerns of investors, or a unit manager who strengthens cooperation with other departments, relationships are vital to success and are uniquely human. Effective reward systems are designed to encourage and reinforce the relationships the organization needs to succeed in a dynamic marketplace.

Integrity. The programs need to function with sincerity, reliability, and trust. If people perceive that rewards are intended to manipulate or exploit them, the programs and the leaders will be resented. If a program is presented in one manner but operates in a different manner, integrity will be eroded. Hence effective reward systems must have a strong level of discipline, commitment, and administrative reliability to them. When a salesperson does not feel that he or she is receiving the proper credit for sales, the entire sales incentive system will be mistrusted. Promises made but not fulfilled by executives also set up situations in which their credibility is eroded. People need to know, have confidence in, and trust that the process by which their rewards are determined and delivered is consistent with its objectives, structure, and philosophy. Then people can focus their energy on achieving the desired results.

Value. The receiver determines the importance and value of any reward. Program designers and executives often ignore this simple, obvious, and profound principle. The value is a function of many things, and economic worth is only part of it. Executives can do a great deal to enhance the value of rewards beyond their financial implications. In later chapters we will examine recommendations to enhance the value of rewards so that they become truly positive experiences.

Engagement. When business plans are made but not communicated outside a small circle, they have little impact on actions. Further, reward systems that are not linked directly to a business strategy, plan, or philosophy may become meaningless ways in which an organization distributes financial resources. Plans need to engage people to understand what they must do and allow them to see how they are progressing and how they will realize something of value.

Putting Principles into Practice

The preceding principles form an acronym—*STRIVE*—that provides a set of criteria for assessing and designing reward systems. In later chapters we examine specific programs and other specific criteria that are relevant to these principles. Readers will be guided through a synopsis of how traditional programs work and will review a set of success criteria and examine what designs and practices need to change. Hopefully, this exploration will spur you to ideas that are appropriate for your particular environment, even though they are not specifically included in this book.

Peter Senge, director of systems thinking and organizational learning programs at the MIT Sloan School of Management, stated in *The Fifth Discipline*, "It is poorly designed systems, not incompetent or unmotivated individuals, that cause 'most organizational problems."[9] Our task will be to examine existing programs and create a strong alignment and a meaningful set of positive consequences to reinforce desired performance.

When programs succeed, we will see that these principles are embedded in how the programs were developed and practices that were applied. When program fails, the root causes may be in the specific nature of the program or that it fails to live up to these STRIVE standards.

Therefore, the challenge to organizations is to develop and use reward systems that support factors that lead to their success in the short term and over time. While environments change and companies with great cultures have not survived, we should seek to give our organizations the best chances possible to prosper. As an organization develops its business plans, systems, and processes for ensuring the implementation of key decisions, it also should examine the systems by which people are encouraged and rewarded for achievement. Do people understand what they need to do? Do people know how well they are doing? Do people have the skills, abilities, and attributes that are consistent with the organization's requirements and values? Do people believe that if they succeed, they will benefit as well? Is the benefit felt on multiple levels so that the commitment of minds and hearts is fully dedicated to the tasks ahead?

Perhaps one of the key attributes of great leaders and great organizations is that they understand this concept and that it is interwoven into everything that they do.

Align Rewards with the Organization's Strategy

When you do common things in uncommon ways, you command the attention of the world.

George Washington Carver

W HEN AN ORGANIZATION sets out to fulfill its mission, regardless of the markets it serves or the work it does, it needs a game plan. This plan may be as simple as a commitment to solve a customer's problem or as complex as a multiyear strategy. A plan enables the organization to focus on what it does best, make decisions, and allocate resources so that it can achieve its objectives.

One of the framers of management as a discipline was Frederick W. Taylor, an engineer who invented carbon-steel machine tools. He became the leading authority on management at the turn of the century.[1] Taylor asserted that there was a best method for organizing work. Organizations that adopted his principles did, in fact, prosper. His principles included the following:

1. *Simplify work by specialization.* By identifying the basic tasks involved in work, reducing any unnecessary movements, and structuring them into related tasks, organizations could achieve incredible efficiencies.
2. *Establish predetermined rules to govern work methods.* This involves determining the standard operating procedures and work processes necessary to complete the needed tasks. As a result, activities can be controlled to minimize variance.
3. *Monitor work activities to ensure compliance.* The principal role of supervision is to ensure that employees follow the prescribed process.

These principles of organizing work helped organizations achieve a critical advantage—the production of a high volume of standardized products or services. The volume reduced unit costs and improved profitability. The success of the United States from the 1920s to the 1970s was based on many of these principles. The output per worker during this period grew at an average rate of 2.3 percent per year, far faster than in any other industrialized country. The basic driver of this success was industry's ability to transform one-of-a-kind inventions into mass-produced products and services and distribute them at prices people could afford. American society embraced this method of production by purchasing the products, which in turn fueled this growth.[2] In this era, the focus of the organization was to control work process so that customers received the desired products at an appropriate price.

As organizations became more successful, the voice and influence of the customers became more distant from the people managing these firms. Executives concerned themselves with the organization's structure, lines of authority, span of control, consistent policies, and financial reporting systems. Demand for products grew, the firms kept doing what they were doing, and shareholders and executives gained a great deal of wealth.

The Emergence of Structured Compensation Systems

As management become more professional, compensation systems developed to support the leading principles of management. The use of discretionary and arbitrary pay decisions created confusion and conflicts that were disruptive to organizational performance. A system of controls was needed for compensation.

From the mid-1950s to the early 1980s, compensation systems such as that of the National Metal Trades, AAIM (American Association for Industrial Management), and the Hay system were developed to standardize decisions on how much money people should make. These systems sought to rationalize and objectify pay decisions.

Such compensation systems focused on the job as the primary unit of value. Job descriptions, a common element in many pay programs, sought to capture the unique, specialized content of the job as well as the authority and accountability assigned to it. They became the basis for allocating dollars spent on compensation and defined status and power in an organization. Job descriptions customarily were used to clarify job responsibilities in the context of the superior's responsibilities. However, whenever a manager wanted to satisfy a frustrated employee, he or she would rewrite the job description.

The use of incentive plans frequently was reserved for top executives or people who did sales or highly routine operational jobs. Usually focused on individual effort, they were either formulaic (i.e., awarded for the number of pieces produced over a standard minimum) or discretionary (i.e., awarded based on how a top executive felt about the worker's performance).

Compensation systems became both a reflection of the organization's hierarchy and a way of reinforcing it. Because pay increases often were associated with specialization and control over resources, these systems acted more to reinforce the terms of the hierarchy than to meet customer needs. Managers were reluctant to implement change until they could see how the new "points," or job levels, would affect them or their people. Hierarchical organizations were appropriate at a time when people generally were unskilled and the work involved simple production. These pay systems were reflections of their times and were accepted as the natural order of things in the workplace. Then something fundamental began to change.

The Shift from Hierarchy to Team

Industry leaders came to face increasing competition from smaller, niche businesses or companies in related industries. The latter companies saw opportunities for gaining market share because the existing providers were neither responsive to the customers nor focused on developing products and services that met the customers' emerging needs. The traditional market leaders were resistant to change and consequently easy prey for these new competitors.

To address these threats to market leadership, revenue growth, and profitability, a new model for leadership emerged that emphasized establishing a clear vision, empowering people, building collaborative relationships, and involving people in direct and meaningful ways. Warren Bennis,[3] John Kotter,[4] and Richard Boyatzis[5] conducted research and developed new frameworks for leadership.

Companies created small business units and supported self-directed work teams within many parts of their organizations. They sought to empower employees to take responsibility for lowering costs, reducing lead times, improving product quality, introducing new products, and providing more responsive services. These were the types of changes that could not be dictated by executives but that required people to do things differently and take personal responsibility for making change happen.

However, many of these change efforts failed. Numerous research studies clearly indicate that only 25 to 35 percent of firms were successful in making this transformation.[6] Companies such as Corning, Kimberly-Clark, Ford, Nucor, and Wells Fargo succeeded in transforming their organizations with new models of leadership. They organized and rewarded employees around key drivers of their businesses and did so as teams. Layers of management and control functions were reduced significantly.

The Shift in Compensation from Status to Results

One of the principal changes that this new organizational model required was a shift in behaviors from protection to collaboration, from passing problems up the organization to solving them directly, from focusing on the number of units produced in a time period to meeting the needs of the customer. Companies invested millions of dollars in training and education, organizational change and reengineering efforts, and reorganizing or replacing staff in critical positions. As mentioned earlier, many of these attempts failed to live up to expectations or to produce the desired return on investment.

Organizations in the 1980s started to extend variable compensation programs to lower levels. They focused reward programs on team results, and they achieved remarkable improvements. The variable compensation efforts at Corning (see www.GoalSharing.com), Allied Signal, and General Motor's Saturn are perhaps some of the most dramatic illustrations of this.[7] Not only did these programs include all members of the organization, but they also reinforced a philosophy of involvement and performance improvement. These programs were important factors in the transformation of these companies (Figure 3-1).

As organizations transformed themselves from hierarchies to teams, they found both positive and negative conditions. Many realized strong benefits from becoming a customer-centered organization and found new capabilities and commitment from their workforce. They increased quality and built more positive organizational cultures. However, for some companies, teams became associated with a lack of personal accountability and slower decision making. Top performers did not receive the recognition they deserved, and lackluster performers shared in rewards they did not deserve. Further, these companies were not able to make the changes they needed to respond to market threats and opportunities.

The Transition from Teams to Networks

These issues have set the stage for a new model of organizations. This emerging model can best described as *network organizations*.[8] Perhaps one of the premier examples of this concept can be found in General Electric Corporation (GE). GE has built a continually transforming

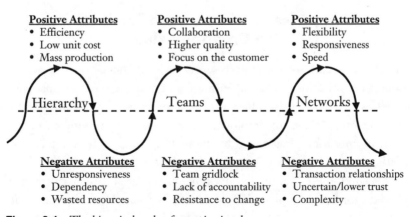

Positive Attributes
- Efficiency
- Low unit cost
- Mass production

Positive Attributes
- Collaboration
- Higher quality
- Focus on the customer

Positive Attributes
- Flexibility
- Responsiveness
- Speed

Hierarchy   Teams   Networks

Negative Attributes
- Unresponsiveness
- Dependency
- Wasted resources

Negative Attributes
- Team gridlock
- Lack of accountability
- Resistance to change

Negative Attributes
- Transaction relationships
- Uncertain/lower trust
- Complexity

Figure 3-1   The historical cycle of organizational structures.

organization with both independent and interdependent business units. It has focused the organization on being the market leader in every line of business in which it operates, and it has created a culture that is intense and involving in a manner that does not diminish accountability for performance. With the clear and present pressure to anticipate and respond effectively to market shifts, GE remains highly competitive.[9]

In addition to notable companies, a new industry emerged rapidly that demonstrated new ways of organizing and creating value. This industry increased the capabilities of organizational networking and attempted to live by the philosophy of what it was creating—the information and communications industry. While many of these firms were awash with venture capital, not all of them should be held up as premiere models. However, the impact of information and communications technology on methods of conducting business will be felt for many years to come.

Information and communications technology is changing the way individuals and organizations communicate, share information and resources, and conduct business. Smaller companies are able to function as well-established companies, and individuals can work with a global network of colleagues to provide services to a common customer while never being part of the same organization. These relationships remain dynamic and come into being continually, evolve, and disband, only to be reconstituted in some other form at another time. There are capabilities now that have never existed, and they will continue to evolve in a manner that will accelerate the pressure and ability to change most organizations.

Compensation Shifts from Productivity to Creating Value

Within this context, we can see several critical changes in the ways in which organizations use compensation and other reward systems. First, salaries are evolving to reflect the value of an employee's work in the marketplace. While the employment relationship is changing continually, payment for services can be defined in terms of the value created rather than the employee's level within the organization.

Second, there is an increasing reliance on variable or performance-based compensation plans. These programs do not increase salaries but rather provide rewards that are contingent on the accomplishments of individuals, teams, or units and/or the organization at large. They also may be based on a special project team, whether it consists of employees, contractors, or others associated with the project.

Third, companies are using more equity-based reward programs than ever before. Since the 1990s, the number of companies using stock options or similar programs for employees other than their top executives has grown from less than 10 percent to over 40 percent of U.S. companies.[10] Further, at present, between 15 and 25 percent of established companies' stock is held by employees and managers of those companies through stock options and employee stock purchase programs. Although there have been major disruptions in the equity markets, the use of equity as part of the employment agreement is likely to continue for a large majority of managers and employees. Further, the impact of equity has changed the mindset of executives and employees and increased the demand for a stake in the long-term growth in value of organizations.

Fourth, companies are making more active use of recognition programs. While these programs sometimes are associated with "tickets, trips, and trinkets," many highly successful companies have used them to build and reinforce a strong performance-oriented culture. Southwest Airlines and Disney are two classic examples of this approach.[11] As we will see in later chapters, the real value of these programs is in how they create personal meaning and value for the worker.

Finally, companies will continue to provide employees with benefits and employee services; such things provide an important level of security and life balance. For example, companies that offer dry-cleaning services, child-care programs, or resources for long-term care of family members or parents are seeking to minimize the everyday pressures people face. These programs will continue to increase employee security and provide resources to address personal challenges. Such programs will be discussed in more detail in Chapter 4.

A Model for Understanding What Influences Organizational Performance

In Chapter 2 we discussed a model of the factors that influence individual performance. We can elevate these same factors to understand the forces that influence how an organization performs, whether it is based on hierarchy, teams, or networks. As with the individual, many cultural, environmental, and physical factors affect how well an organization does. This model presents a simple framework for linking the factors that shape the dynamics within an organization and that directly strengthen or limit an organization's ability to compete (Figure 3-2).

These factors include

> *Strategy.* As with an individual who needs to know what to do, the strategy defines what the organization needs to do to be successful. This element includes the organization's mission and vision, the core values that define its desired character and culture, and the marketplace in which the organization operates. This element articulates the company's business model and clarifies its proposition to serve desired customers. Frequently the strategy is based on a set of core competencies that make the organization unique or attractive to its customers. Finally, this element also defines the organization's long- and short-term plans for growth and success. When the strategy is translated into structure, roles, and accountabilities, this element is linked to with the "focus" element discussed in Chapter 2 for the individual. However, a strategy is only worth the material it is written on until it becomes operational.
>
> *Information.* The second element of the model includes the information the organization needs to process, communicate, monitor, and respond to. Information for many executives has become the

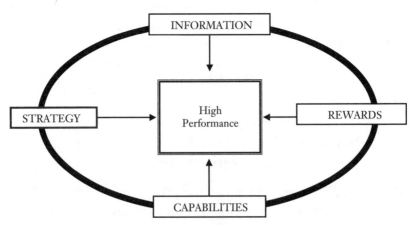

Figure 3-2   Strategic framework: the forces that drive high performance.

"lifeblood" of the enterprise. This includes fulfilling orders, adjusting prices, transferring data, adjusting commitments, and enhancing a product's features. Each year millions of dollars are spent on developing or improving these systems. Email, intranet, and Internet systems provide channels where people share information, obtain information, and link a company directly with its customer and supplier chains. Information helps increase the speed with which the organization can act. Information gives people the market intelligence to develop strategies and plans to improve competitiveness. Information gives people the ability to know if they are on track to achieve their objectives, better meet the needs of their customers, and use resources efficiently. Information can make the strategy and plans come to life, and the lack of sufficient information can severely limit an organization's abilities. Information provides no value unless people do something with it.

Capabilities. This element of the model defines what the organization needs to have in order to implement its strategy. Capabilities can include technology, distribution systems or locations, image and reputation, capital resources, and people. Since this book is about people, we will limit our discussion of capabilities to the talent the organization needs to succeed. Human talent, by its nature, depends on the work and services the organization performs. However, capabilities go beyond technical skills to encompass desired attributes, styles, skill levels, potential for learning, and other competencies needed for success. Finally, the organization may choose to own or use external capabilities through alliances, joint ventures, contracts, and other third-party relationships. However, having a good plan and strong capabilities will not ensure that the organization will move in the right direction.

A Systematic Way to Create Alignment and Deliver Positive Consequences	
• *Systems*	Based on sound principles and effective practices
• *Creation*	Works in the best possible manner
• *Alignment*	Focuses on what the organization needs in order to succeed
• *Desired action*	People taking action because they "want to"

Figure 3-3 What is the purpose of reward systems?

Rewards. In Chapter 2 we discussed how consequences are the most important influence on behavior, but we also pointed out that they cannot function effectively independent of the other elements. Rewards create for the individual an association between the information and the expected consequences. From the organizational perspective, rewards are the systems, programs, and practices that affect what people do (Figure 3-3). They include formal salary and incentive plans, promotions and career-development opportunities, participation in equity or long-term incentive programs, and recognition that people find truly meaningful. They may be informal processes and practices in which people both receive expressions of appreciation and feel internal success for what they have done. These programs can be based on performance as well as membership within the organization. (*Note:* More on this will be discussed in Chapter 4.) In short, these reward systems, processes, and practices affect what people do within the context of the organization's needs and responsibilities. They are the organization's way of systematically delivering positive consequences.

Few organizations realized the potential power of these systems, and if these systems are well designed, the organization, its shareholders, and individual workers receive something of value. A lack of effective tools and methodologies makes this area the least developed of the factors that influence organizational performance. This means that there is an opportunity for organizations to develop high-impact reward systems that are linked significantly to their strategies and that result in improvements in competitive advantage. However, organizations first need to understand how these drivers can affect performance and what set of programs will provide the greatest value.

Many executives focus attention and resources on developing and communicating their business strategy. This is key to providing the direction and game plan to meet customer needs and create shareholder value. Ideally, resources are allocated and structures are created to align with these ends.

Executives also focus attention on assessing and building the capabilities of the organization. This includes investments in technology, training, the hiring of new people, and process improvements. Without strong capabilities, or at least capabilities that exceed those of competitors, the desired results are not likely to be achieved. Further, executives often are highly concerned about information systems, the level of communication and coordination, and knowing how well various units are meeting their objectives, plans, and performance requirements.

When it comes to using systems and processes that create the desired impact on people, executives often devote inadequate attention. There is a common belief that "if we say it, they will do it" or "if we build it, they will come." This is not to suggest that people do not have an inherent desire to do their best; people do not need to be managed with assumptions that they are totally self-centered. However, executives often believe that if pay systems are competitive, the organization will be able to attract and retain the talent it needs. Many executives believe that pay systems are the only truly meaningful reward system and that such systems only need to be examined and reviewed annually during award decision time or for planning changes. The view that reward systems are merely an infrastructure or administrative function means that the organization will not have access to or an understanding of how to truly connect people to its strategy. Commitment and enduring superior performance will be more a function of luck than competence.

Transforming Rewards from Programs to Strategy

This background on how organization and compensation plans have evolved is important because it illustrates the mindset that many executives, managers, and employees have about reward systems. They often use personal experiences to interpret decisions related to their compensation program without knowing why things happen as they do. In today's global economy, the structure of programs should not inhibit the ability of an organization to respond but should facilitate decision making, involvement, and accountability. The strategy—and what the organization needs to do to succeed—should become the predominate force that focuses the activities of the organization. To this end, we need to shift the purpose of compensation from reinforcing one's role in the organization to reflecting the contributions one can and does make.

To implement this concept, the structure and function of reward systems should relate directly to specific elements of the strategy and core values of the organization. As stated earlier and as discussed in more detail in subsequent chapters, each reward program has particular strengths and limitations. By defining what the organization needs people to do to support its mission, values, and strategy, and by using the right program for each element of this strategic framework, we can deepen the connection between people and the organization. A system then emerges as the purposeful interconnection of various programs. Imagine what impact this would have on an organization's ability to compete.

There are well-developed processes for business planning, developing capabilities, and improving information systems. Many people view reward systems as pay and benefit programs that create little value for the enterprise. What is needed is a new framework and a set of tools that executives, managers, and employees can use to strengthen the capabilities, competitiveness, and performance of the organization.

Setting the Strategy and Actions That Are Key to Success

Because organizations pursue different strategies and have unique cultures, they do not have the same reward systems. While there may be similar elements, value is created in how these programs reflect the true character of the enterprise. This means that a reward program and the system of which it is a part need to be uniquely tailored to each situation. A good place to start is with the strategy of the organization.

We first need to understand different the types of strategies. Building on the work of Michael Porter, professor at the Harvard University School of Business,[12] and that of David Norton and Robert Kaplan,[13] it is apparent that there are a number of strategies that organizations employ to create value for their shareholders, customers, and employees. To simplify these concepts, we can identify four unique strategies:

1. *Cost/price leader.* Organizations that use this strategy offer products and services at lower prices than their competitors. These companies need to be experts in operational efficiencies and productivity. The quality of the products and services is similar to

that of competitors, so the customers' purchase decisions are based primarily on price. Companies with this strategy include Wal-Mart, Southwest Airlines, and Costco.

2. *Innovation.* Companies that use this strategy seek to establish market leadership through their innovations, technological advances, and ability to stay well ahead of the competition. Customers buy from these companies because their products and services enable them to remain technically ahead of their competitors. The additional costs provide ample return on investment. Companies with this strategy include 3M, Intel, Apple Computer, and Merck.

3. *Quality.* Companies using this strategy build their reputations on the reliability and quality of their products and services. These companies build systems of controls and quality assurance and may promote these as their competitive advantage. Customers use their products and services because of how well they meet specifications, reliability, and the service standards. These features ultimately enable customers to enjoy lower costs or still fulfill their unique strategic position. Companies with this strategy include Corning, Toyota, Beth Israel/Deaconess Health Care, and Boeing.

4. *Service.* Companies using this strategy promote their ability to understand the needs of customers and to provide products or services that are highly tailored to meet these needs. Customers receive highly customized solutions and form a strong bond with the company over time such that the boundaries are sometimes blurred. Companies with this strategy include McKinsey & Company, Dell Computers, and Carlson Travel Network.

Obviously, companies usually seek to achieve a combination of these strategies. For example, Southwest Airlines seeks to provide both low-cost fares and very high quality and reliable services. Although the service is implied in the fourth strategy, the difference between quality and service is the degree of customization that is provided to meet the customer's needs. Southwest Airlines does not go where each customer wants to go, but it clearly provides superior and entertaining services. At the same time, if an organization does not emphasize price as a primary focus of its strategy, this does not mean that it is not concerned about costs. In fact, such companies understand that their customers seek a high value in relation to their costs and manage their resources accordingly.

People Implement Strategy

These four strategies carry a requirement for people to act somewhat differently from how they have in the past. For example, a company whose competitiveness is determined by operational efficiencies and low-cost production cannot tolerate individuals who continuously redesign the product or reorganize the process. There will be conflicts between actions and costs.

Each strategic approach requires a reward system that is uniquely tailored to the key factors leading to the organization's success. Once a reward strategy has been established in alignment with the business strategy, then specific programs can be developed and managed to produce maximum impact.

To develop a reward strategy, determine what is required for successful performance along each of the following dimensions:

1. *Collaboration.* Should people collaborate with others to meet performance requirements, or should they perform the work as individuals without interference from others?
2. *Expertise.* Should the expertise required to perform critical tasks be shared by many, or is it best possessed by only a few?
3. *Retention and attraction.* Does the organization possess the skills and capabilities to perform critical functions, or must it acquire them from outside the organization?
4. *Time frame.* Should the focus be on achieving immediate short-term results or on investment and development of long-term results?
5. *Action orientation.* To achieve the desired results, should people take bold, dramatic actions based on reasonable risk taking or make continuous improvements that yield dramatic increases in performance over time?

These dimensions can assist the organization in translating strategy into a list of critical actions that people must take for the organization to be successful. The requirements for success as defined by these dimensions should establish the purpose and fundamental requirements for each of the reward programs the company seeks to use. Once the purpose is clear, specific program provisions can be developed and implemented.

Let's examine several case studies to demonstrate the alignment between business and reward strategies.

Case A: The High-Growth Company

In this situation, the company is facing a rapid growth in business activities and needs people to meet the commitments of an increasing customer base. The company assembles very technical products to meet unique needs of customers (i.e., service strategy) and fulfills these orders faster and more cheaply than its competitors (i.e., price strategy). Collaboration is necessary for people to cover for one another and share information and resources so as to meet high demands from the marketplace. Because of this growth, the company will need to bring new people into the organization and assimilate them quickly. Clearly, there are few rules governing actions, but depending on the strategic focus, either operational efficiencies or resource capabilities will need to be developed to increase the ability of the organization to respond to the marketplace opportunities.

In this case, the reward strategy will need to focus on acquisition of talent, encouraging fast and effective actions by people, and building expertise. To be more specific, the salary program will need to apply and use pay guidelines that are sufficient competitively to attract the talent the company needs. The incentive plans will reward short-term key growth-focused results and encourage both collaboration and individual contributions to meet customer demands. Costs will be minimized, yet rewards need to be frequent and have value. Equity-type plans will offset some cash compensation and provide people with the opportunity to share in the firm's successful growth. Recognition programs will keep people excited about the tasks they are performing and the level of success they are achieving. They will emphasize individual and team achievements depending on what is necessary to maintain balance among the other reward programs. In short, the programs need to be simple, sharp, and meaningful, and support growth.

Case B: The Project-Oriented Company

In this situation, the company develops and implements systems for customers and operates with a strong project orientation. The company's success depends on its ability to develop custom-tailored systems that give its customers competitive advantage in process transactions and information (i.e., service and quality strategy). While individuals officially report to managers of their specialty areas, they are accountable to a project manager for their work. Individuals tend to work on only one or two projects at a time, and each project has a variety of expertise levels and areas depending on the customer contract. The projects can range from 6 months to 3 years in length, but they all have short-term milestones to track progress. The company continues to grow in measured ways, based on its customer requirements. Consequently, the company prefers to hire individuals with strong technical abilities at the early stages of their careers and develop and retain them in multiple career paths depending on individual interests and abilities and the company's needs.

In this case, the reward strategy is oriented toward retaining and developing talent to serve the projects and using the project objectives and individual contributions as the primary determinant of performance rewards. Salaries reflect the competencies people have and apply to client assignments; incentives are based on project milestones and individual and team performance. In most cases, the team results are weighted more heavily than individual results. Salaries are determined by the functional or discipline manager (with feedback from project managers), and incentives are determined by the project managers. Thus, the rewards encourage and reinforce the focus on both project deliverables and individual development—both critical to the company's success.

Case C: The Company Undergoing Transformation

This company is facing critical challenges in the marketplace. For many reasons, competitors have replaced the company as a market leader in innovation. The firm needs to rebuild both its internal processes and its reputation (i.e., innovation and quality). Many of its products no longer have a leading-edge quality to them, and the firm is relying increasingly on its service function for profitable growth. The executives and board of directors realize that the business will face certain decline if it does not regain its leadership through new products, innovation, and quality. Management has developed and is implementing a major restructuring and transformation effort before the company passes a point of no return.

The reward strategy is seen as instrumental to a successful turnaround. While the game plan is clear, the key leaders realize that if they do not encourage and reward a new pattern of action, the plan will not succeed. Consequently, they have placed significant emphasis on creative incentive and recognition programs. They have shifted the focus of rewards away from increasing salaries (in fact, they have frozen salaries for all but the most critical talent positions) to a series of organizational and business unit incentive plans. Everyone participates in the incentive plans, with one or two measures tied to organizationwide results. The major weighting of the incentive is linked to individual division or department plans that are clearly tied to the turnaround strategy. For some units, the focus is on quality measures for products and services; other units focus on process improvements that reduce lead times for new products and their associated costs. Units with sales and direct customer contact have plans that are linked to expanding the diversity and volume of new products. While most of the incentives are team-based, the leaders and key managers are heavily involved in recognizing individuals and teams for breakthroughs in innovation and commercializing ideas. The company realizes the critical importance of aligning its turnaround strategy with the messages and methods for rewarding performance.

These case studies demonstrate how companies can build a bridge between their strategy, their current challenges, and the actions of their people. Each firm has placed as much emphasis on how actions are encouraged as on setting the business plans. Most important, these companies have set out to develop very clear and positive consequences for achievements. While their employees are clearly willing to make whatever contributions are necessary, the reward systems add an extra element of reinforcement that cannot be realized through clear plans and timely information. While success is never guaranteed and may be the result of factors outside the control of these companies, at least the companies achieve a competitive advantage.

Create Customized, Systematized, and Personalized Rewards

If you want to make an apple pie from scratch, you must first create the universe.

Carl Sagan

W HEN A COMPANY DEVELOPS a strategic plan, it is often followed by annual operational plans that define how the strategic objectives will be achieved. These plans provide a clear sense of direction for allocating resources and developing programs to strengthen the organization's ability to fulfill its mission. Unfortunately, most companies stop at this point, assuming that once the plans are clear, people will carry them out completely.

Strategic planning can be inspiring and exciting, and it can give people a clear sense of direction. If it is positive, involving, and engaging, strategic planning usually creates enthusiasm. However, if there is little "ownership" of the plans, little clarity about actions, or serious skepticism about what is expected, people likely will do little after the plans are announced.

One of the unique characteristics of a reward system is its ability to steadily maintain employee focus and performance, encouraging employees to find new ways to achieve the results outlined in the strategic plan. Thus, long after the excitement and emotion of the planning process have faded, reward systems can reinforce continued commitment. However, few organizations take real advantage of this capability.

This chapter will outline processes and key areas to consider when updating a general reward strategy to a system of very effective rewards. As outlined earlier, a reward system is the integration of specific programs that encourage and reinforce actions that lead to desired results. After reading this chapter, you will have a clear understanding of what types of reward programs support different strategies and how they can result in enduring achievements.

Steps to Developing the Reward Strategy

In Chapter 3 we discussed the key dimensions involved in translating a business strategy into a reward strategy: work process, expertise, the need to attract/retain talent, time frame, and action orientation. We will build on these themes as we seek to translate the reward strategy into a set of program specifications. While, for some, these principles may be obvious or too conceptual, experience has shown that if one jumps too quickly to an answer, the results likely will be delayed and/or missed entirely.

In manufacturing, rework is considered a sign of poor quality and increases both costs and time to market. Business and reward strategies must be designed to minimize reworking. Many companies find this to be a positive paradox: If one applies thoughtful planning and consideration at the beginning of a process, the desired outcome often is achieved more quickly and with fewer recurring problems.

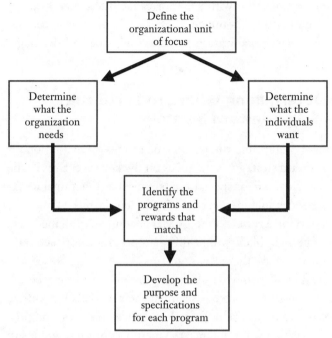

Figure 4-1 Developing the reward strategy.

Developing a reward strategy involves five primary steps (Figure 4-1) These steps are

1. Define the segment for which the organization needs to develop a reward strategy.
2. Determine what the organization needs from these individuals.
3. Determine what these individuals want from the organization.
4. Select the programs that best match the wants of the organization with those of the individuals.
5. Summarize these programs into a systems approach that fits what the organization can and is willing to do effectively.

This is essentially your strategic guide to developing an integrated total rewards system. Many organizations pay little regard to these issues and assign their resolution to someone who is not accountable for implementation. However, if one can develop systems and practices that provide the organization with superior capabilities, then one can gain a winning competitive advantage. In this world of intense competition and change, every organization needs to find a special advantage.

1. Determining Where to Focus the Reward Strategy

The first step is to determine the persons or groups for whom one is developing the reward strategy. Is the focus on the key executives of the organization, the sales staff, or specialized technical or functional workers? Or will the focus include everyone in the company? While one ultimately may develop a reward strategy that encompasses all members of an organization, there likely will be different programs for each population segment. What are these key segments?

This process is similar to basic marketing techniques. In marketing their products, successful companies segment their markets into different customer sets and then seek to provide products, services, and promotional campaigns that will influence the members of these groups to buy the products.

A company that is in the emerging growth stage of its development may find that the priority area of its reward strategy is either with its technology team or its sales organization. The company likely needs to attract a significant number of new people with specialized skills and abilities. At the same time, these individuals need to learn the organization and products quickly, build strong relationships with peers, and do the work successfully. Information needs to get to the sales organization quickly, as well as into engineering and product development. Customer relationships need to be developed and strengthened.

A great deal of care must be taken in selecting and hiring new sales professionals, as well as in establishing a sales process that effectively transitions account relationships to the internal salespeople. The reward strategy for these groups would be entirely different from what might be developed for internal operations or key support staff. Consequently, the organization needs to specifically determine the various groups for whom a tailored set of reward programs will support implementation of the company's strategy.

2. Defining What the Organization Needs to Succeed

The next step involves defining how these individuals support the organization and what they must do to make a difference to the organization's success. In short, this means determining primary roles, accountabilities, and performance requirements. To determine what is important more specifically, consider these dimensions and questions:

1. *Work process.* To what extent does the work require individuals to collaborate and integrate their activities? With whom do they need to collaborate and around what types of issues or functions? Are the situations in which work needs to be coordinated occurring on a periodic basis or as part of one's everyday responsibilities?
2. *Time frame.* What is the performance cycle? Organizations at various stages of development face a wide variety of challenges. For some, there is a primary crisis of immediate importance; for others, it is necessary to continue to improve their capabilities and performance at least as rapidly as their competitors do. The time cycle of the organization therefore has a significant bearing on the types and alternative choices it has for reward systems. This dimension therefore involves understanding the sense of urgency for change, the performance cycles of the business, and the priorities of the strategic plan.
3. *Relationship.* What is the nature of the relationships the organization wants with these individuals? A relationship is often defined by the degrees of awareness, sensitivity, communication, and commitment to the success of others. Relationships are between people. They may be very short term, transaction-oriented or intense, evolving, and highly interdependent. For example, a specialty chemical company that develops highly customized products found that its highest growth opportunity and profitability came from customers for whom it built highly customized solutions. It shifted its strategy from trying to sell to anyone in the market to building strong partnership-type relationships with its key customers. The company shifted its general market sales to an independent distributor network and focused the sales and development organization on expanding

the relationship with key accounts. Had this change not been accompanied by a major change in the company's sales compensation plan and an expansion of the incentive to include the development engineers, this strategy would have failed. Instead, it made a major difference to the company's increasing "customer share" and return on its assets.

3. Determining What People Want

People come to work for an organization for many reasons. Numerous studies have attempted to identify the decision criteria. Clearly, the reward system is not always the dominant reason people take a job. For many, it is the opportunity to work for a leader in an industry or for an organization that provides significant investment in training, development, and career opportunities. For others, the company may be geographically desirable, may provide opportunities for travel or discounts on products and services, or may involve the individual in relationships with other people of similar expertise in the company. Finally, many people are attracted by the compensation, benefits, employee services, and opportunities to receive incentive pay, stock options, or special awards. They become excited by the opportunities that are available to them as well as by the challenge of the work, the work environment, and the vision of the company's leaders.

The focus of a reward strategy needs to go beyond increasing a firm's ability to attract and retain individuals. Rewards must be meaningful to the performers, in addition to those in transition (either joining or leaving the organization).

It is critical to remember a simple but essential principle of effective rewards—the receiver, not the provider, determines the value. Companies often go to great lengths and expense in determining what is competitive in the marketplace but spend considerably little time and money determining if what they have is meaningful to their employees. While it is always critical to make sure that one's compensation and total reward programs are competitive, it is more important that people feel valued by what they receive.

There are essentially three ways to determine what people value. First, try different things and see what gets people to respond. Some organizations use short-term contests or performance campaigns to see what it will take to inspire people. Similar to the Hawthorne experiments on human motivation conducted in the 1950s,[1] one may find that any attention people receive likely will lead to increased performance and morale over the short term. However, companies need sustaining systems of rewards to achieve enduring results.

Second, ask people what they prefer. The Wilson Group, Inc., developed and conducted a "Personal Preference Survey" for a number of clients, and each survey revealed a number of important findings (Table 4-1). For example, through a number of surveys, it was determined that the top five factors of importance to individuals from their employers are

1. High-quality leadership
2. Health care benefits
3. Involvement in decisions
4. Paid personal time off
5. Challenging work assignments

However, on closer examination, it was learned that some of these wants differed based on education level, gender, and age of the individual. The top two factors, quality of leadership and health care, generally were consistent across all groups, except that individuals in their twenties favored career opportunities and training over health care benefits. It is interesting to note that direct compensation was not included in the top five priorities of any employee segment. This is generally consistent with other research on motivation[2] and employee opinion surveys.

When examining the other items on the preference list, male respondents preferred rewards based on individual performance, whereas female respondents preferred team-based rewards. Variable compensation, whether based on individual or team performance, and opportunities to receive stock options were preferred by younger employees more than by older employees (those 40 years and older). Employees in their thirties and forties preferred recognition programs more than did younger or older workers. While the database on which these conclusions are based is not sufficient to represent U.S. employment as a whole, the process of surveying employees to determine what they find meaningful has always yielded important findings.

Finally, a more personalized approach to identifying what people value is to observe what choices they make when they have the freedom

Table 4-1 What People Want from Their Employer

| Rewards Preference Items | All | Educational Levels | | | Gender | | Age Groupings | | | |
		High School and Associate's	Bachelor's	Master's and Above	Male	Female	20s	30s	40s	50s+
High-quality leadership	4.40	4.28	4.42	4.50	4.28	4.47	4.28	4.41	4.78	4.25
Health-care benefits	4.38	4.69	4.17	4.38	4.23	4.47	4.37	4.31	4.48	4.38
Involvement in key decisions	4.27	4.22	4.23	4.35	4.30	4.25	4.31	4.28	4.26	4.25
Paid personal time off	4.23	4.33	4.10	4.32	4.13	4.29	4.19	4.31	4.35	4.25
Challenging work assignments	4.16	4.03	4.25	4.18	4.15	4.17	3.98	4.28	4.35	4.25
Involvement in work-process redesigns	4.15	4.17	4.25	3.97	4.02	4.24	4.13	4.28	4.22	4.06
Regular performance and salary reviews	4.09	4.06	4.02	4.21	3.98	4.16	4.09	4.29	4.04	3.88
Training for future job assignments	4.08	4.06	4.12	4.06	3.94	4.17	4.30	4.18	4.00	3.31
Career advancement opportunities	4.03	4.31	4.02	3.74	4.11	3.99	4.59	3.83	3.91	2.63

Source: Wilson Group, Inc., Concord, MA.

to do so. If the individual enjoys travel or sporting events, rewards that offer these experiences should be well suited. If the individual uses his or her free time to be involved in community, church, or civic activities, giving one the opportunity and resources to pursue these activities likely will be more meaningful than a trip. If an individual pursues creative endeavors in art, music, or woodworking, for example, providing support to these activities as a reward may have a significant impact. This simple, obvious concept also has been well researched.[3]

The fundamental concept is to enable people to earn the things they value for doing or achieving outcomes the organization needs in order to be successful. The person determines the meaning and value of the rewards; the organization determines the basis on which one will receive them. If both get what they want, then rewards have facilitated an important win-win relationship as long as they do not become exploitive to either party.

4. Selecting the Programs That Fit Strategically

Having determined what people want from their employment relationship, a fundamental question emerges regarding what the organization should do. Are rewards only cash compensation? Do rewards include a more challenging job, flexible work schedules, or a simple "thank you" by one's manager? Do rewards include health care benefits, training, access to specialized equipment, involvement in decisions, or membership in task forces or internal committees? Must all rewards be contingent on performance? The simple answer is "yes" because we have defined rewards as programs, processes, and practices that influence the things that people do. However, rewards must not be considered as a quid pro quo or as reinforcing only a transactional relationship.

To organize diverse programs and services, we can view them in categories that reflect their function. This is shown on Figure 4-2.

Organizations provide programs, services, and experiences for a variety of reasons. Some programs can be based on one's membership in an organization, and others can be based on one's performance. By *membership*, we mean that people receive these services or have the opportunity to participate in these programs as a right of joining the organization. People who are not employees cannot receive them. For example, health care benefits usually are provided to all employees based on their joining the firm; they are not reserved for only the highest performers in the company. Some programs may be provided to an individual based on his or her role in the organization; executives receive higher salaries and also may receive supplemental benefits or perquisites (e.g., parking). Because some programs are provided based on membership does not mean that everyone receives them equally. The requirement is that one needs to be in a specific position or meet some other requirement to receive them.

Performance-based rewards, however, are based on actions and results, and individuals may not receive them equally, even those with the same job. Performance may be determined by the achievements of the individual, team, group, division, or even the overall company. For example, when a company has a profit-sharing program for all employees, it is a performance-based reward because the awards are based on the performance of the company even though everyone receives a payout. When a program or service is given regardless of the performance, it belongs on the membership side of the ledger.

The second dimension categorizes programs into whether they provide cash and related compensation or tangible, symbolic, or work-related rewards. Cash-based programs provide payments to individuals, such as salaries, bonuses, stock options, and so on, whereas work-related rewards provide benefits and services that people normally would buy for themselves, such as health, life, or disability insurance. The importance is that cash-based programs can have a material impact on the lifestyle and standard of living of the individual.

Work-related programs and services provide rewards that are symbolic and meaningful to the individual. These are programs that people can share with other employees or teams that have achieved common objectives. The importance of these rewards is how they provide meaningful recognition and appreciation by the organization. For example, recognition programs are regarded as symbolic programs that can fall into either category—membership- or performance-based. If employees receive awards for years of service (10-year, 20-year, or greater awards), then this is a membership program. If there is an employee appreciation day or a companywide party or event, this is regarded as a membership program, even though it may provide opportunities for recognition. Recognition that heralds a team for achieving a major milestone is a performance program. A company that has special pro-

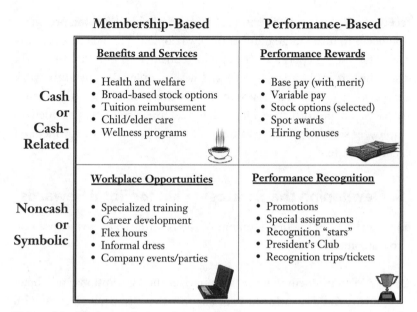

Figure 4-2 Total reward system framework.

grams for sales staff, such as a "president's club" or "winners circle," is fostering a recognition-type program in which the ability to participate is based on one's performance.

This framework provides a way to classify reward programs into four different types based on their focus and structure. Once an organization assigns each of its existing reward programs to one of these classifications, it needs to ask some strategic questions:

1. Where do we place the greatest reliance and dollars in terms of employees, and is it consistent with the firm's strategy and values.
2. Should we lead the marketplace, be competitive, or lag the marketplace?
3. What programs are the most and least effective in creating value for employees?

In addition to these competitive assessment questions, this framework should be used to determine which programs best fit with the requirements of the organization and the wants of the targeted group of individuals. If the organization is seeking to provide a stronger reliance on performance-based programs, then is the program likely to be received with support or resistance by key individuals? If the organization needs to hire a large number of new people while retaining the current staff, then perhaps it should consider programs that will distinguish it in the marketplace and with people who currently work for the company. This does not mean that there should be little emphasis based on performance but rather that the programs provided to employees should be highly valued so that the company can attract and retain new talent.

5. Developing the Strategic Plan for Total Rewards

This final step in the development of the reward strategy is focused on two outcomes:

1. A plan or document that summarizes the assumptions and objectives and a plan for how to support the business's strategy with rewards.
2. A clear definition of the requirements for each of the specific reward programs and how they are integrated into a strategic framework.

The primary value of this documentation is that it provides a basis for assessment, discussion, decision making, resource allocation, and accountability management. The plan also may serve as the standard against which the effectiveness of current programs can be assessed or new programs can be devised and implemented. One of the greatest benefits companies receive from this task is the ability to establish priorities for investment and development as well as the reduction of programs that either are counterproductive or are wasting resources. Alignment between the strategy and the actions of people can strengthen the commitment and ability of the firm to succeed.

If the total rewards plan is limited or a minor element of the firm's strategic plan, efforts to enhance reward systems will not be considered to create value. While the emphasis of the business must remain clearly on its strategic and operational tasks, the reward strategy can define a clear set of consequences for achievement of the key objectives.

Further, this reward strategy can serve to focus executives, managers, and human resource or other professionals on what is necessary to encourage and reinforce the actions needed to be taken by people within the organization. As we saw earlier, the business's strategic plan will serve to provide focus, the periodic reviews of progress and other information systems will keep the required attention on objectives, and the reward programs will sustain the motivation, commitment, and performance of people who are so critical to successful plan implementation. Examples of reward strategies are given in Figures 4-3 and 4-4.

Reward Strategy Case Studies

To demonstrate reward strategies in action, let's examine several case studies. These are actual companies, but their names have been changed. Each company is facing different conditions, and each obviously has established different but strategically significant reward strategies to support the businesses. In addition to the companies' financial, marketing, and operational plans, they have a "people-based plan" that has as much value and importance as the others.

The Case of the Turnaround Company

Brown Electronics Company is fighting for its life. Over the last several years it has faced increased competition, primarily foreign, for its markets. The competitors have been able to introduce similar products at a 10 to 15 percent lower in price. The challenge Brown faces now is a competitive fight for survival.

The overall business strategy calls for multiple efforts to regain Brown's market leadership. The attention will be on meeting the competitive needs of its customers through providing costs and services that are tailored to customers' strategies. This will be accomplished through introduction of new products in specific areas that broaden Brown's product line, reduction of prices (and costs) of the current lines, and strengthening of face-to-face relationships with customers. Further, by increasing services and lowering prices, Brown seeks to retain customers. The implementation of this strategy will involve many members of the organization, not just management, sales, or customer servicepeople.

The implications of this strategic change for individuals at Brown Electronics will be significant. First, there has to be an increased sense

Key Objectives of Reward Programs

Base Compensation System
- Focus on competencies and paths
- Develop and apply
- Be competitive with market

Desired Behaviors
- Focus on the customer
- Personal initiative
- Teamwork
- Business responsibility
- Innovations
- Continual improvements

Variable Compensation System
- Supports team achievements
- Ties measures to strategy
- Focuses on both short and long term

Recognition Management Systems
- Recognize individuals and teams
- Reinforce service-oriented actions
- Be as immediate as possible

Figure 4-3   A reward strategy.

of urgency and responsiveness among staff members. Waiting for someone else to do something will lead to failure. Second, people need to focus on the core issues facing their customers and concentrate on using Brown's products and services to meet customer needs. This will require translating the customer profiles, Brown's competitive strategy, into measures and directives to which each individual can relate. Third, employees need to drive out any waste or low-value-added activities. They must reduce costs and speed up the process of work. Reports or meetings that are not necessary will have to be dropped. Materials and supplies will have to be used carefully to minimize losses.

Fourth, people need to treat one another, and especially customers, as partners. From now on, everyone will be viewed as someone to serve and appreciate. Finally, while the task of a turnaround is challenging, people need to see their accomplishments and feel valued by others. In this way, Brown Electronics plans to create a spirit of change and winning that will motivate its people and enhance performance as an organization.

As an element of this business strategy, Brown's senior management has decided to make specific changes in its reward systems. These changes focus on driving the activities Brown needs to alter its manner of conducting business. The reward strategy will include the following goals:

Salary Programs: **Enable us to attract, retain, and develop the talent we need to succeed**

1. Is competitive (50th to 75th percentile) with leading companies where we recruit for talent.
2. Reinforces roles and accountabilities.
3. Is flexible and supportive of our organization's growth and development.
4. Is responsive to specific market pressures or encourages internal development of talent.
5. Provides salary management guidelines so that decisions are made with confidence, integrity, and speed.

Incentive and Equity Plans: **Create a process to effectively reward people for their contributions to the success of the company**

1. Utilizes company-, business unit/department-, and individual-based variable pay where they make sense.
2. Provides for equity participation in relation to roles, contributions, and long-term impact.
3. Utilizes measures that are clear, strategically focused, and easily supported by our systems.
4. Provides rewards that are meaningful to the performer, consistent with our strategy, and reinforce our culture.
5. Is supported by clear, frequent communication and simple tools.

Benefits: **Provide programs that meet people's needs and are cost effective and utilize innovative programs that make us distinctive as an organization**

1. Be competitive (50th or 75th percentile) with companies our size and where we compete for talent.
2. Provide benefits that are truly meaningful to people, supported by highly effective communication and easy administrative support.
3. Provide some "special" benefits, services, or events that will make us distinctive in the marketplace and consistent with our culture and values.
4. Provide benefits that are cost effective from both an individual and a company perspective.

Recognition: **Utilize effective practices that are supported by innovative programs that reinforce our desired culture and make us a special place to work**

1. Reinforce individuals who make us more competitive, efficient, and important to our customers.
2. Reinforce teams that make us more efficient, lower our costs, and prevent mistakes.
3. Utilize a variety of programs, events, and activities that keep the process exciting.
4. Ensure that the process is fiscally responsible, administratively easy, and documented.
5. Utilize programs that are focused, flexible, and fun.
6. Facilitate communication, involvement, and high responsiveness to support the culture that we desire for the future.

Figure 4-4 Philosophy and purpose of key reward programs.

1. All levels of the company will identify and focus performance measures on the key factors of the organization's success that people can implement: product costs, delivery performance, responsive customer service, and new products that provide more complete solutions.
2. The reward strategy will emphasize variable compensation for organizationwide and team performance. Base pay increases will be used to reward selected individuals who make major contributions to the team or company. Performance management will be the process to integrate activities in setting goals, charting improvements in critical areas, and celebrating achievements that strengthen Brown's relationship with customers.
3. There will be less concern about the external competitiveness or internal equity of the company's pay rates as long as they remain within generally accepted parameters in the marketplace.
4. The company will increase the payout frequency of the incentive system to four times a year in line with the increased sense of urgency. This means restructuring the incentive plans so that each quarter stands on its own and there are no payments for cumulative performance. Make each quarter a battle that has to be won.

The Case of the Rapidly Growing Firm

Armistead Beverage Products is enjoying the benefits of a market that is coming to its door. Armistead's products began as specialty items in convenience and small grocery stores, but changes in consumer demand have made them increasingly attractive, and the company is experiencing record-setting growth.

The challenge to Armistead is that competition is also increasing, particularly from major market players (Coca-Cola, Pepsi, etc.). Armistead does not have the marketing resources to withstand a direct attack on its market position, so it needs to remain flexible, responsive, and quality-focused. It also needs to develop a reward strategy that will retain the qualities of its current culture while enabling it to attract, retain, and manage new people.

The essence of this challenge is to support the firm's growth while retaining the values that have made the company distinctive in the market.

Armistead's key success factors require a continual focus on the customer and continual improvement in the work process, maximization of current resources and minimization of new costs, assimilation of new people into the firm's culture, an emphasis on individual efforts, and a focus on teams that work strongly together and produce desired outcomes. The corporate culture itself needs to develop and change without creating the weight of traditional bureaucratic organizations.

Armistead's reward strategy seeks to accomplish three major objectives. First, it must be sufficiently competitive to enable Armistead to attract and retain the talent it needs. This will entail creating a combination of base pay, incentive pay, and equity-related programs tailored to attract the expertise needed and make the firm clearly superior in the marketplace. Armistead needs to provide average levels of base compensation but significantly higher incentive opportunities than its larger competitors.

Second, Armistead needs to ensure that the base-pay program and the incentive program do not reinforce a bureaucratic philosophy of management and do not become an entitlement. People must not become complacent about the rewards they receive. The measures must focus on customer requirements, not on the subjective needs of managers. The feedback process must be real time, not delayed to tie in with annual events. The data must provide people with the information necessary for them to respond to rapidly changing conditions. Finally, the firm needs to reinforce actions that enhance the firm's competitiveness. This effort will focus primarily on special teams but must ensure that teams value their individuals members. In this way, Armistead can leverage all the talent potential of the firm to compete aggressively with others who may be larger or have deeper pockets. While bureaucracy and controls may entangle competitors, Armistead will be different.

The Case of the Renewal Company

Pierce Manufacturing Company has a long history of quality products and industry leadership. It is a large company with manufacturing and customer centers located throughout the world. Although it enjoys a dominant share of its primary markets, erosion is occurring in many of its key market segments. Competition is appearing within its industry as well as from new entrants to the market. Pierce's top executives are realizing that if the firm does not increase its rate of improvements, it will soon face major problems. Although the firm has an established vision statement and has made significant investments in total quality management efforts, only modest improvements in results have been seen.

To meet the challenge, Pierce's executives have developed, in combination with several special task forces throughout the organization, a strategy to improve the competitiveness of the firm and to move the company back to its position as a market leader in its primary segments. The strategy entails focusing on core strategic business units (SBUs) and developing specific investment, marketing, and organizational plans around them.

The executives have decided that a new reward strategy is necessary to reinforce these change efforts. The implications of this strategy for behaviors will be quite important. First, corporate executives need to let go of their traditional approach to control. They need to focus on encouraging the SBUs to formulate and execute strategies to build their businesses into primary market leaders. Investment decisions need to be made according to what will benefit the SBUs and in turn create synergy across lines of business. Second, managers need to take greater risks and challenge the assumptions of past practices. If the firm is to regain its competitive strength, some actions must be retained and others changed. Each SBU needs to determine this difference and support the changes required. Finally, the firm must integrate new investments in technology or work processes to build its competitiveness quickly. This means reducing the walls that divide divisions, minimizing internal competitiveness, and focusing on serving the changing needs of Pierce's internal and external customers.

The firm's executives have decided to decentralize the current control-oriented pay system in the divisions. Each division will develop its own reward strategy and programs to support its business plans. The corporation will manage general employee benefits, such as health and retirement plans, but each division can be as creative as it wants around special employee services, such as child care centers, special leave policies, and so on.

Although each SBU will create its own reward strategy, there will be some common themes. First, incentive plans will be developed around the key success factors of each SBU. In most cases, the measures will include factors related to product quality, customer satisfaction, and expense control. Some divisions will create incentive plans for new product introductions, delivery times, and customer service. Second, the base-pay plans will seek to address individual performance. While most divisions will focus merit pay around individual contributions to team performance, a few divisions will develop pay-for-competencies-employed programs. In these cases, the firm will seek to reward employees for increasing their skills as new technology, process manufacturing, and product development strategies are implemented. Finally, the performance management process will become the centerpiece for managing performance on a day-to-day basis. The focus will not be on appraising performance but rather on providing people with the measures, feedback, and reinforcement they need to excel in their work. In this way, Pierce is making the process of change and renewal real, positive, and meaningful to its employees.

Summary

A reward strategy is a process by which a firm translates its competitive business strategy into a series of programs and initiatives that will have a positive impact on human behavior. A reward strategy that focuses only on establishing a desired position in the external marketplace will not be effective in driving needed change. Only when the strategy defines what new behaviors are needed and builds systems and practices to reinforce these behaviors do the desired changes become real. The reward strategy provides an overall architecture or blueprint to guide changes in pay and performance management systems. In this way, people can both see and feel a difference in their work environment. The change in performance, coming about from a change in daily actions, will produce the results necessary for the firm to survive and prosper. Behaviors are the raw materials for implementing a competitive strategy, and reward systems are the core tools needed to create the conditions where people take the initiative to change. Reward systems help employees know what to do and why they should do it. Reward systems also help an organization marshal the resources of its people to create a win-win experience for all.

Be Careful What You Measure and Reward

Measures give relevance to rewards;
rewards give meaning to measures.

Thomas B. Wilson

IN PREVIOUS CHAPTERS we reviewed the factors that affect the performance of both organizations and individuals, as well as different models for defining an organization's strategy and the importance of translating them into a meaningful focus for the organization.

The fundamental purpose of measurement systems is to provide the translation mechanism between what an organization needs to do to be successful and the actions people need to take to make it happen. Measures are based on information systems or at least the assessment, observation, and feedback on how well something produced meets the needed specifications.

The performance of people often defines an organization's competitiveness in the marketplace. However, customers define the success of an organization by deciding whether to do business with the company or with one of its competitors. This means that performance is determined fundamentally by whether the needs of customers are being met. In today's marketplace, customers have more choices than ever. If an organization is able to institute measures that reflect the needs of its customers and if its people act accordingly, the organization clearly will have a competitive advantage.

This chapter examines ways to develop performance measures that focus on the needs of customers and thus increase an organization's value for its shareholders and other stakeholders.

Traditional Approaches to Performance Measures

Conceptually, performance measures are supposed to reflect an organization's strategy and key drivers of value. However, many such measures wind up being used for controlling the operation or as a "game" to enhance the wealth of selected individuals. For example, such measures as error rates, number of units per time period, customer complaints, scrap rates, absenteeism, and government or safety compliance encourage managers to find problems in current performance. Managers, naturally, respond by seeking ways to exert greater control over the operation and its people rather than taking actions that will engage people in taking responsibility for improving performance. As a result,

1. Performance measures are used to identify problems and highlight the points at which performers are not meeting standards.
2. Performers are required to complete reports to senior managers but get little or no feedback from them. Thus the information goes "upstream," and the performers see little in return.

It is not surprising, therefore, that performance measures have acquired a bad reputation. For example, when a company announces that it has hired an external consulting firm to develop performance measures and systems, the response is likely to be one of fear and concern among the performers involved. Few people look forward to implementing new measurement systems. Performers may ask publicly or privately, "Will this effort identify what we are not doing right, and/or will it simply require more work for us to collect and provide data to management? Will it lead to layoffs and/or some other punitive action?"

Dr. Edwards Deming, who is best known for his development of statistical process control techniques in total quality management (TQM), stipulates as one of his key points: "Eliminate work standards (quotas) on the factory floor. Substitute leadership. Eliminate management by objectives. Eliminate management by numbers, numerical goals. Substitute leadership."[1] His reasons are very clear. Managers often use measurement systems to control and punish workers. The normal response is to avoid being measured, seek ways to do just enough to get by, and negotiate with the manager. These are low-value-added activities because they emphasize the relationship between the manager and the performer rather than focusing on improving the work and better serving the customer. Subsequently, both managers and employees resent being measured at work.

The performance achievement model and the leadership approach presented in this book seek to change this association. Measures should be used to engage people at all levels in the business of the organization and create many opportunities for rewards and positive reinforcement. As Deming points out, the emphasis must shift from setting standards to using measures to monitor and manage work activities. Going one step further, we can use measures to build the bridge between the strategy of the organization and the people who bring it into reality.

Many executives are concerned about providing too much information to their employees. They hold certain beliefs about employees' response to data. These include the following:

1. *Employees won't understand or care about the information.* They won't have the sophistication to comprehend the data or use them effectively. They won't even be interested in them, so it will be a waste of time.
2. *Employees will use the information against management.* Once they figure out how much profit is really being generated by their performance, they will want more of it. They will seek more resources for their business unit or more compensation for themselves.
3. *Employees will give the information to the competition.* If employees really understand the competitive strategy of the business, they

will somehow leak it to a competitor, who will then use the information against the company.

These assumptions have some merit. Employees will not understand the data or care about them unless the information is presented in terms to which they can relate. This makes it the executives' responsibility to translate corporate measures of economic returns, market share, and product positioning into terms that employees can understand. An initial process of education is required before employees can fully relate to the numbers that executives deal with on a daily basis.

InterMetro, Inc., a manufacturer of industrial shelving products, provided a series of infomercials for its workforce on understanding product costs, gross margin, customer returns, and production forecasts as part of its biweekly business updates. It took approximately 3 months before management could use a common set of concepts and language to discuss the ongoing state of the business. The process was based on the need to create economic literacy in the workforce. This information was part of the feedback process in support of the company's goal-sharing program and has become a very important element in building the desired partnerships within the workplace.

Management's concern that the information may fall into the hands of competitors is usually unfounded. More competitive information is lost by way of executives and senior technical contributors who are hired by competitors than by way of disgruntled members of the workforce. In most cases, little useful competitive information is provided through such sources. Further, the success of a competitive strategy lies more in the execution of a company's own efforts than in knowing about a competitor's plans. The information provided to employees through performance measures is seldom of interest to competitors except in terms of benchmarking performance levels.

For all these reasons, the focus of performance measures needs to shift from one of withholding and controlling to one of providing sufficient information in a timely and understandable manner so that performers take decisive actions responsibly. Measures need to become a scoring system for understanding how well a strategy is being implemented or achieved. Finally, executives should not protect employees from bad news but rather use such situations to refocus or mobilize people to greater levels of performance. This will happen when measures are associated with support and reinforcement, not blaming or hunting for the guilty party.

Developing a New Purpose for Performance Measures

Performance measures, in their most fundamental state, translate the strategic requirements of a business into actions that people can take. In this context, they serve several important purposes:

1. *Measures provide the focus for taking action.* When performance measures are effective, people know what to do. They bring the vision into focus. They bring the strategy into everyday consciousness. They identify the critical priorities of the business. They define what is expected and what will be inspected. They become the basis on which people take, or do not take, certain actions.

2. *Measures provide the basis for monitoring work activities.* Measures provide the information necessary to supply feedback to the performer. They enable performers to know whether or not they are taking the correct actions. Further, they provide a basis for establishing desired performance levels. Measures need reference points, such as historical or baseline performance, competitors' benchmarks, or corporate objectives. These reference points provide meaningful milestones or calibrations for monitoring activities. The desired end point is reached when the performers themselves track, monitor, and display their own performance data, making them more immediately useful, usually more reliable, and surely more meaningful.

3. *Measures provide the basis on which the organization rewards performance.* Measures that are used to threaten people will result in situations in which people avoid or manipulate data. They may indicate that certain performance levels are impossible to reach or that certain activities cannot be measured reliably. When measures are used for rewards and learning, people are more likely to appreciate them because they associate them with gaining something they want or value. These gains may be external, such as praise from managers, peers, or customers, or internal, such as

the inner satisfaction of seeing a process take shape in some desired fashion.

This process is clearly reflected in our use of measures for personal, non-work-related activities. Most sports activities, for example, such as golf, bowling, baseball, and tennis, have scoring systems built in; the measurement system defines the game. For other activities, such as cooking, sewing, painting, jogging, hiking, fishing, and skiing, we use different kinds of measures and define success in terms of exceeding our own "personal best" level of performance. When measures are linked with reinforcing progress, they become natural to the activity and desired by the performers. Imagine if an organization had the same level of excitement and enthusiasm about setting certain goals as a sports team (and its fans) does about scoring points.

Measurement systems are an integral part of any purposeful human activity. They need to be used in ways that create a rewarding environment to encourage performers to go on striving to do their very best. In the work environment, the focus of these measures needs to be on meeting the needs of customers.

Developing Performance Measures That Link with the Strategy

A great deal has been written over the years about performance planning, management by objectives, and results. It is beyond the scope of this book to provide an in-depth description of various models or steps. However, several important elements need to be used to create meaningful measures. Further, a planning framework, with a clear understanding of the terminology, is important to support rigorous goal setting and measurement processes.

Figure 5-1 displays a flowchart with key planning process elements. There are five steps:

1. *Mission, vision, and the value proposition.* This first stage defines the reason the organization exists and its business model to create value for its customers and shareholders. Statements relating to these elements are enduring and provide a long-term perspective for the organization and its activities.

Figure 5-1 The link to strategic drivers.

2. *Core organizational values and culture.* Every organization has a culture that is a function of the norms, styles, and informal manner in which it operates. It provides the code of ethics and defines the true character of the organization. It provides the environment that distinguishes the organization from others and makes up its enduring qualities. Organizations that have a culture and operating set of values that are in alignment with the strategy and key success factors are always stronger in times of change and turbulence.

3. *Strategic initiatives and operating plans.* These are the plans that the organization uses to guide actions, make investment and resource allocation decisions, and fulfill its mission. There are both short-term (quarterly or annual) plans and long-term plans (3 to 10 years). These plans may exist at the corporate level and translate down to business units, departments, and groups. Or the plans may be a "rollup" of operating companies into an overall enterprise. The outcomes of this phase may be a comprehensive strategic plan with specific objectives and commitments or informal, presentation-type plans with key points and objectives. The important output of this stage is a set of plans and directions that provides people with the focus they need to make decisions, allocate resources, and perform.

4. *Measures, goals, and milestones.* This stage is merely a next level down in the detail and specifications of the operating plans. Depending on the details of the strategic plans, these measures, goals, and milestones can refine and define what is expected. They indicate what will be monitored to assess the progress for implementing the strategy. They can be goals for divisions, units, or groups; milestones for projects of a particular function or area; or projects/programs that involve multiple areas of an organization in implementing key initiatives.

5. *Accountabilities, roles, and tasks.* This stage allocates the responsibilities for plans and activities so that groups and individuals are clear about what they must do and how they can contribute to the overall strategy of the organization. These provide short-term focus and are specific and action-oriented. They may define accountabilities that are unique to a particular individual or team or define how various accountabilities are shared across different functions of an organization. In short, this stage defines how the organization's strategy will be implemented "on the street."

Developing Performance Measures That Focus on Customers

Most traditional approaches to performance measures center on finding the factors that reflect the firm's strategy, that encompass what a person can control, or that create mechanisms to direct and control the work. When measures are oriented toward meeting the needs of customers, there is less concern about control and more focus on serving others. For many people, this is inherently a more meaningful process.

One approach builds measures and plans based on the customer. The model shown in Figure 5-2 describes a four-step process that begins with understanding the customer and ends with understanding what people need to do within the unit or target group. A measurement process that is focused on meeting the needs of customers will greatly increase an organization's chances of success.

The first step involves developing a customer profile:

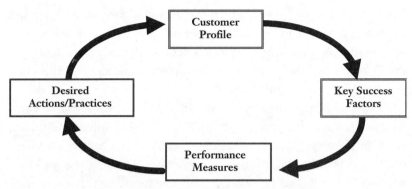

Figure 5-2 Establishing measures that drive success.

- Who are our customers?
- What do they want?

All groups within an organization have customers. The customers may be internal or external to the organization. This analysis should reflect a horizontal line of sight in the organization. Senior executives or shareholders are beneficiaries of the effort; they receive something of value in return for providing sponsorship and capital investments. However, they should not be customers. This is not to say that profitability and shareholder return are not important. They are a measure of success for the entire company and should be a concern for all. The question is, Does the company exist to generate shareholder value or to serve customers? We would suggest that organizations exist to serve customers so that shareholder value is created.

After identifying the customers, it is possible to identify or describe what the customers want. What exactly does the customer need from the unit's products or services? The requirements may include factors related to quality, delivery performance, reliability, low price, functionality, responsiveness, special design, and so on. A useful task in developing measures is to verify these requirements with customers or those with direct knowledge of customer needs.

The second step is to summarize the needs of the customers in terms of the key success factors (KSFs) of the unit. Most groups have multiple customers. KSFs are defined by assessing the risks and interdependencies in customer-supplier relationships. KSFs reflect the priority dimensions that determine whether the unit is successful. They are based on an understanding of customer wants as well as on the group's *core competencies*—the work the group does particularly well. KSFs are the link between these competencies, customer needs, and the value proposition of the organization.

The third step involves identifying the indicators that show whether or not the group is fulfilling its KSFs. These indicators, called *performance requirements*, should clearly relate back to customer needs and provide the information necessary for the group to know whether or not it is successful. Performance measures often are found in this step.

The fourth step involves identifying what behaviors on the part of the group are necessary to fulfill the performance requirements. These behaviors (which may include starting or increasing certain actions and/or decreasing or eliminating certain others) should be identified as specifically as possible so that the members of the group fully understand what they need to do to be successful in serving customers.

These four steps are illustrated in Figure 5-3 as a customer analysis for the Materials Management Department at St. Elizabeth Medical Center, a leading health care organization in Boston, Massachusetts, and they usually provide all the information necessary for selecting performance measures. The critical considerations in selecting the right measures include assessing both the environment and the opportunities for performance improvements. When clear, independent measures cannot be identified, the group may be too dependent on others to achieve specific results. In other words, the performance of the unit depends more on factors in its environment than on the actions taken by people within it. It also can happen that the measures are appropriate but that the unit does not have the ability to track or perform the necessary actions. In either case, there is clearly a need to develop a deeper understanding of the performance requirements of the unit.

The Why and How of Performance Measures

Once an organization or unit has defined the requirements for performance, it is important to know exactly how to achieve them. This process, which is shown in Figure 5-4, links the desired results to a cascade of value-creating activities. The answers to the core question—

Customer Profile

Who	*What They Want*
Nurses	Supplies available when needed
Managers	Delivery of products as requested
Purchasers	Accurate inventory information
Executives	High level of service, minimum costs

Key Success Factors

Supplying the hospital's units so they can do their best

Keeping inventory levels to a minimum to improve cash flow

Matching actual inventory supplies to the general ledger

Ensuring that nursing and unit managers feel we are highly responsive to their needs

Performance Requirements

Fill rates equaling 95 percent (based on inspection of supply centers)

Inventory turns 14 times per year (to improve our cash flow)

Accuracy of inventory counts within 2 percent of accounting records

Nursing units that are satisfied with their supplies and our responsiveness

Turnover rates of our staff members being minimized, below hospital norms

Behavioral Requirements

Being on time on the job all the time

Being responsive to calls for assistance; communicating a sense of urgency

Coordinating the use of supplies with other areas of the hospital

Handling all materials in a safe manner

Going out of our way to communicate our courteousness and helpfulness to our customers

Making sure we account for all inflow/outflow of supplies so our records are accurate

---

Figure 5-3 Customer-focused performance measures.

How should this desired result be achieved?—form a flowchart that links results to actions. Once this first level of results is defined, the same question—*How* can this be achieved?—should be asked about each subordinate result, and the process should be continued until each of the desired actions, behaviors, or tasks has been sufficiently defined.

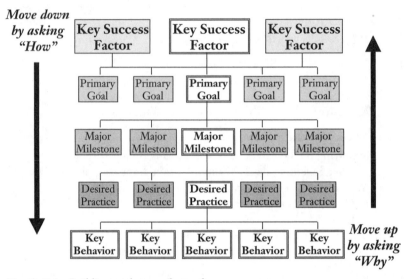

Figure 5-4 Building a value tree for performance measures.

The process can be verified by selecting a task or result and then asking: *Why* should this be done? The answer should lead one to the next level of the hierarchy. If intervening variables are discovered when one asks why, they either should be added to the next level up or take their place as an additional layer in the action-planning flowchart.

This process is similar to a Pareto analysis, root-cause analysis, or cause-effect diagram. The focus, however, is on the *value tree of actions* necessary to accomplish a desired end. By asking how and why, one can outline the tasks needed to achieve the required results and then pinpoint the measures needed to monitor the progress of performers in achieving them.

When to Use Results and When to Use Process

In some cases it is more important to focus on the actions that contribute to the desired results than it is to focus on the results themselves. While a results orientation is always critical to success, there are situations where the process is as important, if not more important (Figure 5-5).

One should focus on *results* when the following conditions exist:

Focus on __PROCESS__ when:	*Focus on __RESULTS__ when:*
• New skills or behaviors are required • Current performance is a long way from goals • There are many intervening variables • There are long time delays • How to achieve the goals is not exactly clear	• People are highly competent • Current results are relatively high • There is a direct relationship between the effort and achievements • Progress can be monitored frequently • People know what they need to do

Figure 5-5   Where to focus: process or results.

- The current results are at a relatively high level, and the desire is to encourage continued improvements.
- The results are clearly improving, and the desire is to reinforce this progress.
- The performers are highly skilled and competent to perform the tasks necessary to achieve the desired results.
- There is a high correlation between the actions people take and the results they achieve, reflecting the group's degree of control over the performance factors.

On the other hand, one should focus on *process variables* when the following conditions exist:

- The current performance is a long way from the goals.
- New skills and behaviors are needed to achieve desired results.
- The results are very delayed, or there is a long interval between what people do and the opportunity to measure the results.
- There are many intervening variables or forces outside the influence of the performers that affect the results.

If external factors are greater than internal factors, the measures should focus more on the specific actions people take or on the progress they make in the key result areas.

What It Takes to Make a Performance Measure Meaningful

Traditionally, performance measures are selected and used to focus the efforts of group members. Results-based measures are effective when they are

1. Objective
2. Outcome-oriented
3. Time-specific
4. Within one's ability to influence
5. Achievable and challenging

Consider these criteria: When measures are outcome- or results-oriented, they usually encourage people to focus on *what* is to be done. In cases in which there is a clear relationship between action and result, this is appropriate. However, *how* one achieves desired results is often left undefined.

When there is a single achievement level for a goal (i.e., pass or fail), people perceive this as an implied threat. A high-stretch goal indicates that the probability of achievement is remote. In such cases, the measures defining what the performers must do and do not show how well they are doing or improving.

Measures that reinforce desired performance should fit the following criteria (Figure 5-6):

Positive. Measures should be expressed in terms that the team members view as positive and create opportunities for tracking and celebrating progress. The terminology used should underscore the process. Instead of measuring late shipments, measure on-time

- **P**ositive
- **R**eliable
- **O**bjective
- **A**ction-Oriented
- **C**ontrollable
- **T**imely

Figure 5-6 Criteria for effective measures.

delivery; instead of measuring error rates, measure flawless rates or 100 percent accepted rates; instead of measuring amounts of cost reductions, measure the amount of savings achieved.

Reliable. The measures and methods of capturing the data should be consistently accurate and verifiable. These criteria should reflect both the nature of the data-collecting process and the administrative feasibility of providing the information. Further, administrative systems should be viewed as supporting elements rather than as restrictions and demands with which the measures must comply.

Objective. Measures should reflect the work that is actually performed. Judgments by a single individual can be biased or distorted by recent events. An assessment based on perception data collected from a large number of people who have received or observed the group's performance has considerably more credibility and objectivity. The measures need to reflect what is actually done, quantitatively or qualitatively.

Action-oriented. Measures need to reflect the aspects of work that the performer can do something about to achieve desired progress. If people actually can achieve the result by doing nothing, you do not have a good measure. For example, reducing waste can be accomplished by doing no work. The goal should be how to use 100 percent of the materials.

Controllable. Measures need to describe work or tasks that are within the influence of the performer. Although very little is actually within one's control, select measures that are to a high degree within the individual's or group's ability to affect. The reason is simply that the organization is preparing to pay additional compensation or rewards for achieving desired performance. It should know that what it is paying for is truly achieved by the performers. This ensures that the return on investment can be determined accurately.

Timely. Measures and feedback should reflect actions that can be determined on a timely basis, depending on the overall time frame of the business cycle—monthly, quarterly, annually, or longer. The measures should tell performers if they are not being successful in sufficient time to allow them to respond. Although there is little hard scientific evidence, our experience indicates that the performance data should be reviewed at least three to five times before an incentive payout is determined. In other words, if one has a quarterly incentive plan, the data should be provided to the performers at least monthly. If it is an annual plan, then quarterly or bimonthly feedback of progress is essential.

These six criteria produce the acronym *PROACT,* a shortened form of the critical word *proactive.*

The Types of Performance Measures That Make a Difference

Performance measures come in all shapes and sizes. A significant industry has evolved around the task of defining the performance measures that are right for a given business, as well as creating systems to integrate the activities of the business. The issue facing many executives is not the lack of measures but the lack of reliable data and their alignment with the strategy of the business.

Organizations often have a strong set of measures for assessing productivity, costs, and return on investment. These frequently are more suited to manufacturing or operational activities with clear and definable tasks. Measures become less clear, reliable, and attractive when they address the services of the business, the satisfaction of its customers, or the value that is created by functional departments or cross-functional efforts.

AT&T places significant emphasis on aligning measures with the competitive strategy of its business divisions. The company calls these measures the "Golden Threads" of the business. The hierarchy of measures model discussed earlier, the hows and whys, enhances the ability of a firm to trace measures through the organization. This is significant because when measures are clearly aligned with the key factors of a firm's success, they gain strength and importance to the people whose actions determine the performance.

One of the more useful tools in creating a portfolio of performance measures is the "balanced scorecard." R. Kaplan and D. Norton developed this concept, and it outlines the process of using a variety of measures within a strategic framework.[2] While organizations develop a variety of measures, they tend to fall into the areas of finance, internal business, innovation and learning, and customer satisfaction. Specific measures are then developed in each of these areas and monitored on a regular basis. This balanced scorecard approach expands the focus of executives from simple profitability, gross margin, and return-on-investment indicators of performance to the key drivers of the businesses success.

To be consistent with the framework outlined earlier on what drives individual and organizational performance, we can examine, as Kaplan and Norton have done, the requirements of the business to create value for customers and its owners or stakeholders. This framework and a set of associated measures are displayed in Figure 5-7. This model looks at performance measures from several perspectives. These are

1. *Resource-focused.* These are measures that imply the use of or the benefit received from the resources of the organization. These are measures that reflect the value that the organization creates, the return that is realized by shareholders or owners, the efficiencies of the organization, and the metrics related to the use of resources. In each of these categories, the organization has expended resources to achieve a result or desired outcome.

2. *Process-focused.* These are measures that relate more directly to "how things are done" in the organization. These measures determine how well the organization is meetings its market needs and opportunities and the needs of its customers. They also highlight the measures that build the capabilities of the organization to achieve future market requirements from its human resources and organizational practices.

3. *External-driven.* These are measures that reflect the marketplace in which the organization operates. The success of these measures is generally due to the effectiveness of the organization in serving its customers and other constituencies in the external market. If customers value what the organization provides, it receives financial returns and customer satisfaction.

4. *Internal-driven.* These are the measures that are more likely in the control of the organization and build the capabilities and functionalities that often enable it to achieve favorable results in the upper-quadrant areas (financial and customer metrics).

These dimensions form a framework for understanding and developing performance measures.

	Resource-Focused	Process-Focused

External-Driven	*FINANCIAL METRICS*
	Value Creation
	Revenue growth
	Revenue (product) mix
	Profit margins
	Revenue per employee
	Economic value added
	Market capitalization
	
	Shareholder Return
	Return on equity/
	  assets/capital
	Cash flow return on
	  investment
	Earnings per share
	
	Total shareholder return
		CUSTOMER METRICS
		Time to Market
		On-time delivery
		Cycle time—external
		New product development
		
		Customer Satisfaction
		Market share
		
		Customer feedback
		
		Account penetration/
		  no. of services
		Customer retention
		Quality of customer treatment

Internal-Driven	*OPERATIONAL METRICS*
	Operational Efficiency
	Budget to actual expenses
	Product/process quality
	
	Reliability/rework
	Accuracy/error rates
	Safety rates
	
	Cost per unit/transaction
	Resource Utilization
	Process improvements
	Inventory turns
	Cost reduction
	Project/plan
	  implementation
		CAPABILITIES METRICS
		Human Resource Capabilities
		Employee satisfaction
		Turnover/absenteeism/
		  safety incidents
		% implementing PM process
		Succession plan utilization
		% of employees with requisite
		  competencies
		
		Internal Effectiveness
		Service/quality index
		Cost of time per hire
		Project/plan implementation
		Response time to resolve
		  issues

Figure 5-7   Four categories of performance measures.

Financial metrics relate to the revenues, expenses, assets, asset utilization, and return generated from operations and investments. These are the measures that are used most frequently by organizations and reflect the true work of business.

To be specific, one of the measurement tools that has gained popularity in companies that are asset-intensive is the application of economic value added (EVA). In brief, EVA is determined by measuring the difference between net operating profit after tax and after the weighted cost of capital employed by the firm. The capital is defined by the total debt and equity of the firm, and cost of capital is determined by cost of debt (i.e., effective interest rates) and the cost of equity. The firm's historical performance generally is examined using the analytical tools of EVA and may be compared with companies in the same industry or with similar profiles. This provides executives with a framework to determine the true value that is being created by the organization through the application of its current operating and invested capital. This measure has been used determine executive compensation at several major companies, including Coca-Cola, AT&T, CSX, and Wal-Mart.[3]

Operational metrics show how well the organization is doing its activities on a day-to-day or short-term functional basis.

Customer metrics are often regarded as leading indicators of financial measures. These measures document how well the organization is doing in serving the needs of its customers and achieving the desired position in the marketplace. For many companies, for example, their success is defined by how well and how quickly they bring new products to the market and beat the lead times of their competitors. Companies are facing increasing pressures to reduce the lead times and ensure that customers receive the products or services when they need or want them. This has been a primary strategy of General Electric under the leadership of Jack Welch.[4] These are also the types of measures that rebuilt Sears into a market leader.[5]

Capabilities metrics are similar to Kaplan and Norton's "innovation and learning" sector, but in this case they are measures that reflect the current and future abilities of the organization to meet present and future needs. They include both people capabilities and internal process capabilities that produce directly or indirectly the outcome measures in the other sections of this framework.

In each quadrant, there are types of measures and examples of measures. The task of the organization is to examine which of these (or others that reflect the organization's mission and strategy) are the most directly linked to implementation of the company's strategy. The measures provide dimensions for which performance can be monitored and actions adjusted if progress is not satisfactory. They also provide the feedback systems the organization needs to reinforce progress, success, and learning.

One highly effective way to display measurement feedback is to use a focus board. In essence, this is a display of four to seven critical dimensions of performance for a business unit, such as a plant, division, project team, or company. These dimensions are listed across a large board. Under each dimension are the goals, measures, projects, or other reactions that support performance improvements. Further, some organizations use these boards to display progress and results. They may show charts, photographs of key players, comments from customers, and so on. Hence these boards create a visual display of the primary drivers of the business and create opportunities to reinforce the progress and the performers.

Once again, their alignment with critical competitive strategies and their meaningfulness to and association with formal and informal rewards for an organization's members determine the value of performance measures.

How to Make Performance Measures Meaningful

Executives and managers often are very preoccupied with performance measures. There is a belief that if one gets the performance measures right, the right actions will follow. Organizations often spend thousands, if not millions, of dollars on developing performance measurement systems. Measures are used to provide managers with the information necessary to take action. Often employees view such actions as punitive. When new systems are effective, people will start to respond to the new information in the desired ways. When desired performance is not realized, managers tend to increase the pressure in various ways (by yelling louder, for instance).

We can understand the role of measurement and feedback systems when we view them from the perspective of the performer. If a team is made aware that late shipments are a serious problem for the customer, measuring on-time performance will not cause resentment. Measures used to enhance workers' understanding of quality—in relation, for example, to completion of a report, production of a component, or handling of a sales call—empower those workers to focus their skills on achieving the quality desired. Measures provide meaningful and immediate feedback to performers so that necessary actions can be taken.

Without such information, the quality of the product or service produced may be inconsistent.

From a manager's perspective, performance measures can become a vehicle for communicating what is important about the operation of a given unit. Whether linked with the strategic plans that guide an organization, with product-development schedules, with productivity levels, or with costs, performance measures provide an important means of communicating with the workforce.

If performance is not at the desired level, a manager can take action to improve understanding of the goal and measure or pinpoint the problems or barriers to performance. These corrective steps will work if the performers associate these tasks with achieving more desired consequences. They will fail to work if, after providing the additional reports or collecting more data, the performers hear nothing about the results. Without any response as to whether the information was of any value, was correct or incorrect, or was even read by anyone, performers will see the measurement system as just adding unnecessary work. In the behavioral science research literature, this process is called *extinction* (see Chapter 2). The natural response to little feedback or positive/negative consequences is to gradually stop doing the action or finding other ways to reinforce one's own actions internally. Where once the activities were viewed as important, the measures and actions have lost their meaning because people did not see any consequences resulting from their actions.

To keep measurement systems from becoming associated either with extinction (no one cares) or with compliance (do just enough to get by), they need to be supported by meaning, high-impact rewards, and recognition. Ideally, these rewards will be associated with the work itself. Natural consequences are similar to intrinsic rewards— meaning that the performers find great satisfaction in their work. Measures can make this possible by providing performers with new information that enables them to greatly improve the quality or value of their work. The external sources for positive feedback can come informally from one's supervisors, peers, employees, or customers. In such cases, measurement systems become associated with developments that enrich the value and contribution the performers associate with the work they do.

To summarize, performance measures can accomplish several important tasks:

1. *They add importance to the work.* After a work process, procedure, or desired practice is explained to performers, measures aligned with the process, procedure, or practice priorities can provide necessary information on how well the employees are performing in these areas. The measures demonstrate that the actions or results support the strategy of the company. They give concrete reality to the directives given to individuals or work teams. If something is worth doing, it is worth measuring.

2. *They provide a source of feedback to performers.* Performance measures are meaningful only when they generate useful feedback. In fact, it is difficult to separate measures from feedback. In this context, feedback is not a judgmental assessment of performance but actual, real-time data about work done. Measurement information that is not given to the performers involved is a waste. While managers may be the beneficiaries of the information, the performer is and should be the primary receiver of the measurement information. (In our experience, misdirection of feedback is the root cause of the inability of many organizations to realize any value from measurement systems.)

3. *They create opportunities for providing rewards and reinforcement.* Compensation or recognition programs are the most important element of effective measurement systems. Measures provide the link between desired performance and additional pay and rewards. In goal-sharing or team-incentive plans, they define the results the team must achieve to receive incentive payments (see Chapter 10). In individual pay-for-performance programs, they define the expectations and contribution requirements. In special recognition programs, they form the basis for giving recognition (see Chapter 12). In pay-for-competencies-employed systems (see Chapter 7), they form the basis for assessing competencies and rewarding growth. In short, they define the difference between real reinforcement and general "atta boy/atta girl" responses.

Summary

Under the old management paradigm of control, the role of the manager was to use measurement and information systems to find out which employees were not performing their assignments correctly. Information was used to play "gotcha" with the employees. In fact, many of today's employee safety programs work by encouraging employees to report on their coworkers—a way of using fear to manipulate behavior in the workplace. This is not collaboration, and it does not create flexible, responsive, and competitive organizations. People may in fact simply complain, feel helpless, or employ their talents and energies outside the workplace. A job becomes just work.

Performance measures in a collaborative environment are used to provide performers with information on progress as quickly as possible, to empower them to correct their mistakes or celebrate desired achievements, and to create opportunities for communicating the value and importance of their efforts. Measures are important to everyone in the organization, not just management. They will enhance the view that one's work creates value, contributes to something important, and provides individuals with something they value for what they do, thus providing a new and meaningful use of measurement systems.

II

Implementing Innovative Reward Strategies

REWARD STRATEGIES that remain simply innovative ideas do not serve organizations. Results come from ideas that are put into practice and integrated into an organization's way of doing business. If this is done effectively, such ideas change the organization in directions that support its strategy, stakeholders, and future. Moreover, there is probably no change that has more impact on an organization than that which influences the actions people take.

The purpose of the chapters in Part II is to provide an in-depth examination of specific reward programs. This information will enable you to assess the structure of current programs, as well as determine how they operate within your organization, and to identify areas that need to be reinforced, changed, or discarded. Further, we provide guidelines for designing or redesigning programs, checklists and tools for adapting to your own environment, and many case studies.

Chapters 6 and 7 examine base pay or salary programs. We will look at how they work and how they should work, and we will outline several alternative approaches from which you can determine which program will work best for your organization. Chapter 8 looks carefully at the performance management process. Although this process can help you to integrate a variety of reward programs, it is presented after the chapters on salary programs because of the link often made between salary increases and performance management programs. We will see that performance management can and should extend its impact well beyond just determining pay increases.

Chapters 9 and 10 explore variable-pay programs and how they can and should be used to drive dynamic performance. We will examine a number of programs, as well as best-practices research and success criteria. Chapter 11 covers what needs to occur "between the paychecks," otherwise known as recognition of performance. We will examine a number of principles, best-practices research, and applications of these programs to different work situations. These programs often are simple to design but are a greater challenge to implement and sustain on a consistent basis. Chapter 12 is devoted to stock options and other equity sharing tools. In short, equity programs, whether they are "real," meaning they use restricted stock, stock options, or similar inducements, or "simulated," meaning they use various phantom, long-term cash incentives, or similar approaches, have become a major element in the employment proposition. One needs to know the terms and tools that are currently available and examine a variety of case studies or applications on how they work. While the laws in this area differ greatly from country to country and continue to change in response to various high-visibility events, these programs are likely to remain an important element of total compensation.

Some of the ideas presented in Part II may be regarded as traditional, whereas others may be viewed as novel or outrageous. We find that innovation is a relative term—meaning that it all depends on the frame of reference of the person considering the ideas. The various approaches presented here are provided with the expectation that each person will identify specific ideas on which to build programs or practices that will result in the changes that will lead to success.

If you are not in a position to make the changes outlined in these pages, the information should serve as an educational resource to aid you in becoming aware of how and why specific programs work the way they do. Perhaps in this material you will find new ways to use existing programs in innovative and significant ways. The power and impact of these programs are not based on their design but rather on how they are put into practice. This section should provide an in-depth understanding of how you can make better use of what you have or build the support you need to spur necessary change.

6

Make Salaries a Defining System of the Organization

The greatest waste in America is failure to use the abilities of people.

W. Edwards Deming, *Out of the Crisis*, 1986

V IRTUALLY EVERY ORGANIZATION has a base salary program for compensating its employees. These programs provide employees with paychecks of a fixed amount at regular intervals. Base salary programs are the foundation of the economic contract between individuals and their employers.

The salary/wage is a primary element of the discussion when a new employee is hired and when a person is promoted to a new position. This frequently defines the size of the job in relation to the new employee's previous experience. The pay levels are often set through a system of market pricing, job evaluation, and salary administration.

Base pay accounts for most of an organization's compensation expenditures—as high as 50 to 70 percent of its total costs in some companies. Hence these programs are important elements of costs and the ability of the company to attract and retain talent.

In this chapter we will examine how current base pay systems function, assess their effectiveness, and examine alternatives to enhance or reform them. Among these alternatives will be both simple and sophisticated approaches to addressing the fundamental flaws in base pay systems.

There is perhaps no other reward system within an organization that has caused more agony than base pay. In many organizations, no one seems satisfied with his or her current pay level. There are continual pressures to increase pay levels, either to keep pace with inflation or to increase the economic well-being of employees. There are equal pressures to reduce them, through salary cost controls, minimal increases, or headcount reductions. Pay increases often become a process in which work is reorganized or relabeled to justify a desired adjustment. Managers and employees often feel frustrated by the meager increase available in salary budgets, and compensation managers are often rewarded for their ability to control these costs.

Increases in base pay become annuity costs to the organization; they compound year after year. Table 6-1 shows how a $30,000-a-year salary can grow to $38,289 in just 5 years at an annual increase rate of 5 percent; this is a 28 percent increase in costs and represents the effects of compounding pay increases. If the productivity of the organization does not increase by the same amount, payment costs lower gross margins or place pressure to raise prices. Both options will reduce the company's ability to compete in the global marketplace.

There *are* solutions to this complex array of issues. To find them, however, we need to understand how typical base pay systems work. We can then target specific strategies to enhance the value and return on investment in these expenditures.

Overview of Traditional Base Pay Systems

The purpose of a salary program is to enable the organization to attract and retain the employees it needs to conduct its business. (It is sometimes referred to as "show up" pay because, without it, people most

Table 6-I   The Compounding Impact of Base Pay Increases

Year	Base Pay	Pay Increase (5%)	% Increase since Year 1
1	$30,000	$1,500	--
2	$31,500	$1,575	5.0%
3	$33,075	$1,654	10.3%
4	$34,729	$1,737	15.7%
5	$36,466	$1,823	21.6%
6	$38,289		27.6%

likely would not show up for work.) Such programs are often based on the pay levels of the marketplace. Salary surveys provided by consulting companies and industry associations offer much of this information. The market price for a job is then established, based on a comparison of the levels paid by other companies for jobs of similar scope, the organization's desired level of competitiveness, and the amount the organization can afford to pay. Consideration of these industry-established pay levels is particularly important for organizations hiring a great number of people or vulnerable to losing critical talent.

Edward Lawler of the Center for Effective Organizations at the University of Southern California and author of many books on compensation systems voices a commonly held belief that employees value themselves in relation to the marketplace.[1] If a competitor organization offers more money to an individual, the employee likely will change companies. While people often do have a sense of their worth in dollars, Lawler believes that employees have a full understanding of the marketplace pay rates and frequently seek to test the waters regarding pay opportunities. With the rise in availability of salary data on the Internet, this task is becoming easier to accomplish; hence he recommends that base pay levels be based on a careful examination of competitive market data.

Employees use a variety of sources to determine the fairness of their pay. Some people always compare themselves with someone who is higher up or paid more and then use this information as a justification to feel dissatisfied. Others see how far they have come or compare themselves with their parents and feel satisfied (sometimes). While pay satisfaction is interesting, there is no clear evidence that it has any impact on behaviors (except at the extreme levels). Instead, pay dissatisfaction is often more a reflection of a lack of positive feedback and reinforcement in the workplace. Consequently, many executives and compensation professionals address the wrong problem when they provide more pay to reduce dissatisfaction. A more effective approach would be to increase the amount and impact of performance-based rewards and recognition systems to enable people to feel valued by their contributions.

The conventional wisdom is that if an employee is generally satisfied with his or her job, a competitor needs to offer between 10 and 15 percent more pay to get him or her to switch jobs. If this guideline is correct, the effective application of rewards can give an organization a competitive advantage by raising the perceived value of the rewards without increasing the costs. If the organization succeeds in helping its employees feel important for their work, it can spend less to *keep* them than other firms would need to "buy" their talent. If employees are very dissatisfied or feel stuck in their current roles, the cost to retain them will be high; if employees feel rewarded and valued by the organization, the total costs will be much less. This means that compensation and reward programs can provide a real return on investment (ROI).

In addition to market data, many organizations use some form of internal comparison to rationalize their overall pay levels. Chapter 1 discusses the way traditional systems of job evaluation tend to mirror an organization's command and control of bureaucratic values. Organizations usually implement a job evaluation system in reaction to a compensation system that is viewed as out of control. The compensation system is then redesigned to ensure that pay practices will be seen as fair from an internal perspective, and this enables the organization to relate external market data to its internal pay levels.

The Need for a Structured Pay System

Let's examine how base pay systems operate by reviewing two brief case studies. They describe different situations with different issues but essentially the same approach to base pay.

Case I

Walden Widgets Company (a fictitious name but a real company) has been growing rapidly. In the past 3 to 4 years alone its employee population has grown from 125 to over 350 people. When the company was small, the president herself interviewed and made the final selection decision on every employee. As the firm grew, the managers interviewed and hired their own employees. As the organization grew still further, *their* managers interviewed and hired employees. With each hiring decision, compensation was established on the basis of what the individual wanted and what people were currently paid in the same department.

In the last few years employees have began discussing their pay with one another, and many have become very angry. In some departments, employees were hired at rates equal to or above those of others who have long service with the company. The marketing and sales employees have all received higher salaries than others in operations, finance, and emerging functions. As the organization grew, people promoted in some departments received large pay increases (as much as 15 to 20 percent), whereas others received much less (3 to 6 percent). The employees know which senior managers offer big salaries to their employees and which ones do not.

The frequency and severity of the complaints have increased. Employees have sought transfers or threatened their managers with quitting. In some cases, the managers have responded with pay increases; in others, they have not. The managers have become distrustful of one another because of these "deals." Salary ranges were created, but there has been no rationale for why people are put in any particular grade. Managers say that their pay system is based on the market, but the company does not participate in any surveys. The company is facing internal conflicts and morale issues because of its informal pay systems.

Case 2

Security National Bank (also a fictitious name but an actual organization) is made up of a confederation of 12 small to midsized banks. The chairman seeks to merge the affiliate banks into a single organization in order to increase the bank's overall ability to compete with other major financial institutions. The integration will involve a functional-based organizational structure, the centralization of certain operations, common product prices and credit policies, and centralized advertising and promotion. To support this strategy, a single salary program has become an effective way to create a "one organization" spirit in the bank. However, the current senior and middle managers are reluctant to give up their ability to set salaries or make promotions based on their own criteria. While this concern is well understood, the human resource function has been charged with using the development of a new total compensation framework, including salaries for all employees, that reflects the overall organization's principles and values.

How Salary Programs Usually Work

In both these cases, the organization is trying to create a single system of compensation in which the emphasis is on *internal equity and building an integrated organization*. By *internal equity*, we mean that individuals with similar levels of responsibilities and impact on the organization have similar compensation opportunities. Job evaluation is the process that assesses all jobs with a common set of criteria and relates them together in a ranking structure. This measurement process is in total points or grade levels. For example, jobs with 500 points are at a similar level, and that level is lower than jobs with 800 points.

The evaluation of the job usually is based on information contained in the job description, which is commonly prepared by the supervisor or manager of the position or someone in the compensation department. Some organizations have adopted questionnaires that involve job incumbents in describing the job responsibilities, and then the supervisor reviews the questionnaires. The intention is to decentralize the effort and involve employees in the task. Most job descriptions require the following information:

- Title of the job
- Title of the position to which the job reports
- Summary of responsibilities
- Budget, staffing, and other dimensions that the job controls and affects
- Primary accountabilities and responsibilities
- Decision-making authority
- Overall hiring requirements for knowledge, skills, or certifications

This information is then compared with the job-evaluation criteria to determine the appropriate level for the position. The job description also can be used for clarifying performance expectations, identifying dimensions for performance evaluation, developing selection criteria, and describing career paths. However, few organizations use job descriptions for more than communicating general accountabilities of the job and determining the salary grade level assignments.

The criteria used in most of these job evaluation systems fall into four basic areas:

1. Knowledge and skills:
   - Technical know-how
   - Specialized knowledge
   - Organizational awareness
   - Educational levels
   - Specialized training
   - Years of experience required
   - Interpersonal skills
   - Degree of managerial or supervisory skills
2. Performance effort:
   - Diversity of tasks
   - Complexity of tasks
   - Creativity of thinking
   - Analytical problem solving
   - Physical application of skills
   - Degree of assistance available
3. Scope of responsibility:
   - Decision-making authority
   - Scope of the organization under one's control
   - Scope of the organization where one has impact
   - Degree of integration of work with others
   - Impact of failure or risk associated with work
   - Ability to perform tasks without supervision
4. Working conditions:
   - Potential hazards inherent in job
   - Degree of danger that can be exposed to others (e.g., handling toxic materials)
   - Impact of specialized motor or concentration skills

- Degree of discomfort, exposure, or dirtiness in doing job
- Impact of work on personal relationships (i.e., travel)

The job-evaluation process sometimes involves applying a selected number of these factors to the position and determining an overall score for each. These scores are then weighted in a prescribed fashion to reach a final score. This process occurs in a variety of settings: (1) a group of people in a committee, (2) a small team of experts from the compensation department, or (3) through computer scoring of a questionnaire.

Regardless of the method used, all jobs within the organization are scored using the same criteria. This makes a rank order of the positions possible. This ordering of the positions into a series of grades or levels of pay can be compared with jobs within the same level and with available market data to determine the salary range that is most appropriate to jobs on each level.

Design and Market Pricing Techniques

Salaries are administered using a variety of decision tools. The first is the salary range. This range defines the minimum and maximum the organization is willing to pay for jobs of a specific nature. Positions with a similar job evaluation and marketplace reference have the same salary range. This salary range provides the guidelines necessary for the organization to manage compensation costs. Individuals at the lower end of the salary range are considered *learners*, and individuals at the upper levels are considered *high performers*, in that the organization is paying a discount or a premium, respectively, for their efforts. Individuals paid at around the middle of the range (also known as the *midpoint*) generally are considered *fully competent*.

Problems emerge when the actual performance of individuals is not consistent with their positions in the salary range. The customary practice is to make a salary adjustment if the person is paid below an appropriate level for his or her performance or to freeze or limit pay increases for the person who is considered overpaid for his or her performance or job function. In this way, the salary range can serve to control compensation costs relative to a midpoint or control-point level.

Many organizations use a salary-increase matrix to administer salary increases. This matrix (Figure 6-1) is usually divided into three or

	1	2	3	4	5
120–112	0%	0%	2%	3%	4%
112–104	0%	3%	4%	5%	6%
104–96	2%	4%	5%	6%	8%
96–88	3%	5%	6%	8%	10%
88–80	4%	6%	7%	10%	12%

current salary as a percent of the midpoint (salary range position or "comp- ratio")

individual performance rating

Figure 6-1   The traditional salary increase guide.

five vertical and horizontal sectors, with one dimension being levels within the salary range and the other being levels of individual performance. As shown in the figure, the largest pay increase goes to the individuals who are paid low in the salary range and are high performers. Individuals who are high in the range but are performing below standard receive no or little pay increases. Consequently, the matrix manages compensation by limiting pay increases above the midpoint of the range. This process of relating the salary increase to the performance and the position within the salary range is referred to as *pay for performance*.

If an individual is promoted to a job or a new job is created that is in a higher salary range, the individual's pay (before a promotional increase) is lower in the new salary range. Depending on the number of levels the promotion or new job reflects (frequently there is a one- or two-level difference), the person is usually eligible for a higher pay increase; if the person receives a promotional increase in pay but still remains in the lower portion of the new salary range, he or she will receive a higher salary increase at the next review, depending on the performance rating.

These tools—job description, job evaluation, salary ranges, salary-increase guides, and so on—comprise the elements of traditional base pay systems. While many organizations have added new features to a number of these, the fundamental premise reflects the following:

1. The organization pays for the job, not the person.
2. Internal equity is determined by a common set of job-evaluation factors or internal comparisons of responsibilities.
3. External competitiveness is achieved through the salary ranges and pay-increase policies.
4. Salaries are administered relative to the midpoint of the salary range, reflecting the level as the appropriate amount for a job that is performed in a fully competent fashion.
5. The job description is the foundation for the system, and the salary-increase guidelines and job-evaluation process control the compensation expenditures of the organization.

What Is Wrong with This Process?

This summary describes the traditional process for determining and managing base salaries. These practices were established during the 1950s and 1960s and are used by thousands of organizations. Watson Wyatt, a compensation and benefits consulting firm, reports that over 98 percent of *Fortune* 500 companies have a similar form of merit-based compensation system. An entire industry of compensation consulting firms has grown up around these principles, and organizations spend millions of dollars each year on services to support these systems. Given the amount of money that organizations spend on compensation for their employees, it is no wonder that internal expertise is developed and external expertise sought to ensure that dollars are spent wisely. But are they? Let's examine some issues that have emerged as a result of current practices.

In Chapter 1 we discussed the emergence of a new philosophy of management that places the customer at the center of work activities and focused on increasing the value of the firm. Whether the customer is an external user of products or services or an internal user, organizations are integrating customer- and value-based metrics into performance assessments. Traditionally, however, organizational structures have reinforced the manager as the customer, fragmented work, and emphasized cost controls. As organizations attempt to realign their activities with a customer-oriented horizontal rather than vertical perspective, conflicts have arisen with the compensation systems.

To understand these conflicts, one needs to look at each element in the traditional compensation system. The first is the job description. The standard description asks people to document certain aspects of their jobs that reflect the control and specialization paradigm. These include

- Whom you report to—strengthening the idea of hierarchy
- What resources (people, budgets, etc.) you control—reinforcing the point that the more you direct and control, the more valuable your job
- The unique responsibilities of your job—implying that the more responsibilities that are yours alone, the more important your job is
- The decision-making authority—reflecting the idea that the more authority you have, the more important your job is

Thus, from the very start, the next-level manager is designated as the customer, and performing a set of upwardly focused responsibilities fulfills the job. Where is the customer? What is the value-added nature of the function? How can the talents of the individual be reflected in valuing the importance of the position?

In many organizations, job descriptions are documentations used to assign a job to a salary level. One frequently finds people searching for the magic words that will provide the desired result or using impressive-sounding phrases that are more fiction than fact. Job descriptions can provide the performer with an understanding of the job requirements, but they have few meaningful and immediate consequences (except for job evaluation). Overall, job descriptions are either used insufficiently or associated with negative reinforcement (i.e., "do just enough to get by").

An examination of the salary-administration process reveals several interesting competition-oriented practices. First, the salary-increase guide provides pay increases based on individual performance and the level within the salary range. Since few people are rated at the highest level and fewer people are rated below competent or midlevel, most employees are rated at average or above-average performance. Therefore, if one wants to maximize pay increases, one needs to be promoted continually or have the job upgraded so that one's pay remains in the lower quadrant of the salary range. Employees and managers in a large publishing company with such a system, for example, often were heard to remark that once you went above midpoint, you were "dead in the water" when it came to salary increases.

Second, following the job description, when any individual receives more than the average salary increase, someone else in the group has to receive less because there is usually a fixed budget for salary increases. For example, if an average-pay-increase budget for a group of 10 people is 5 percent and one person gets 7½ percent, the extra 2½ percent will have to come out of one or more of the others' increases. Hence members of the team are encouraged to compete with one another to receive a higher performance rating. This win-lose game reflects an inherently competitive pattern of management that subtly undermines the spirit of collaboration.

Today's organizations need innovation, calculated risk taking, teamwork, and a spirit of willingness to share ideas and information to surmount competitive challenges. Many pay systems that encourage internal competition reinforce information hoarding, risk aversion, and suboptimal performance.

Finally, performance typically is evaluated on the basis of individual achievements. This assessment should reflect a full year's performance, but in most cases it takes into consideration only the critical incidents in the preceding 2 to 3 months. The value of earlier achievements is often forgotten or discounted. Furthermore, the achievements of the individual are often weighed more heavily than the achievements of the group of which the individual is a member. Individuals seek recognition, and managers frequently seek to use salary increases to recognize their top performers.

If salary increases are higher than guidelines dictate, the manager often needs to justify this action to some higher authority. If no salary increase is provided, then documentation is necessary here as well in order to protect the organization from being sued for wrongful treatment. Therefore, to avoid an adverse consequence in either situation, the manager will provide pay increases within a moderate range. The manager then will explain to the higher performers that "the system" will not allow a larger pay increase but that they will be recommended for a promotion or job upgrade.

As organizations reduce levels of management, combine salary ranges to create broad bands, and reduce the amount of money available for merit increases, the salary-administration program has lost its impact on performance. Employees continue to want and expect regular pay increases, and managers seek to do what they can. We find ourselves with an engine that is without gasoline and unable to drive performance.

Applying the Success Criteria: STRIPE

Let's examine the traditional base salary program against the criteria of an effective reward system. In Chapter 2, we outlined the STRIVE criteria as they apply to all reward systems. When we focus on base pay plans specifically, a similar set of success criteria—STRIPE— should be used in assessing the effectiveness of current programs or in developing a new one for the organization (see Figure 6-2).

Strategy

Most base salary programs have few areas in which a clear line of sight can be established between the strategy of the company and the role one performs. The structure of the salary program often determines how salary dollars are allocated. Thus, it is imperative that the criteria used reflect the fundamental requirements of the organization. These criteria could include the desired level of competitiveness in the marketplace for talent, the level of responsibilities and capabilities to perform the work, and/or the key competencies or characteristics the organization needs to promote among the employees. Base pay plans therefore need to be seen as strategic, not just the infrastructure within the organization for allocating payroll dollars.

Timeliness

As a manager, one of the most frustrating experiences involving salary programs, especially in large corporations, is the time it takes to determine an appropriate salary for an individual. Whether you are hiring a new employee, transferring in an employee from another area in the company, or promoting an individual into a new or existing job, time is critical. However, most base pay systems have such a complicated process

- Strategy
- Timeliness
- Reliability
- Integrity
- Personalization
- Equitability

Figure 6-2 Success criteria to assess reward programs.

of controls that the experience is often more frustrating than fulfilling. In successful base pay programs, the guidelines for pay levels are clear, the reference information is easily available, and the decision process is simple and reinforcing.

Reliability

Much has been said about how current salary-administration systems are being undermined by the practices of managers. What is quite interesting in many companies is that this practice is reinforced. Compensation departments are required to be customer-focused, and many line managers are interpreting this to mean that they now have the authority to do what they want. The challenge is to redesign the system so that it works to meet the needs of its customers, line managers, employees, and shareholders.

Finally, current practices require a significant number of staff members to keep job descriptions and evaluations up to date, analyze market survey data, and plan, budget, and control the salary increases. As compensation staffs are reduced, the process of administering pay in the traditional manner is becoming more difficult. Consequently, highly successful salary programs are supported by technology that provides for easy access to information and effective decisions.

Integrity

If the salary system can be manipulated easily, the desired results can be achieved. However, results in this context undermine the intent and design of the salary-administration system. From a performance standpoint, if the employee clearly understands the performance expectations and perceives them as achievable, there is an opportunity to reward desired performance. The fallacy is that the performance is often evaluated only on an annual basis, encouraging participants to apply extra effort only as they approach the review date. Results achieved earlier in the performance cycle frequently are forgotten or considered not sufficiently challenging to be worth a reward. Clearly, the message is that as the review date approaches, the employee must look very busy, act as if the assignment is monumental, and complete it in time so that the evaluation of performance can be "properly" considered.

Personalization

In most organizations an odd paradox exists. From the employee's viewpoint, the salary has great meaning. It not only provides for some level of secured income on which to live and function, but it also defines the "value" the organization places on the role performed, and it may be the basis on which benefit programs and other features of the company are based. From the organization's viewpoint, the salary program is an objective, independently operating system to ensure that pay is consistent with the internal and external market. Conflicts arise when these viewpoints are not in alignment and people do not understand the basis on which they are paid. In successful base pay systems, employees understand how and why they are paid as they are. Although they may not agree with the decisions, they at least understand them. Further, the pay opportunities are linked to an increase in the employee's capabilities, thus providing greater value to the organization. Pay then provides economic and symbolic value to the individual.

Equitability

Although there is a myth that people should not discuss compensation, it is in fact discussed, compared, and examined a great deal. Pay is viewed as equitable when the individuals concerned see that the differences in pay are based on clear differences in roles, responsibilities, and market areas. An individual who wants to earn more income needs to acquire additional skills, perform at a higher level, assume greater responsibility, or find another employer. Further, although people often compare themselves to references that are higher than the current position and thereby draw inappropriate or personally hurtful conclusions, the organization needs to seek to establish the right level of equity in pay relationships based on its philosophy. Finally, there has been much legal and social turmoil on drawing the differences between equity pay and pay that is equitable. If an organization establishes a policy that it will compensate individuals differently based on the external market, responsibilities, and/or performance, then it needs to have a decision process that ensures that the decisions are made properly. This process may adversely impact certain groups, but the policy and implementation of this policy may be the right thing for the organization.

In summary, the question is not why current base salary programs are ineffective but rather why we ever believed they would work to drive desired performance. Based on this analysis, it seems clear that base salary programs are not effective at reinforcing the desired behavior. In many cases, they actually undermine the process of change; at best, they are neutral. Thus pay for performance, using this type of system, simply does not exist—as managers and employees have been telling executives and compensation professionals through various employee opinion surveys for some time. This leads us to two questions:

1. If the base salary program does not work as a system to pay for performance, what is its purpose?
2. How can we make base salary programs more effective in reinforcing desired behaviors?

Redefining the Purpose of Base Salary Programs

Given the challenges facing today's businesses and the changes they are instituting, the fundamental requirement is to redefine the purpose of the base salary program. Chapter 3 outlined the critical decisions involved in developing a rewards strategy. Within this context, we need to formulate a new purpose for the base salary program. Once it is identified, we can select and develop a system that not only reflects the fundamental requirements of the organization but also is meaningful to those whose behaviors we seek to influence.

A useful construct is to draw parallels between compensation programs and financial management practices. In finance, two key concepts are used for displaying financial structure: balance sheets and profit/loss or cash-flow statements. In this context, the purpose of base pay is to enable the company to attract and retain talent and to encourage the development and application of competencies that create value for the organization and its customers. This means that salaries are similar to asset entries on the firm's balance sheet. These are the dollars the organization uses to generate growth and gain a return on investment. On the other hand, variable pay encourages and rewards short-term performance. It is similar to the revenue and expense entries of the income statement. It relates to the dynamics of the organization and how it generates profits—returns that exceed its costs.

The base salary program can support an organization's ability to compete by providing it with the people capabilities it needs. Each organization serves a customer and has a unique set of competencies and strategies to give it a competitive edge. Some experts in the field refer to this as the *core competencies* of the organization—the things the firm does particularly well and that provide it with an advantage in the marketplace.[2]

It will be important to go beyond the core competencies and reflect what the organization requires to implement its basic business strategy —*how* it will be successful. While key success factors usually are conceptual and strategic in nature, they need to be translated into a set of criteria that will form the basis for the investment of compensation dollars. In this manner, compensation becomes the resource the organization uses to gain market leadership or fulfill its basic mission. Compensation reflects the real value of the human assets of the organization—its true "balance sheet."

When this point of view is compared with traditional thinking about base salaries, one should note the absence of the external marketplace or the emphasis on internal equity. An organization that is not able to provide an attractive place to work for a reasonably competitive pay level will not be able to acquire the talent it needs to do its business. Consequently, it will not have the abilities needed to be successful. In our experience with consulting to hundreds of companies, the external market needs to be a centerpiece of the pay system only when the firm is actively engaged in attracting or retaining its human resources. When this is a key success factor, pay levels should operate well above the norm and be a key element of the employment proposition. When the firm has to operate with minimal costs, pay levels should be below average market values. In this case, other reward systems enable the firm to attract, retain, and motivate critical talent. Hence the marketplace is a tertiary reference for the base pay system and for the employees. The pay system needs to be geared more toward direct support of the talent strategy of the organization.

Further, internal equity is not a primary focus for most reward systems. When people complain about the lack of fairness in the current compensation program, they generally are reflecting either a lack of understanding of how other systems work or a sense of not being valued and reinforced by the organization. Traditional compensation systems seldom satisfy either of these concerns. In a reinforcement-enriched environment, people are not concerned about what others get; they feel valued for what they personally do and are pleased to see others succeed as well. Further, as will be discussed in Chapter 7, new approaches to establishing base salary levels need to be highly visible and well understood by managers and employees. Internal equity need not be an issue if it is defined in a manner in which it can be understood and applied with integrity.

The old thinking holds that internal equity is based on seniority and job responsibility. The new thinking is based on concepts of talent, growth, and performance and uses internal equity to reflect on individual capabilities and accomplishments. With this in mind, Chapter 7 will examine alternative approaches to developing a reward-oriented base salary program.

7

Designing Base Pay: Choose Your Approach Wisely

Those who say it cannot be done should not interrupt those who are doing it.

Chinese proverb

A BASIC PREMISE OF THE STRIPE model of base salary compensation design, outlined in Chapter 6, is that there is no common system for all organizations. Therefore, the purpose of this chapter is to examine several alternative approaches to salary programs, each with particular advantages and disadvantages. The task is to select the approach (or approaches for a complex situation) that best fits the needs of your organization and then modify and adapt it to your organization's particular requirements.

Five approaches are as follows:

1. Market-based career development model
2. Company's core values to determine job importance
3. Pay for competencies employed (PACE)
4. Team performance–based salary increases
5. Variable merit pool

Market-Based Career Development Model

The current approach to job evaluation reinforces the concept of hierarchical control. In order to increase one's pay opportunities, one needs to expand the scope of control as well as authority. Obviously, this runs counter to what many firms are attempting to implement in order to increase their flexibility and competitiveness.

An alternative is to change the method by which jobs are priced and pay opportunities are determined. This approach establishes a market price for a job based on the rates of pay for similar positions in the marketplace. The relationship to the market—pay at market level or higher or lower than market level—is established based on what is needed to attract people to or retain them for the organization. The pay rates become guidelines for managers to use in hiring, career development, and rewarding performance. Further, the number of grade levels is reduced, providing salary ranges geared more toward fundamental differences in roles within the organization. The result is a broad salary range or a specific target rate of pay for each position.

The following will illustrate this briefly. A large technology company reduced the number of grade levels for its exempt professional employees from 18 to 5. The salary ranges were increased from 50 percent (from minimum to maximum pay level for the range) to up to 150 to 200 percent. The levels were defined as

- Basic, entry-level contributor
- Proficient, highly competent performer
- Performer with mastery of the role requirements
- Technical, functional, or business unit leader

Within these levels, managers set target salaries based on market information for individuals with similar backgrounds and responsibili-

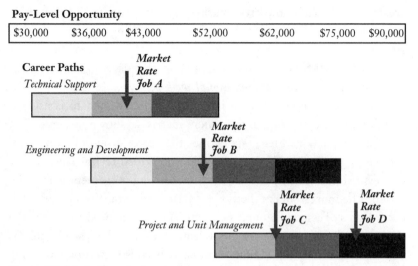

Figure 7-1 Market-based salary ranges.

ties. The managers were given market data and the responsibility for administering salaries as appropriate to attract, retain, and reward their staff. They had to operate within a compensation budget, but how the dollars were allocated was based on managerial judgments. This model is illustrated in Figure 7-1.

In order to provide target pay guidelines, the market needs to be defined using a variety of sources. First, the external market can be defined as what other organizations pay people with similar roles and responsibilities. In organizations experiencing rapid growth, understanding the competition and establishing a competitive advantage are keys to attracting the talent needed for the firm. Second, the external market can be defined by the geographic area or the industry in which the organization operates. The industry is the best reference point for setting salaries if compensation costs need to be closely aligned with those of competitors. Unfortunately, many executives confuse the compensation marketplace for talent with the business marketplace for customers. Third, while the industry market may be a useful benchmark, another consideration is to examine where people come from and where people go. Further, the marketplace for talent may not be just external. Many organizations rely on promoting people from within and acquire individuals externally only for certain roles or functional areas. This is often the true marketplace for talent, and the company should understand this marketplace in setting its compensation strategies.

A useful tool for determining the real marketplace for the organization's talent is to use a *human capital movement matrix*. This matrix is rather simple to conceptualize but requires sound data to construct. Developing a human capital movement matrix, as shown in Figure 7-2, can aid this analysis. First, one defines the target group of employees, such as engineers, marketing professionals, skilled technicians, and so on. Second, one defines the scales for describing movement within the group. The most frequent method is to use salary grade levels, although other forms of assessment may be useful. Third, one needs to define the time period for assessing the movement of people; usually this is between 1 and 3 years. Finally, the matrix is constructed by indicating the number of people who started in one level and ended in another level during the prescribed period. There are columns for noting the levels at which people were hired and left the organization (through transfers, exits to competitors, or exits to others). This displays an analytical map of the movement of people in the organization (see Figure 7-3).

The analysis of these data can provide several very valuable insights. First, one can clearly identify the sources of new employees, where they entered the system, and where they were promoted to higher levels. Second, one can clearly identify where the most vulnerable leaks are in the

Hired	10%	30%	12%	5%	15%
16	0%	0%	0%	60%	10%
14	0%	0%	45%	30%	7%
12	0%	70%	10%	0%	35%
10	60%	25%	10%	5%	10%
	10	12	14	16	Terminated

Where people started (job level) (vertical axis label)

Where people ended (job level)

Figure 7-2 Human capital movement matrix.

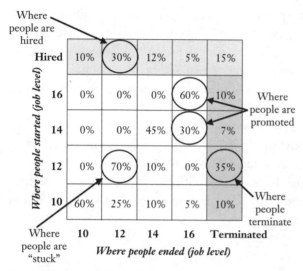

Figure 7-3 Analyzing the human capital movement matrix.

system. Where are terminations most likely to occur? Third, one can identify where the stuck jobs are (i.e., where people are not moving beyond a certain level) and even pinpoint the primary source of talent. The analysis can go as deep as needed to understand the flow of human resources and the critical issues surrounding attracting and retaining talent.

Companies active in the areas of human resource planning and development have used this human capital movement matrix to identify the sources for talent (internal and external) and the jobs that are characterized as "dead-ended." The implications of compensation design are very powerful both for defining the marketplace for talent and for understanding how competitive compensation levels need to be. Based on these data, the reward strategy can be established in a more systematic manner.

Use of Core Values to Determine Job Importance

Companies that adopted job-evaluation systems developed in the 1950s, 1960s, and 1970s were reinforcing the philosophy of management that was prevalent in those days. However, as we move into a globally competitive marketplace, the requirements for success have changed. A management philosophy is emerging that focuses more on value for the customer and promoting organizational quality, flexibility, and speed. Retaining the philosophy of command and control, job specialization, and hierarchical relationships inhibits organizations from addressing current challenges.

To support the change in philosophy, the organization can adopt a new framework for establishing pay levels that reflects the firm's core values, competencies, and value-added functions. This involves asking new questions about the design of work processes and determining worth from a customer-focused, value-added perspective.

The methodology begins with a different approach to job descriptions. Instead of asking the standard questions (Whom do you report to? What resources/people do you control/impact? What is your decision-making authority?), ask

- Who are your customers, and what do they need?
- Who are your suppliers, and what do you receive from them?
- What value-added activities do you perform to produce what end results?
- What are the key requirements for your success?
- What are the primary indicators or measures of your performance?

These questions provide a method for defining roles within a customer-focused context and emphasize new patterns of behavior. This information also can support a role-assessment process—not a job-evaluation system—that reflects the factors truly important to the firm's competitive success.

This process can be implemented in three steps. The first is to define the factors and sets of behaviors that best reflect the values, core competencies, and key success factors of the business. These should be those for which the organization is willing to provide more compensation. The more they can be measured in actual results, the easier the assessment process will be. Examples may include

1. Integrates with customers:
   - Understands needs of the external customer
   - Uses a sense of urgency to meet customer needs
   - Integrates feedback from customers into operations

- Positively impacts customer's ability to achieve/retain competitiveness

2. Integrates with critical suppliers:
   - Translates the firm's needs to external suppliers
   - Ensures that suppliers' services are aligned with the firm's needs
   - Integrates capabilities and performance of suppliers into operations

3. Establishes focus for others:
   - Ensures that work has a clear purpose and is linked to primary objectives/mission of the unit
   - Exercises discipline to keep activities working in concert with unit objectives
   - Communicates to others the purpose, rationale, and requirements for success

4. Uses resources effectively:
   - Determines priorities in relation to customer needs, organizational goals, and operating values
   - Ensures that resources are used in the most efficient manner possible
   - Establishes clear, specific measures to track progress
   - Uses the firm's resources to create greater value
   - Determines resource requirements necessary to achieve key goals

5. Empowers others:
   - Verbally expresses trust and confidence in the abilities of others to succeed
   - Encourages others to take calculated risks to achieve desired ends
   - Encourages individuals and teams to set their own goals
   - Aligns the work of individuals and teams with organizational priorities
   - Allows others to decide how tasks will be accomplished
   - Sets, maintains, and monitors work activities

6. Implements organizational strategies:
   - Seeks innovative ways to achieve objectives with fewer resources or less time
   - Collaborates and integrates work with others

- Participates in interdisciplinary efforts to achieve goals
- Keeps others informed of key events in a timely fashion

The second step is the assessment process, which should be carried out by a panel of experts using a comparison or Delphi decision-making methodology. In this technique, a set of core positions is evaluated by comparing the factors with each of the role definitions or positions. The task is to determine whether the position in question is the same, higher, or lower than a comparable position for a given factor. This process is best implemented with a process that facilitates the decision-making process. The result is a rank order of all the positions based on the criteria. Not only is the order important, but so is the relative scaling of the positions in the dimensions.

The third step involves analyzing and clustering the ranking of the positions into levels consistent with their patterns. The positions are reviewed for quality assurance, and additional positions are integrated into the framework by comparing job families or positions with similar functions. No attempt is made to draw cross-functional comparisons beyond the core benchmark positions. The end result is a set of levels that reflects the values and philosophy the organization needs to support its strategic direction.

Several risks are inherent in this approach. First, the factors need to be clearly defined and understood by the panel of experts. Second, the source documents for the assessment—customer-centered role definitions—need to provide the information necessary to make a sound judgment. Third, since this process establishes the firm's importance for the roles, the marketplace values need to be incorporated into salary ranges for the positions once the rankings are complete.

Pay for Competencies Employed (PACE)

Job-evaluation systems allocate pay based on the content of the job and the market. Little or no value is placed on the quality or capabilities of the people performing the function. This is usually addressed through the salary-administration process. An increasing number of companies are experimenting with pay systems based on the talents of the individuals and the way they are employed within the work setting. We refer to these as *pay for competencies employed* (PACE) *plans*. They are similar to pay for skill plans, pay for knowledge plans, and career-based pay plans in that they focus on the talent of the individual. This approach is different because we need to examine the application of that talent to work.

WorldatWork (formerly the American Compensation Association) recently conducted a study of these plans and discovered that although they had been developed for operational (usually manufacturing) employees, their underlying concepts were being used for professional service functions such as information systems, engineering, legal services, consulting, and accounting.[1]

Further, a similar study on the application of competencies to pay systems shows that companies usually seek to link competencies and compensation when the skill mix of its workforce is not consistent with the emerging requirements. In many cases they seek cross training by employees so that several individuals can do the same job. This is most appropriate when many people can share the work tasks; this approach improves the productivity of the unit. Often bottlenecks develop in operations as work waits for people to get to it. PACE-type pay programs serve to reduce these bottlenecks by rewarding people who have and apply cross-functional skills. Companies also use this form of compensation when they are undergoing significant technological change and when routine jobs are being eliminated. This process encourages people to expand their knowledge, skills, and abilities in order to perform more advanced jobs.

The primary advantage companies seek with PACE-type programs is an increased flexibility by the workforce to respond to changes in the way work is performed. Companies are also seeking cost reductions because they need to use fewer people to perform more functions. While this is often the way such programs are sold to senior management, the WorldatWork study concluded that few firms realize significant cost savings through downsizing.[2] Perhaps the greatest advantage of PACE-type programs is that they enhance employee capability and performance so that a firm gains greater return on investment from its compensation dollars.

The disadvantages of PACE-type programs are often due to the way they are designed. Such programs often raise employee expectations for continual pay increases. Further, the cost savings suggested earlier are seldom realized. The firm may experience higher actual labor costs in the effort to gain greater productivity, but unit costs may decline. If such performance improvements are not soon realized, this type of pay program is not a worthwhile investment. These are the primary reasons why this form of pay program is disbanded.

These systems require the organization to invest in training and development for employees and to use the skills employees have acquired. If the nature of work does not provide or even require these new skills on a regular and extensive basis, the system may not be appropriate. Further, once the pay system is in place, employees want to receive the necessary training and development. This training may come from more seasoned employees, online educational programs, or special programs conducted by the organization. Regardless of how the training is provided, employees want to take advantage of the opportunities presented to them to expand their abilities and increase their earnings.

Finally, administering such systems with integrity and reliability is an important undertaking. Depending on the extent of the assessment process, records will need to be kept on each employee's evaluation and development. Management will need to ensure that the program is applied consistently to employees who clearly demonstrate the application of increased abilities to their work. This investment will need to be considered in the overall cost and return-on-investment requirements of the system.

One application used by some companies is to pay the individuals more while they are performing the higher-skilled job and then return them to a base rate when they perform their basic job. However, companies such as Pepsi-Cola, Motorola, and Texas Instruments dropped these provisions because they found the administrative requirement too cumbersome, they added very little value, and they were not justifiable in terms of cost. Furthermore, this created confusion on the part of the employees and tended to strain their relationships with management. Frequently, tasks were labeled as new but were performed in the same old way. The audit and control functions created more barriers among employees than they eliminated. The method now used by these companies is to increase a worker's pay after he or she has clearly learned and applied the new skill over an extended time period (3 to 9 months). Hence these pay plans differ from promotions because they pay people *after* they have demonstrated the skill, whereas with promotions, people are paid *before* they become fully competent in a new role.

The Value of the Competency-Based Pay Program

The primary value of pay programs linked to competencies is the ability it provides the organization to manage its inventory of talent and encourage the development of its people consistent with the business requirements of the organization. There are several primary advantages to this approach. The process enables the compensation system to be very personalized. People sense a greater control over their pay and associate the assessments with opportunities for development and rewards. As managers reinforce individuals for their learning and use the system to provide focus and objective feedback, the system works to motivate people to excel in their development. When turnover occurs, individuals seek to recombine work responsibilities to create greater opportunities for development and increase productivity. The return on investment from PACE-type programs is realized through improved performance, decreased unit costs, and reduced staff levels. This enables the firm to be more competitive.

There are disadvantages as well in the requirements of management. A highly reliable competency-based pay plan requires a lot of effort and expertise from both the line and human resource functions. The competencies need to relate to core business requirements and be clearly understood and validated. Also, the program requires managers to become more active in managing the assessments and developing their employees. Employees need regular review sessions in which they can see their progress and plan new activities to acquire new skills. Third, there are risks of discrimination for people of diversity; the competencies need to be available and applied fairly to all. Fourth, these plans do not fit well in functions that are highly specialized, that have few employees, or that provide limited opportunities to combine work. For example, corporate legal functions (not private law firms) or other specialized functions within a firm may have difficulty justifying the costs of this kind of plan. Such PACE programs are also difficult to create for managerial roles unless the firm is committed to developing the role of general manager within the organization. Finally, there may be situations in which the skills and competencies are no longer needed by the organization because of changes in technology, strategy, or the marketplace or because people have achieved high capabilities but there are few opportunities to employ their skills. This is a basic misalignment between capabilities and requirements (supply versus demand). In such cases, the firm may have high-priced talent that is no longer needed. A period of retrenchment and retraining may be required.

In short, the business defines the talent and competencies it needs to succeed in a complex, competitive marketplace. The marketplace and the desired competitive position of the company determine the opportunities individuals have for compensation. Yet it is what the individual learns, develops, and applies to the company that determines "how much" one should be paid. The individual increases his or her value to the organization by increasing and employing the competencies that the organization truly needs.

Team Performance–Based Salary Increases

Perhaps the easiest change to make is in how salary increases are determined. Traditional approaches compare the individual's performance with the level in the salary range (note the salary-increase guide described earlier). An easy alternative is to change the dimensions on the decision matrix. Instead of using the salary-range position, use the performance of the team. Individual performance would be based on how well the person contributed to making the team successful. The actual increase may be modified if a person is particularly low or high in the salary range, but this is done for equity or market adjustment, not based on performance (Figure 7-4).

In addition, the decision-making process can be expanded to include the team as well as the manager. This is sometimes referred to as a *360-degree review* or a *multirater review*, in which feedback on an individual's performance is gathered from all those affected by the individual's actions. While traditional practices place the manager in the sole decision-making role, an alternative would be to seek input from the team members in making salary-increase decisions. Obviously, this feature requires teams that can honestly and with integrity differentiate among the performances of individual members. This decision can be made as input to the manager who has final decision-making authority or can be delegated to the team. Another alternative is to use the manager to coordinate the collection of assessment feedback from multiple sources and to share all this with the performer. The conclusion will be a clear performance standing that is not based solely on the manager's judg-

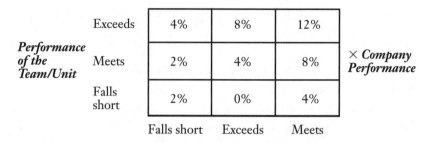

Figure 7-4   Team-based salary increases.

ment. The decision on salary increases should be made after the *team's* performance has been determined and the range of pay increases is known.

This new matrix approach has several simple advantages. First, it uses the performance of the team directly in considerations on salary increases. This encourages the individual to work for the team's success as well as his or her own success. Second, it removes the salary range as a major determinant of an employee's pay increases. This reduces the pressure to seek promotional increases in order to provide higher pay increases. Equity adjustments can still be made, but as a separate decision independent of the reward decisions.

The primary disadvantage is that the matrix does not control compensation expenses. Expense controls need to be put in place so that pay increases do not become excessive, particularly when salaries approach the maximum of the salary range. Although this may be viewed as a drawback, it does have the advantage of removing pay-increase decisions from salary levels and ranges. We feel strongly that one should use the correct tools for the correct application and not seek to use a single tool for multiple, conflicting needs. Stated another way, one should not use the salary-increase process to both reward performance *and* control costs. Use it to reward performance, and use the budget and financial controls to manage costs.

Variable Merit Pool

One of the principal problems with current merit pay systems is that they are fundamentally a zero-sum game. If one member of a team is to get more than the budgeted percentage, then someone else has to get less. This fundamentally conflicting situation seldom encourages superior performance but rather promotes suboptimal performance. This is so because the amount of money available for merit pay is fixed. Why does it need to be fixed?

An alternative is to make the merit pool variable based on the performance of the team, division, or company. Then individuals will receive a merit pay increase that is a share of a company pool. This encourages a mutual interest in increasing the size of the pool through improved team or company performance. The increases could be the same for all team members or differentiated by level of contribution to the team's performance. Increases could be the same dollar amount, the same percentage of current salaries, or allocated by where individuals are currently paid relative to their salary range or market. The objective is to transform merit pay from a zero-sum game to one based on a common fate.

A midsized manufacturing division of a large industrial company adopted this concept. The company planned and budgeted for a 5 percent average pay increase. It established specific performance measures for the four key divisions and adjusted the merit budget allocation based on both company and divisional performance. The company instituted a common salary increase date 45 days after the end of the fiscal year. In the initial year, the company achieved its goals slightly ahead of target, and, therefore, the merit pay increase was adjusted to 6.5 percent. Of the four divisions, two fell below the target, and their merit adjustments were reduced to 4 percent. Another was on target and received 6 percent. The fourth was significantly above target and received an average of 8 percent. The pay increase for each person was determined to meet these budget allocations. Any dollars not allocated were used for making special market adjustments where needed.

The primary lesson to be learned from this company's experience is how to align merit pay with the success of the company and each division. Rather than being viewed as an exercise in budgeting and justifications, people saw how their combined efforts would be rewarded. All staff members better understood divisional objectives and performance, a fact that contributed to acceptance of the diversity in merit increases. Actual pay increases ranged from zero for the team and individuals who simply did not perform well to 12 percent for the high-performing team and individuals. This process significantly reduced the we/they conditions between employees and managers and gave real meaning to the performance objectives.

Summary of Alternatives to Salary Programs

We have described five approaches for a base pay system and how people receive pay increases. They range from very simple programs to plans requiring extensive development and implementation. Each is more effective than traditional methods employing a pay for performance philosophy. By using methods that fit with the reward strategy of the organization, base pay systems can be transformed from delivery systems for cash into actual reward systems. Each of these alternatives changes the basic premise of management. Base pay systems focus on the talent assets of the organization and can grow as the capabilities and performance of the organization grow. The primary advantage of these techniques is their ability to make pay systems more personalized and more directly supportive of the organization's key success factors. The responsibility of the organization is to create opportunities and reinforce the process. The responsibility of the individual is to seize the opportunities and make even greater contributions to the organization. In so doing, base pay systems can form the foundation for a comprehensive system of rewards.

Manage Performance Instead of Appraising It

Performance appraisals are one of those special human encounters where the manager gets no sleep the night before, and the employee gets no sleep the night after.

Thomas B. Wilson

T HROUGHOUT THIS BOOK we have explored how a company can increase its competitive advantage substantially by finding and changing the way it influences how people within the company take action. One of the key variables in improving individual and organizational results is an effective performance management process. In fact, performance management has been described as a tool to help create major culture changes within organizations. Yet it is an extremely challenging task to build *and* sustain a performance management process that is viewed as adding value for all the parties involved—managers, employees, human resources, and executives.

Background of Performance Management

Traditional performance appraisals consistently have gotten a bad reputation. In a performance management survey by the Society for Human Resource Management (SHRM) and Personnel Decisions International (PDI), 32 percent of human resources (HR) professionals responded that they were unsatisfied with their performance appraisal system.[1] Some of the challenges cited that make the performance appraisal program ineffective include

- Many executives do not support performance reviews or even complete performance appraisals of their staff. Yet information about who the performers are in the company can be of significant value to the company.
- The performance appraisal system is not valued in the company by employees, managers, or executives. They do not see it as their own system but rather as a bureaucratic process required by human resources.
- Users find it difficult to create goals and objectives and/or to identify appropriate measures. For some functions and job levels, it is difficult to create meaningful goals that are sustained throughout the year.
- People are not trained in how to write or communicate performance information to employees. Often employees need training on their roles and must be encouraged to contribute more to their own reviews.
- The system requires too much time to complete primarily because written performance appraisals and the discussions can take many hours for those with limited capabilities.

If performance appraisals are ineffective, their relationship to the total rewards systems has an even greater impact. In Chapter 4 we said that people perform better when they know how well they are doing as individuals and as members of units and of the entire enterprise *during* the performance period. They can then act on this feedback prior to the end of the performance period so as to improve their performance. This involves both measurement and feedback on progress (creating and assessing performance goals). This chapter contrasts the elements and issues of traditional performance appraisals with a new approach that includes the purposes and objectives of performance management, as well as best practices and a new methodology for developing a better process. Because performance appraisals are so difficult, the key objective of this new methodology is to enable managers to earn the right to *not* do performance appraisals again—but with the caveat that managers demonstrate that they manage performance on a real-time basis! What does this mean? We will examine how to shift the focus from opinion feedback to self-sustaining data feedback, from evaluating performance to reviewing it, from making decisions about pay to using a variety of rewards, and from appraising performance to managing the drivers of high performance.

Case Study: "Normal" Performance Appraisal

As Charlene Wilde's job anniversary approached, her manager, J. Charles Marsh, began preparing for Charlene's performance appraisal. Charles knew that the appraisal needed to be submitted to Human Resources by Friday or Charlene's merit pay increase would be delayed.

To begin the process, Charles pulled together a variety of data. First, he retrieved Charlene's annual performance goals and her last year's performance review. Second, he obtained the new performance management review form and the employee self-evaluation form from Human Resources. He gave the self-evaluation form to Charlene to complete prior to their meeting. Third, he scheduled a meeting with her for about 2 hours on Thursday morning in his office. Finally, he combed through his department's performance records for any information about Charlene's specific performance results.

Charlene had worked for Charles for approximately 2 years since his transfer to the Marketing Department. Charlene was a product manager for one of the firm's major lines of business. She had been in the department for approximately 3 years and had shown significant potential. She and Charles had a good relationship, with strong mutual respect for each other's talents—his in marketing and hers in technical product knowledge and work commitment. The previous appraisal had identified several areas that needed improvement, and these would be considered during the appraisal discussion.

For 2 hours on Tuesday evening Charles prepared the performance review. He liked the narrative part of the form and was able to describe

Charlene's achievements accurately. He also was able to identify priority areas that he felt "needed improvement" and to summarize Charlene's overall strengths and potentials. On Wednesday Charlene gave Charles her self-evaluation highlighting her quantitative results. She did not refer to the chaos she had created in the engineering group, the conflicts she had caused in manufacturing, or the problems she had had with other product managers and several regional sales managers. Charlene was very results-oriented and always made her specific product financial and market-share targets. Neither the form nor the financial system enabled Charles to back up his concerns about Charlene's relationships with other departments.

The performance evaluation discussion began as usual with general conversation about work, special projects, and the company. When Charles and Charlene settled into the specific discussion of Charlene's performance, Charles reviewed each of the objectives and the results accomplished. The data on the financial targets were very clear, and Charlene had met all the objectives. Performance on the more process-oriented objectives was substantiated, supported by letters, comments, and critical incident reports that Charles had collected during the year. Charlene was very surprised by much of the qualitative data and challenged many of the conclusions. She was clearly expecting a "distinguished" performance rating and a very high pay increase. Charles rated her as a "strong performer" (a 4 on the company's 5-point scale). He concluded that while she had reached all her primary goals, she had caused numerous problems that Charles had had to address in other areas of the company. Her single-minded focus on results was preventing her from gaining support and commitment from other members of the organization. Charlene thought that she was doing what Charles wanted, but Charles felt that he had too often had to clean up after Charlene's encounters with other people in the organization.

Following the performance appraisal, Charles completed the forms, obtained Charlene's signature, and turned it all into Human Resources. Once the forms had been received and approved, Charles was given the okay to process Charlene's merit pay increase. He told Charlene the amount of her pay increase early the following week, and Charlene clearly was disappointed. The overall company limits to base pay increases (between 0 and 7 percent, with an average of 4 percent) were less than in previous years. Charles explained the policies to Charlene, showed her the salary-increase grid, and stated that she had received an above-average rating compared with others in the department. Although this was reassuring, Charlene felt that Charles did not fully appreciate her achievements.

What Goes Wrong and Why

For many people, this case study sounds familiar and looks normal. In fact, some may regard this story as a generally positive one because many managers have experienced problems that were a lot more challenging that those Charles faced. However, this case study demonstrates that performance appraisals ultimately set up a win-lose situation, especially where the ratings or raises must follow a prescribed distribution. The result is a discouraged worker who sincerely wants to do a good job.

As discussed in the introduction to this chapter, there are many reasons why performance appraisals fail, including managers not being trained, lack of executive commitment, the system requiring too much time, and managers and employees finding it difficult to develop effective goals. Longenecker and Goff's study of performance appraisal systems gives additional reasons for why such systems fail to accomplish their objectives[2]:

- Managers lack sufficient information to judge performance accurately.
- The goals and standards are unclear and subjective.
- The system makes employees defensive.
- The process is not taken seriously.
- Managers do not prepare adequately.

The Purpose and Objectives of Performance Management

SHRM conducted a performance management survey in 2000 in which respondents were asked to rank the most important objectives of a performance management system.[3] Rank ordering has the following objectives:

1. To provide feedback to employees about their performance
2. To clarify the organization's expectations of employees

3. To provide information to employees about their development needs
4. To identify development needs
5. To gather information for pay decisions
6. To gather information for coaching
7. To document performance for employee records
8. To gather information for promotion decisions

These objectives are consistent with the four drivers of human behavior that we have been discussing throughout this book—focus, feedback, competencies, and consequences (see Chapter 2). Performance management can become an essential ingredient in an integrated model of high performance. Let's look at the drivers of the process in more detail.

Focus

A primary objective of performance management is to provide employees with an understanding of the strategies, directions, accountabilities, and tasks of the organization they support. By clarifying the organizational expectations of the employee, performance management answers the question, "What should I do?"—along with when, how often, and in what way. Although this is one alternative, far too many managers rely on outdated and static job descriptions to provide employees with direction instead of clarifying expectations within the framework of the organization's business strategy. When the performance management process and documentation are used instead, each employee's expectations are clarified in a very individual way and with the amount of specificity needed to fit that employee's needs or situation. The skilled leader also will know how to find the right balance between giving employees sufficient focus to take desired actions and providing room for creativity, innovation, and initiative.

Feedback

The second objective is to provide employees with the information they need to know if they are performing their responsibilities in a way that is consistent with what is required for success. By providing feedback to employees about their performance on a frequent basis through a variety of channels, managers can help employees understand what is expected of them and how they are doing and can provide them with time to adjust their actions in order to maximize their contributions and rewards and avoid negative consequences. Managers tend to take notice of this objective most when they discover that well-documented performance appraisals are needed as defense against litigation over an involuntary employment termination they absolutely needed to make. This also satisfies the need to document performance for employee records in order to reduce the risk of and defend legal actions.

F. Balcazar, B. Hopkins, and Y. Suarez have conducted some very interesting research on the impact of feedback.[4] After examining more than 126 different research-based applications of feedback to determine the factors that enhance its effectiveness in affecting human behavior, they concluded that feedback alone does not uniformly improve performance. Rather, when feedback is combined with objective-setting and consequences, it has a clear and consistent impact on behaviors.

Competencies

Employee development and coaching result in an enhancement of employee competencies. This third performance management objective includes identifying development needs and gathering information for training and coaching. Competencies are considered part of the forces of human behavior because they provide the abilities of an individual to take desired actions and shape expectations and decisions.

Consequences

The final area includes promotions, pay-increase decisions, and other actions related to rewards for performance. The performance appraisal often creates a link between performance and rewards that results in advancement and promotions, selection for training and development, merit pay increases and other salary administration actions, discipline, and termination. More contemporary alternatives are to link not only these rewards but also other forms of compensation. Together, both positive and negative, these are the consequences in the human behavior model discussed earlier in this book. Although the results of performance assessment should be the basis for gathering information for pay decisions, when the process has gone wrong, the order is reversed so that the primary content of the appraisal is a discussion of how much the pay increase will be. This then can be a discussion that is not very meaningful to the employee. This approach also has resulted in employees who are overly focused on the change in salary as opposed to feedback from or goal setting with the manager.

These four drivers of behavior function as a system or process in which each element gains strength and value from the others. Research clearly demonstrates that each of these factors cannot operate alone as an effective tool for managing performance. Focus provides the direction, feedback provides the sense of progress, competencies provide the knowledge, and consequences provide the reasons for action. In developing a new or enhanced performance management process, it is helpful to organize the tasks with the four forces that drive behavior clearly in mind and to understand what the organization is especially strong at and areas where it needs improvement.

Best Practices in Performance Management

This section explores best practices in the performance management process and specific alternatives. We find that performance management best practices are universal, regardless of industry. Longenecker and Fink[5] researched performance appraisal systems in 28 U.S. manufacturing and service organizations and reported consistent best-practice results:

- Clearly defined objectives
- Easy-to-use forms, procedures, and criteria that are job-related and performance-based
- Extensive input by managers and employees early in the design of the performance management process
- Clear goals and expectations
- Ongoing informal appraisals, feedback, and coaching
- Consistent and uniform application throughout the organization
- Manager and employee training on the process and their respective roles

Based on the many research studies on the process and the performance models presented earlier in this book, there are eight key best practices that create highly effective performance management systems.

I. Providing Ongoing Performance Monitoring, Feedback, and Coaching

Traditional appraisals tend to examine performance over a relatively long period of time: 1 year. They assume that performance is consistent over that time and that the results are within the control of the performer. However, there is constant change both internally and externally that affects the focus of the job and the person's ability to achieve goals and meet performance standards. With a once-a-year feedback process, performers have to wait out the whole year to hear that they need to improve on something they could have improved on long ago. Or they receive positive recognition for their results and behaviors long after the events occurred.

The reality is that people want to know how they are doing as they are doing it. Making workers wait for some annual event is not an effective way to help them sustain or improve performance. With more frequent feedback and tracking of performance, employees can make changes to improve or continue to do the things that the manager wants. This is not only fair for the employee but also beneficial to the performance level of the organization. The more specific and timely the information, the better the information will be appreciated. In fact, information that is collected and displayed by the performer is often much more effective than that generated elsewhere in the organization.

Organizations that support frequent tracking and feedback create processes and tools that allow people to monitor performance quickly and easily on an ongoing basis. Our experience in working with organizations on increasing the frequency of performance feedback has shown that effective managers frequently have created their own tools and processes. Such managers also tend to schedule ongoing one-on-one meetings on a regular basis with each of their employees to discuss their performance. Electronic tools also allow managers to record and monitor events, goals, and behaviors. This is an example of finding best practices right within one's own organization just by asking the most effective managers what they do to provide feedback and then looking for ways to replicate it organizationwide.

The frequency of feedback is a critical dimension in its effectiveness. How often is frequent? Ideally, it should depend on the nature of job. Feedback that is daily, weekly, biweekly, or monthly has the most value to performers. For example, project-oriented jobs can be monitored on completion or at milestones. Either the employee's manager or the project manager can provide feedback and coaching. Many organizations that are in the business of conducting financial audits or research and development projects have gotten this down to a science. They review all members of a project team at critical milestones and at completion of the project. Production or service-oriented jobs often have team goals and objectives. Both the goals and the results then lend themselves to easy review in a team meeting that can be followed up with brief individual employee discussions regarding individual contributions to the work. This is an opportunity to review contributions as well as criticisms. Critical reviews usually are conducted in private so that a clear message many be sent, such as, "Although our project team achieved its goals and then some, others had to cover for your frequent absences in order to make it possible." This is best not said in public. For jobs with ongoing responsibilities or long project cycles, a time frame can be set for regular feedback sessions, such as at the end of the month or quarter or at least twice a year. The challenge is to find the frequency for feedback that is most suited to the job and function.

2. Setting Challenging but Achievable Standards That Reflect the Nature of the Job and the Values of the Organization

Employees want and need to understand what they should do to improve organization performance and their own contributions. Yet employees often want to discuss results without regard to the process or efforts taken in reaching them. In addition, when the results are poor, employees want to discuss the effort expended with the claim that the results were outside their control. Managers often are faced with a choice between examining the results and examining the behaviors that achieved those results. Both results and behaviors need to be included in the development of standards, and they must be specific to each employee's role and reflect organizational values.

Employees should know what is expected of them at the beginning of the performance period, and the goals and measures should be reviewed for adjustment on a regular basis. This accommodates change beyond the employee's control and reinforces the employee's alignment with the external environment and group goals (department, business unit, or company). These results are the "what" the employee is expected to produce. As described in Chapter 5, for the performance objectives and measures to be effective, they need to be

- Written based on a specific time period and have a due date
- Measurable or observable by both the employee and the manager
- Focused more on results than on activities
- Challenging but achievable
- Not overly influenced by things outside the employee's control

A criterion for effective performance objectives is for the manager and employee to discuss and agree on them at the start of the period. Employees want to be involved in ways that help them understand what is expected of them and why. Having employees initiate the development of objectives in the context of the group's overall objectives enhances the "ownership" of the tasks. The agreement by manager and employee enables more consistency, objectivity, and credibility of the criteria.

The second element of effective performance criteria is a description of appropriate behaviors and skills that need to be demonstrated when achieving results or the process of achieving results. When employees are very results-oriented, they focus on achieving high levels of the "what" but may discount the "how" of going about obtaining results. The "how" can make a significant difference in the overall outcomes, such as the impact on customers, coworkers, and subordinates, when driving results. Managers may be reluctant to be specific when it comes to behaviors because they appear too difficult to measure and usually pit one person's opinion against another's. The performance management process should reflect the key results needed (i.e., objectives and measures) and the important behavioral and skill variables that define true success and high performance for the employee. Many of these behavioral measures will reflect the values of the organization and the ways in which objectives need to be accomplished.

Competencies take behaviors one step further. They are defined as a combination of observable and applied knowledge, skills, and behaviors that enable employees to be successful in their jobs, ultimately resulting in a high-performing organization. Competencies describe the "how" of adding value and achieving success, not "what" is achieved.

3. Managers and Employees "Own" the Process

In traditional performance appraisal, performance reviews are imposed on managers by human resources. It is seen as human resources' process rather than as a tool for managers and employees to create and sustain high performance in the organization. Employees want to have an opportunity to understand and possibly influence decisions that affect them. They are one of the key customers of the performance management process. Employees should be highly interested in improving their performance and developing their competencies to make them more marketable both inside and outside the company. Managers should understand that since managing is one of their primary responsibilities, performance management as a process is as important as budgeting, capital planning, and workflow design. When performance management is an ongoing process and managers have the necessary training, the process progresses with ease. It comes down to how an organization manages activities and performance on an ongoing basis, not as an annual ritual conducted by managers. In addition, managers are more inclined to see such a process as a key tool and build some of their own "style" and needs into it as a companywide process. Key leadership competencies also can be included for those in certain roles, such as the ability to provide feedback, the ability to translate goals into clear actions, the ability to set and link individual goals, and the ability to provide performance reviews and discussions on time and frequently. A similar competency can be developed for nonmanagement jobs centered around being involved in the process in order to capture employee ownership of the process.

4. Executives Are Involved in the Process and Model Appropriate Behavior

In traditional performance appraisal systems, executives want performance management for everyone else but feel that it is not needed for them, as giver or receiver. Most executives receive bonuses as part of their total compensation, and these bonuses require the development and assessment of goals and measures. Such executives feel that this is all that is needed in executive performance management. Yet outside directors on public company boards have begun to focus recently on executive assessment and are developing their own processes for assessment and reviews. In a traditional model, executives give and receive very little feedback and have limited development actions. As if this were not already a difficult situation, their actions are multiplied many times over and become the model for others. There are always exceptions for the few that rise above this pattern.

Consider the actual situation in a division of a major financial services organization. In this division, different from the other divisions, all voluntarily terminated employees had a similar response in their exit interviews in human resources—they received very little meaningful feedback as part of their performance appraisals. One day the head of the division was quitting the company and consented to an exit interview. His comments were, "I never got any meaningful feedback on my performance while I was here at this company." This is the same complaint that most members of his division had expressed previously. Although the division head wanted feedback on his performance, he did not receive it. Because he did not receive it, despite wanting it, he did not provide feedback to his subordinates, who in turn had trouble passing it onto the next level. This is called the *multiplier effect*, and it means that the ineffective practices of key leaders frequently are multiplied throughout an organization with obvious negative consequences.

In our new model, executives are engaged in various elements of performance management every day. They hold briefing and discussion sessions with individuals and groups, they seek to learn and promote the desired actions of their people, and they are not fearful of providing too much praise for those whom they know are setting the right examples. They understand that in order for others to understand and accept a certain behavior, they need to model the behavior. When they do, the impact of their leadership changes the organization. In addition, they will be the spokesperson and sponsor for the process. Other executives may start to assimilate the process and actions into their practices, asking their managers to provide information on employee performance, holding their managers accountable for going beyond the minimal level, and ensuring the quality of the information being delivered to employees. For a new performance management process, this means that both the design and implementation of the process begin at the top of the organization.

5. Train Managers and Employees in All Aspects of the Process

We have learned that a set of behaviors, however new, will not be put into practice until a person is thoroughly familiar with those behaviors and how to put the into action. The quality of performance management is a function of four factors: Managers know what to do (clear process and guidelines), know whom to do it to (receive effective training), monitor how well they do it (through feedback and reviews of the practices), and provide meaningful consequences (hopefully positive for doing it well). Sound familiar? Experienced and new managers alike need frequent training, feedback, and coaching—starting with performance management 101 through 205. A series of these sessions should cover the following topics:

- An overview of the approach, process, and criteria
- Understanding how to apply the criteria
- Identifying appropriate measures and writing effective objectives
- Providing qualitative and quantitative feedback to employees
- Conducting meaningful and productive discussions with employees
- Dealing with difficult performance issues
- Linking performance management to multiple rewards
- Using the company's tools or resources effectively

Employees also need to be trained in their roles in and accountability for the process. In addition to having a strong knowledge of the process and criteria, performers need to be trained in how to develop objectives and measures, how to evaluate their own performance using the criteria, how to discuss their performance with their managers, and how to initiate a discussion with or confront a manager who is not fulfilling his or her performance management responsibilities.

The trainers of the organizations who deliver the performance management curriculum need to be experienced managers and must be qualified to train, demonstrate, and provide examples to others. They need to be able to provide real-life examples of how to handle the many concerns about performance management. One strong leadership-oriented company selects individuals for key leadership positions partly based on how well they teach and train other managers in sessions such as this. The executives have found that the performance management process not only challenges individuals to teach and coach others but also is an excellent opportunity to test their commitment to the company's values. This company has no difficulty in getting aspiring managers to teach their performance management sessions.

In traditional performance management, there may be one class to introduce a process change and then no additional training. The session is short and information-based, and like getting a flu shot, employees hope that it will be over soon. Newly promoted or recently hired managers come into the organization with a lack of knowledge of the company's desired practices, or they display the practices of their previous employer. The human resources department or its designated vendor is the sole sponsor of the training. Once in a while an executive may show up to introduce the class for support. One should not need to question why the performance management process is not viewed as an important process of leadership—one should wonder why it was ever thought to be so.

6. Assess and Refresh the Process Periodically

The performance management process should be assessed periodically for its effectiveness in meeting its objectives. The frequency with which you review the process depends on the amount of change that is going on inside and outside the organization. Several experts recommend an annual review based on the number of changes occurring in the external environment. Further, a great deal of knowledge on the best practices and innovations to improve the process can be identified and expanded through this refreshment process.

There is so much change occurring within organizations these days that management processes and tools need to be reviewed and adjusted to retain their alignment and value. However, there is a point at which too frequent and too significant changes can result in a lack of credibility for the process. Changes should be realigned carefully and should be consistent with company needs as well as manager and employee feedback during assessment.

7. Align with the Culture and Values

The link of all rewards processes to company culture, business strategy, and the types of employees has been repeated throughout this book for a variety of compensation programs. Performance management is no exception. The criteria used for performance feedback, assessment, executive commitment, and involvement are the actions that reinforce the organization's cultures and values. Rewards can be more effective if they are based on true achievement and an understanding of what determines real performance.

8. Move the Focus Away from the Overall Rating

Ratings continue to be used for assessments of the individual components of a performance review. However, there is a concern that a summary or an overall rating does not have value. The lack of rater reliability and the negative impact such an overall rating may have on employees are two of the primary reasons for not using it. Without a rating, the manager is then left to find a way to summarize performance and tie it to rewards in a meaningful way that is specific to employee needs. However, if all elements of the performance management process are fine-tuned as suggested in the other best practices, pay and other rewards decisions should be relatively simple.

In a traditional system, employees do not listen and managers frequently ramble, hurrying to get to the overall rating and new base salary. Elimination of this distraction helps place the focus on content and frequently allows the discussion to address performance with ease.

A Process for Developing a New Approach

Successfully replacing the performance appraisal with performance management involves following a best-practices process for redesign. Our experience is that not all development efforts yield the same results, primarily due to the uniqueness of the business and the commitment of its participants and executives. However, it is necessary to amend and adapt the details of this process to be consistent with one's culture and values. For example, a participatory process works in many settings, but in some environments there is a need to complete the process quickly because of significant time demands. This results in limited participation by business area managers as compared with, say, a university setting, where there has to be even more participation in order to build commitment.

A process that has minimal impact on an organization is likely to be simple to design and implement. The performance management process, when used to its full potential, is not easy to design or implement. Its potential effect is achieved by making the process simple and logical to understand and implement, but such a process must be based on sound principles of effective leadership, systems integration, business management, and human behavior. To aid this process, we have outlined below the eight major steps for developing a performance management process suited to an organization's unique requirements. These eight steps are shown in Figure 8-1.

Step I: Assess the Current Needs and Performance Appraisal Process

This step involves building a business case for change based on input from employees and managers about the process, external research, and business needs and strategy. There are several ways to obtain the input needed. The following is a comprehensive list of possibilities:

Figure 8-1 Performance management design wheel.

1. Managers are accountable for timely and thorough performance appraisals.
2. Executives feel that high performance by employees can be a source of competitive advantage for our company.
3. Our current performance appraisal process was developed based on employee and manager input.
4. Our performance appraisal measures both my results and the behaviors and skills I demonstrate to obtain those results.
5. My overall performance rating reflects my performance.
6. Poor performers must improve or will be terminated from employment.

Figure 8-2 Sample assessment questionnaire.

- Individual interviews of executives
- Focus groups of managers
- Focus groups of employees
- Surveys completed by managers and employees
- Individual interview of managers

The common theme of the questioning, regardless of the medium, is, What do you like about the current process? What would you like to see change? What would the ideal system look like once implemented, and why? Figure 8-2 illustrates a more specific list of questions for an employee survey. Once this assessment has been completed, the information should be summarized to be used in building the objectives, approach, and purpose of the new process.

Step 2: Define the Approach, Purpose, and Objectives

This section attempts to determine a philosophy of or approach to performance management by describing the purpose and objectives of the process. Earlier in this chapter the general objectives of performance management were covered. By reviewing the feedback received from executives, employees, and managers in this earlier step, it should be relatively easy to craft meaningful company-specific objective statements. Examples include

- "Provide employees with regular feedback on how well they are improving and guidance on ways to improve performance."
- "Support managers in their responsibilities to provide employees with clear feedback on current performance and ways to improve their contributions to department, division, and company results."
- "Provide executives with reliable information on how people are performing in relation to their responsibilities and enhance the ability to develop capabilities, retain highly talented individuals, and reward people commensurate with their performance."

Step 3: Obtain Senior Management Perspective and Commitment

This step involves creating the business case for changing the performance management process so that it has more impact on the company and gains the full support and commitment of executives for the new approach. It is often effective to present a summary of the results of the assessment and clear descriptions of the approach, purpose, and objectives. This presentation should demonstrate how the new process will have a measurable and important impact on the business. The discussion that follows should both provide feedback and test the degree of support for change. It also will provide the framework for developing the specific details of the process so that when the final recommendations are made, there will be strong support. If a representative sample of executives has been interviewed as part of the preceding step, there should be support for a strong commitment to the changes in the process. However, if viewpoints were very different during the executive interviews, this step will be key to proposing and confirming a winning approach to performance management.

This is also a good time to suggest and gain agreement on the following:

- The philosophy and desired outcomes of the performance management process

- The appropriate number of times and the time frames performance reviews should be conducted
- Application of the process to merit pay decisions, succession planning, training and development priorities, and staffing decisions
- Identification of executive team members and other members of the organizations who can be involved in developing or reviewing the specific details of the process and any concerns or objectives for their involvement

The next step to designing a new performance management approach is best accomplished when a representative group of managers is involved in reviewing, developing, and finalizing the new model of performance management.

Step 4: Develop the Performance Criteria and Measures

Performance criteria and measures are the elements by which the performer is assessed. This is the heart of the process and defines the foundation on which feedback information is collected and provided to employees and decisions are made. These are the tasks or levels of performance used to gauge whether or not a person has achieved his or her goals. The purpose of assessment is to provide clear and specific information to the performer on how he or she is doing—what he or she is doing well, what he or she needs to improve on, and what he or she needs to do to improve performance. The other processes linked either directly or indirectly to an employee's overall performance, such as merit pay increases, succession planning, development, and so on, are also a consideration for the purpose of efficiency and consistency.

Step 5: Designing the Process and Tools

This section explores the tools and documents that will be used during the process. These are best discovered by asking a series of questions and considering the alternatives:

How often should feedback be provided to employees?

- Once a year
- Twice a year
- Four times a year
- If more than once a year, should there be one formal session and the remainder shorter sessions?

Who will provide the information to be used as the basis for feedback?

- The employee's manager only
- Two levels of management
- Project leaders
- Peers
- 360-degree or multiple raters

Figure 8-3 provides a list of opportunities and situations in which performance review can occur beyond the normal or expected annual review.

- The employee's involvement in a special assignment has just ended.
- The employee has just reached a milestone in a project or completed a project.
- An internal or external customer has just provided specific feedback to you (either formally or informally) on the employee's behaviors or results.
- It has reached a point where you have observed a significant change in employee performance—either improvement or decline.
- There is a change in goals and/or measures—added, removed, or reprioritized.
- If none of these events or circumstances has occurred, a performance discussion should occur between one and four times outside the annual performance review.

Figure 8-3 The frequency of performance assessment outside the annual review.

What should be the timing of the annual salary review?

- All staff members reviewed during the same month (i.e., common review, also known as a *focal review*)
- On the anniversary of the employee being either hired or promoted to the current position
- Different review schedules, based on employee type (e.g., exempt, nonexempt)

Table 8-1 provides a list of differences between anniversary and common reviews. Although many companies use common reviews, other companies feel that with an increasing emphasis on performance management and the availability of electronic tools, they can do reviews on employee job anniversaries or more frequently.

Table 8-1   A Comparison of Focal versus Anniversary Reviews

Criteria for Effective Goals	Approach	
	Focal	Anniversary
Quality	Multiple at same time	One at a time/multiple overtime
Consistency	Relative comparison = consistent ratings	
Clear basis for decisions	Maintain internal equity	Absolute ratings
Timeliness	Have to submit at once	Managers who are late damage any positives
Degree of change needed	Things are still the same	Positive indicator that this process is different
Administrative ease/efficiency	More efficient when done at same time	Least disruptive to ongoing business; requires more adminstrative support
Encourages frequent feedback		More likely

What is the employee's role in performance management?

- Complete self-assessment
- Draft of personal measures and goals
- Identification of development actions

What is the manager's role in the program?

- Collect all the information necessary
- Prepare all documents and feedback sheets
- Initiate assessment process
- Determine when and where to conduct the review
- Gain approvals from next level of management (prior to or after key decisions)
- Make recommendations on pay actions, development plans, and performance goals
- Determine the person's performance (rate, rank, or both)

Are there any differences in the process based on job or type of job, such as exempt versus nonexempt, manager versus individual contributor, part time versus full time?

- Different measures (results and/or competencies) to be used
- Different timing for performance reviews
- Different approval and review processes

What are the tools and/or systems that will be used, and how will they support the process?

- Goal setting and/or competency feedback worksheets
- Self-assessment form same as manager's assessment form
- Separate development form
- Salary action or other decision form
- Separate interim review form

Automation is a key to making the process and tools easy to use and monitor. Choices include developing one's own automation tools or purchasing an outside system. If you decide to purchase a system, plan for time to select the system and about 90 to 180 days to implement it. There are many systems to choose from, so one should be clear about the purpose, process, and requirements for information and documentation prior to purchasing such a system.

From the best-practices section, one of the most significant impacts is the frequency of providing feedback to employees and linking this feedback to both goals and positive consequences. This can be accomplished by using one major review (annual) and interim reviews (quarterly). The focus of the interim review is to encourage meaningful discussion between employees and managers on what has been done and what needs to be done for the next period. This will help provide the feedback and focus needed for the employee to work to his or her greatest potential.

Step 6: Establish the Link to Total Rewards

This is the pay component of the performance management system. In many organizations, the amount of a pay increase is based on the performance rating and the salary range of or market price for the position. There are few issues in performance management systems that generate more controversy than merit pay. There are four main concerns:

1. Giving pay increases to individuals when their performance is really a function of a team's results or the workplace systems.
2. Giving more pay to some people and less to others on the same team, thereby undermining the cohesion and equity of the team.
3. Making pay-increase decisions with little reliable data from someone, such as a manager, who has little firsthand, objective information on the individual's performance.
4. Having sufficient funds to reward the eagles of the group very well and restricting the pay increases of individuals whose performance was not adequate.

The central question is, Should merit pay increases be included in the performance management process? The answer depends on what you want the process to do. If the purpose of the performance management process is to focus activities, facilitate feedback, and encourage developmental actions, pay should not be part of the process, at least during the performance discussion. Instead, individuals should have their pay adjusted based on external market conditions, overall team performance, or personal achievements that are developmental in nature. If the purpose is to recognize and reward individual performance, then pay should be linked to the assessment of performance and discussed during the performance review meeting.

If merit pay is linked to performance management, then what is the best approach? The traditional approach is to use the merit rating to select a pay-increase percentage. The higher the rating, the higher the percentage until the employee's salary is out of range for the position; then merit bonuses are used in lieu of salary increases. An alternative would be to focus attention on the salary-performance relationship. Overall performance levels can be aligned with an employee's salary range or, if there is no salary range, with a market reference point. Then, if the employee is not paid consistently with a salary that reflects his or her position, pay can and should be adjusted to this point as a reasonable response and within budget restraints on salary increases. If the person has reached his or her targeted salary based on performance, then he or she will be eligible for a merit bonus, not a merit increase. The types of rewards we have been discussing in this book are base salaries, variable pay, long-term incentives, and recognition, including promotions and special assignments. Traditionally, merit increases have been based on the annual performance review and the rating. In the new performance management model, the rewards linked to performance management need to include all forms. New variable-pay systems also may use the performance rating to determine individual awards, such as when a group incentive plan uses the performance rating as a multiplier of group results. This enables the organization to reward both the group's performance and the individuals who made the greatest contribution. In other cases, the objectives and measures may be the same between base and variable pay systems. The variable awards can be paid out during the first half of the year, and the merit awards can be adjusted during the second half. For companies with interim reviews and recognition programs, it may make sense to recognize results from the interim review. It is important to not do this every time so that people do not come to "expect" the rewards and disassociate them from the performance achieved. Such rewards are to be used ideally when results are outstanding or show significant improvement at the end of a project or performance period.

Step 7: Review the Process for All Legal, Policy, and Systems Requirements

If rewards and employment decisions are based on performance, there needs to be a way to determine an individual's performance. In addition, it is important that the performer being evaluated is being judged based on criteria that are job-related. Therefore, the traditional approach of incorporating an employee's job description into performance appraisal criteria was developed. This approach was derived at about the same time as Civil Rights Act and Title VII were put into law. They specifically state that employers cannot discriminate in employment decisions on the basis of race, color, religion, sex, or national origin. Congress went on to add age discrimination in separate legislation. Further, a series of court cases have clearly linked the process of performance appraisals with discriminatory decisions and have stipulated requirements for their conduct [e.g., *Bito* v. *Zia Company* (1974), *Griggs* v. *Duke Power* (1971), *Wade* v. *Mississippi Cooperative Extension Service* (1974), *Albermarle Paper Company* v. *Moody* (1975), etc.]. Thus the job description became the foundation document to ensure the all performance decisions were based on job-specific criteria.

The practices that evolved, which can be assessed in terms of their effectiveness, are directed at protecting individuals from ineffective management practices. The overall objective is to provide employees with a process that helps them understand the requirements of their role, gives them feedback on their performance, and rewards them for their achievements. These principles are consistent with best practices in performance management systems. The challenge lies in creating a process that is meaningful to the performer within the context of today's newly competitive workplace.

Step 8: Obtain Final Approvals and Plan and Implement the Changes

At this point in the development or revision effort, the new process will be defined, measures and tools for assessing performance will be developed, and all the related policies, decisions, and systems will be developed. Because the process began with articulating the philosophy, applications, and requirements with the top executives, the designers of the program should present it to the top executives and obtain final agreement about it. The importance of this process was addressed earlier, but in essence, the process will not work without commitment by top executives, use of the information for decision making, and clear, practical, and useful tools. Before the implementation plan can be engaged, therefore, executive review and approval are essential.

Because implementation usually requires advance notice in order to coordinate the distribution of materials, the scheduling of time and facilities for training, and so on, it is advisable to start planning implementation at the onset of the design project and update it once the final performance management process has been determined.

The implementation plan usually starts with establishing the date by which managers and employees will start using the new process and then working backward to plan the other steps. With regard to timing, a development schedule that is too tight will create issues in the buy-in and confidence-building process, and the implementation actually will take longer than expected. The following implementation steps should help ensure success for the program.

Establish the Implementation Objectives

It is important to put as much effort into implementation of the program as into development. Therefore, it is helpful to start out with objectives. Examples of implementation objectives include

- Employees understand the new performance management process.
- Managers understand and can easily use the new performance management process.
- The performance management process is ready for use as of [date] with the merit increase effective on [date].

Announce the New Performance Management Process

Prior to the start of the new performance management process, employees should receive a thorough explanation of the objectives, key elements, process steps, time frames, and any special features that differentiate the process from past practices. This will help employees become involved in process, and it will indicate what they can expect from their managers (this also helps managers apply the process more consistently). During the initial assessment and development effort, employees should have received periodic updates on how the process was working. Thus, when they see the final product, they will understand that the changes are real and important to the organization. While employee commitment is not a critical requirement for success, in companies that have successful performance management programs in place, employees feel a direct involvement in the process.

Pilot or Test the Program

When full executive commitment cannot be achieved or there is serious resistance by managers and/or employees to the new process, it may be best to use pilot engagements before taking the process company-wide. A test run of the tools and the process may help reduce concerns and demonstrate the value during implementation. At the very least, several employees and managers should try completing the tools and provide feedback on what works well and what requires adjustment. The firm's executives are often the ideal test market so that the process can be tailored to their styles and they can demonstrate to one another the value and importance of the process.

Provide an Overview Presentation

Once the program has been approved in its final format by key executives, it is important to start introducing the program to managers. The agenda of presentations and communications should be focused on an overview—such as what has changed and why and how the program will be implemented. It should allow for dialog so that managers can ask the questions they know will be on the minds of their employees.

Next, employees should receive the same overview, and their managers should be prepared enough to help clarify the information and answer employee questions. An important detail in these overview presentations is to have them presented by key executives and other participants in the design process. This should help create ownership and commitment by managers and employees.

Use Manager Training to Build Understanding, Skills, and Support

Manager training and distribution of supporting materials constitute the next step in the implementation process. The goals are to provide managers with an in-depth review of new process, criteria, and supporting materials and to develop their skills in setting objectives, providing feedback, assigning consistent performance ratings to employees, and training on automation tools or software applications. If a new merit pay process is to be introduced, then this also would include reviewing the criteria and process for making pay decisions.

Final implementation is now ready to begin. In other words, it is time for employees and managers to start the process with an assessment of the last performance period and to set new objectives and measures for the next period. The tools need to be in place on the company's intranet, and any forms of automation should be functional.

Employee Training

Employees can benefit greatly from learning how to develop objectives and measures and from understanding how to use ratings and what their roles and accountabilities are in the process. The manager training should be more of a time commitment than the employee sessions. Managers also will feel more comfortable knowing that their employees understand the new program.

Evaluate the Initial Implementation and Its Ongoing Effectiveness

The final step in implementation, and one that is often forgotten, is to conduct an evaluation of the program. This can and should be done in two parts. First, after managers and employees have had an initial experience with the new process, it is necessary to conduct focus groups, surveys, or interviews with key managers to gain their feedback and observations about the process. It is likely that their reactions will be both positive and negative, and as in any system in which new skills need to be learned, there will be resistance and comparisons with past practices. Then, after managers and employees have completed several interim updates and an annual review (if included in the process), it is necessary to collect additional feedback in the same manner as at the beginning of the development process. Specific questions, often with rating scales, on the program's value, steps, and tools should help determine if the program is meeting its objectives. It is also important to collect commentary on what managers and employees like about the system and what should be changed. In addition, the distribution of ratings and rewards should be analyzed to determine if there it has achieved performance and reward differentiation. Other indicators of the program's impact, such as retention rates, rates of internal promotions and career advancements, and the impact on key performance measures directly related to the process, should be documented. The key is to demonstrate that the value produced far exceeds the time and effort invested.

Performance management is therefore unique to every organization, or at least it should be. It should create opportunities to strengthen the relationship between employees and the organization, thereby reducing undesired turnover. It should focus people on both what they are to achieve and how they should achieve it, thereby improving performance at the "grass-roots level" of the organization. It should ensure that rewards are allocated according to performance and applied in meaningful ways, thereby reducing an entitlement mentality and encouraging people to feel valued for what they accomplish. Finally, the process should develop people into both high performers and leaders within the areas to which they are committed in their careers, thereby enabling the organization to achieve a greater competitive advantage in those areas where talent makes a difference.

To see how a process can be developed and implemented based on the unique needs of an organization, we will explore a case study involving the Nelson Enterprises (an actual company but with a fictitious name).

Case Study: A Team Approach to Performance Management

Nelson Enterprises, Inc., has adopted a different approach to performance management. The purpose of its program is to facilitate feedback and reinforce performance on a real-time basis and in particular to emphasize the contributions of individuals to their teams. While annual reviews have been the traditional method, the chief executive officer (CEO) and senior managers wanted a process that was real time and could drive both the critical strategic measures of the company and its desired values.

The company is facing a business environment in which it needs to continually release new products and services that are suited to its clients. Working in teams is critical to this business imperative, for the company has found in the past that individual heroes resulted in a suboptimal performance compared to the company's competitors. However, the executive team realizes the importance of individual contributions and has developed a performance management process that reinforces collaboration and contributions by individuals. The success of the company depends on an "all hands on deck" sense of urgency.

In terms of process, each major team within the company establishes performance measures on an annual basis in concert with its group managers. These measures may be modified on a semiannual basis, but most target annual goals. Some measures concentrate on results, such as delivery performance, product/service quality, and costs, and others focus on special developmental projects to improve the capabilities of the group or companywide critical initiatives. Once the goals are set, the team discusses how it will achieve maximum results and assigns accountabilities to individuals and subunits. Each measure has a continuum of performance levels, and the team uses a performance matrix, as discussed earlier. Furthermore, Nelson Enterprises developed a personal performance checklist of the critical behaviors necessary to support a team's performance.

Monitoring results and providing feedback are very important to each team's success. Each team monitors certain measures on a weekly and monthly basis, and others are analyzed on a quarterly basis. The teams openly display charts in their work areas, and the measures, the creativity of the charts, and progress are frequently the basis of great discussions. Each team examines its own performance, analyzes any barriers to success, and scrutinizes the contributions and commitments of each individual member. Periodically, the group manager attends the review meetings to assess team progress, encourage and reinforce team efforts, address team concerns, and determine what assistance the team may need to achieve its maximum potential.

Every 2 to 3 months team members complete the personal performance checklist. The process is relatively simple. The individual, in collaboration with his or her group manager, selects five people to conduct an assessment of the individual's contribution. Usually these people are other teammates, but they may be customers or other members of the division. The individual completes a self-evaluation, and the group manager completes one on each person. The group manager then collects the checklists and summarizes the results. He or she then discusses the results of the feedback with the individual and plans appropriate actions to either improve performance or change the perceptions of others. In some of the more developed teams, individuals use these groups to discuss strategies for improving their effectiveness with the team. Some teams chart the overall scores of their members as a measure of the team's overall effectiveness.

The teams and group managers use the overall performance data in two very important ways. First, they track how things are going and identify barriers to their continued growth and improvement. Second, they use the data to celebrate victories. In addition, each team has access to a fund for recognizing its own performance and that of other individuals or teams throughout the division. The quarterly and semiannual reviews are often marked with some "crazy" event (e.g., an ice cream party or a trip to a theme park); the monthly and quarterly individual reviews are seen as an important part of the process of reinforcement and development.

Increases in pay are determined through a variety of vehicles. First, the size of the merit pool is determined by the semiannual and annual results of each division. This determines the average size of the awards available for pay increases. Second, team performance determines the pay opportunities for each individual. In high-performance teams, individuals may have a 2 to 4 percent higher pay-increase opportunity than the corporate guidelines. Individuals on poorly performing teams may have few, if any, pay-increase opportunities. Individual awards are determined by the group manager based on several inputs. He or she solicits inputs from the team on the performance ratings of each individual, examines the performance levels and growth of each individual on the personal performance checklists, and considers the internal relationships of pay. The pay increase is determined based on these factors. However, since this is only on annual event, the performance trends usually are well known to the individual, and there are numerous opportunities for individuals to be recognized for their performance. Often, very little importance is attached to pay adjustments. Other divisions of the company have adopted pay-for-competencies-employed types of programs, and pay adjustments are based on the increase in applied skills. It is quite interesting to note that no one really feels that the performance management process is too time-consuming or that pay is too limited, or no one blames anyone else when he or she does not achieve targets. There is an unusual sense of personal accountability and commitment to the goals the groups and teams establish. Simply stated, the people at Nelson Enterprises are clearly focused and committed to the company's success.

Summary

The answer to resolving these issues does not lie in producing a new form. Nor is the answer to be found in more training for managers or more policies or control procedures to increase the frequency or firmness with which certain actions are taken. The problem with performance appraisals is that we ask managers to do more work than is received in value for employees, the manager, or the company. It is time to consider alternative approaches to performance management that can help both performers and the company to realize high performance.

How Variable Pay Connects the People and the Strategy

If you are trying to change the way you run a company, one of the most visible things you have to change is the way you compensate, reward and recognize people.

Paul Allaire, CEO, Xerox Corp.
Harvard Business Review, October 1992

COMPANIES HAVE BEEN INCREASING the use of variable pay programs in the United States and throughout the world. A recent survey of reward practices by WorldatWork[1] (formerly the American Compensation Association) reports that approximately 66 percent of U.S.

companies use variable pay beyond executive levels; this is an increase from 59 percent in 1995. These programs include sales commission and bonus plans, individual bonus plans, and group and team incentive plans.

The focus of this chapter will be to review the primary benefits and issues of these programs and discuss alternative approaches.

To provide a definition, variable pay plans are compensation programs that deliver lump-sum payments to individuals based on their performance of predetermined objectives of the organization, business unit, and/or individual.

For our purposes, the terms *variable, incentive,* and *bonus* will be used interchangeably. This should provide the framework for how organizations can use such programs to create value and growth. Differentiation will be made by the types of programs.

Types of Variable Pay Plans

Variable pay programs come in many forms. There are 11 different applications that have unique characteristics and requirements. These are

1. *Profit-sharing plans.* Perhaps the oldest and most widely used method, this type of plan shares a portion of a company's profits (above certain planned levels) with its employees. Approximately 20 percent of U.S. companies have this form of pay program in place.[2] Profit sharing has great appeal because of its simplicity and the extent to which it reinforces the positive role of top executives. Many large firms use the profit-sharing payment as a method for making contributions to employee defined-contribution retirement plans or 401(k) plans. In such plans, the dollars are the employer's contributions to employee retirement accounts and are not given to them in direct cash payments. Smaller companies use profit-sharing payouts as a form of companywide bonus plan, and these payouts are made directly to employees. Usually these programs work best when the organization is small and people can relate their performance to the profitability of the organization.

2. *Executive annual bonus plans.* In these plans, senior executives receive a payment based on individual and company perfor-

mance. Such programs are separate from equity-based programs that use stock or stock-related awards.

3. *Management bonus plans.* In these plans, middle and upper-level managers receive annual payments based on their performance, which usually is determined by a set of objectives or discretionary assessments of performance by top executives. Similar to executives, the payouts may be based on company, division/business unit, and/or individual performance against objectives. Typically, companies use a "management by objectives" approach to plan and evaluate individual performance.

4. *Individual bonus plans.* These are bonuses paid to nonmanagerial, professional staff for meeting personal objectives. Similar to management bonuses, these payouts are derived from company, business unit, and/or individual performance against objectives.

5. *Sales incentive plans.* These are incentive programs that are linked to the tasks of the sales force within the organization. The payouts are usually based on the dollar volume of units sold, the revenues of specific products or services, or other direct sales performance measures. The salesperson may receive a commission (i.e., a predetermined percentage of every unit/dollar sold) or a bonus based on achieving a certain level of sales or other performance objectives.

6. *Sales management incentive plans.* These programs link the manager's incentive payout directly to the performance of his or her sales staff. This can include an override based on the production levels of the staff combined with personal performance objectives that are tied to objectives such as customer retention, market share, introduction of new products, and so on. The overall principle is to tie the manager's incentive to the performance of the sales staff and the priorities of the business.

7. *Individual piece-rate incentives.* These incentive programs focus on the tasks of operational employees and involve paying them a predetermined amount of money for each unit of work they produce. The units of work can range from products made, such as the number of golf balls produced by an assembly line, to operations performed, such as the number of orders processed by a mail-order company. The time frame is usually weekly or monthly and operates in a way similar to a sales commission plan.

8. *Goal-sharing/team incentives.* In these incentive programs, the payout is based on the performance of a group of individuals, such as a business unit, department, or plant. Usually several measures relate directly to the functions of the group and may include an overall company measure. The payouts are provided equally to all members of the business unit or team.[3]

9. *Gain sharing plans.* These programs usually involve operational employees (i.e., direct and indirect labor) and provide payments based on the achievement of performance levels above a predetermined baseline. Their function is very similar to a profit-sharing plan, only the payout is based on a unit such as a plant or department. These programs are sometimes referred to as *Scanlon plans, Rucker plans, Improshare plans,* and *GainSharing plans.*[4] The payouts are usually based on a direct economic outcome, such as units of output, increased profitability, or decreased unit costs, and are paid evenly to eligible employees.

10. *Project-based incentive plans.* These are variable pay programs tied to the performance of a project. The metrics are based on project outcomes and milestone performance. Payouts are made to all members of the project at the time the project is completed. At the end of the project, the program is terminated.

11. *Key-contributor incentive plans.* These programs often focus on individuals regarded as special talent to the organization. For example, a professional service company developed a variable pay plan for individuals involved in managing key client relationships and providing technical training to new customers. If certain profitability targets were achieved, the selected *key contributors* would receive payouts tied to overall team and individual performance. These plans are usually applied to new product development teams, scientific and technical staff, and others whose talent as individual contributors is viewed as an essential asset of the company. They are different from project incentives because they focus on group performance factors.

Excluded from this list are discretionary bonus plans in which there are no predetermined performance expectations, spot award programs in which employees are not told in advance the results that will determine the award, and retention bonuses that are paid if individuals remain employed with the company for a specific time period. While the programs involve lump-sum payments, they are not based on pre-determined performance. Further excluded from the foregoing definitions are programs that relate to providing equity or company stock based on performance; Chapter 12 is dedicated to these plans. The focus of this chapter is on the advantages and issues of these plans and the design principles to make them effective.

Primary Advantages and Issues

The purpose of variable pay programs is usually to:

1. Create a stake in the performance of the organization
2. Encourage a performance focus, either for an individual or for a team
3. Support change efforts within the organization by linking their success to the payouts
4. Increase company competitiveness and total compensation
5. Shift more compensation costs from fixed to variable expenses

There is clearly a growing interest in instituting variable pay programs, but there are several very serious concerns. First, some executives argue, "Why pay more?" In other words, employees are paid a salary to perform their jobs. Why should they receive additional compensation? The answer to this question may be philosophical or practical. From a management values perspective, variable plans can, if designed and managed effectively, provide a reward tied to performance levels that most likely would not be achieved otherwise. They can reinforce new behaviors by encouraging employees to perform in a manner that is consistent with the growth and success of the company. If the same performance can be achieved without such plans, the firm obviously should pursue that course. However, in many firms these plans dramatically facilitate the performance achievement.

The second concern usually centers on setting or tracking performance measures. There are many jobs for which it is difficult to measure performance in an objective and reliable manner. It is perhaps more precise to describe this as a concern about the cost-effectiveness of performance measures. The organization should set priorities about what it believes is necessary to drive desired performance. While measures could be established on these factors, it would be too costly to collect and validate the data. A good illustration is the efforts many organizations have taken to measuring customer satisfaction; the factor is vitally important but too expensive to measure frequently.

A third issue is the general resistance to incentive plans because of bad previous experiences. Executives have been known to reject these plans because of an experience they had with another company many years before. While this concern is important, one needs to examine what happened before and what can be done differently now. If an executive had an essentially positive experience with incentives, this, too, needs to be examined for its key learning points. Without such examinations, the organization may be unnecessarily avoiding a reliable process to support critical organizational performance. Hence, change may not be encouraged just at the time when it is most needed.

A fourth concern involves the opportunity for improvement. Some executives and advisers are concerned about the impact on employee relations when performance reaches a limit. They are worried that the absence of incentive payments will make employees angry. Performance levels usually are increased each year unless there is a change in the market or strategy. This is an important concern, but the programs and measures should be established to exist for 3 to 5 years; usually there is enough changing during such a time period to eliminate this concern.

A fifth issue is the impact of employees feeling that the measures are not in their control or that their suggestions for improvement are not implemented. There is ample evidence of organizations in which employees sought to make changes in the business process, but managers and supervisors did not support them. To implement some suggestions may have required additional investments, but the funds were not available or the cost of change was perceived as greater than the potential benefit. This criticism may or may not be justified. If employees view the program as merely a process to get them to work harder (not smarter), then they will have a negative response, and it likely will be justified. Successful plans encourage meaningful collaboration between managers and employees. The important change to continue to encourage is dialogue and deliberation about what is cost-effective and realistic for the organization.

Finally, there are concerns that people will become fixed on earning their incentives and will not implement changes or take actions that do not directly support the incentive program. This is an important concern and reflects programs that use only one or two measures and make limited use of other reward programs. One of the primary reasons for an incentive program is to drive total organizational success. An organization's success is seldom determined by only one or two metrics. Further, the process does not reduce or minimize management roles. Working with the program is not *additional* work; this is *the* work of the managers.

Case Study: A Typical Management Incentive Program

A midsized consumer products company has had a management incentive program for over 10 years. The purpose of the program is to reward individuals for achieving key objectives. All middle and higher managers participate in the plan. The target payout varies according to the individual's level in the organization, as shown below:

- Chief executive officer: 60 percent of base salary
- Vice presidents: 40 percent of base salary
- Directors: 25 percent of base salary
- Managers: 15 percent of base salary

The company needs to reach at least 95 percent of its planned profit levels in order for the incentive plan to be funded. Once this threshold is achieved, each manager is eligible to receive his or her target payout modified by individual performance (± 25 percent). Individual performance is based on results against objectives established between each person and his or her manager or on an overall assessment of the individual's performance. In some cases, the objectives are tied to project outcomes or financial objectives (e.g., growth in revenues, expenses to budget, etc.) for the individual's functional area. If an individual does not have objectives or if conditions change significantly, the performance assessment is based on a judgment by the executive. Finally, the performance assessments and bonus calculations are determined at the end of the fiscal year and approved by the chief executive officer (CEO) of the company. The CEO uses this opportunity to modify the payouts based on his personal assessment of individual performance.

One of the interesting issues in this company is that the executives are reluctant to extend incentives farther down in the organization. They highlight many of the issues discussed earlier in this chapter, and they believe that their incentive program is an important pay-for-performance program.

The participants regard the plan as discretionary in that they feel that they have little control over the payouts. In terms of payout results, the bonus plan has paid out in 9 of the last 10 years. Most managers receive within 5 percent of their target level. Over 90 percent of the participating managers receive their bonuses annually. While there is always concern about whether the 95 percent profit threshold is met, especially during the third and fourth quarters, most managers have come to expect their incentive payment. Frequently, the chief financial officer (CFO) will make the necessary adjustments so that the company achieves the threshold. Finally, these payouts have enabled the company to achieve a sixtieth percentile in the marketplace for total compensation.

What Is Wrong with This Process?

This is a typical management bonus plan. While the payouts are supposed to reflect performance, they seldom vary much from target. Should one therefore assume that this company is successful and meets all its targets? This program really should be regarded as an *entitlement* bonus plan. The participants have lost the contingency connection between the payouts and their performance.

Let's examine the plan based on several criteria of an effective variable pay plan. When we examine variable pay plans, there are unique specific criteria that define their success. Similar to the STRIVE criteria discussed in Chapter 2, the criteria for an effective variable pay program is presented below. By understanding these factors, we can understand why some succeed and others fail.

Specific—Do People Understand How to Maximize Performance?

While individual performance objectives exist for some managers, many do not have objectives, nor do they relate to the key factors of the firm's performance. The objectives are based on personal negotiation between the manager and his or her executive. This reflects a traditional boss-as-the-customer relationship. Furthermore, while the profit budget has been established as a common goal, most executives believe that they have little true impact on the results, except for keeping their department's expenses within budget. This feature of the plan does not have any significant influence on individual performance but does serve to fund the plan. The real determinant of the payout is the evidence the manager can produce to demonstrate his or her achievement on personal objectives.

Meaningful—Are the Payout Levels Sufficient to Influence Behavior?

While the levels of payout are probably meaningful, the company is not getting a desired return on investment. In this organization, the incentive compensation payouts exceed $2 million. If a manager asked to spend a similar amount of money on a project, the top executives would require a lot of hard evidence to justify the return on investment of the expense. Yet they do not demand the same level of rigorous return-on-investment analysis for the incentive plan. There are few areas of the business's expenses that top executives act so cavalierly about.

Achievable—Are the Goals Challenging as well as Possible to Achieve?

The performance objectives are achievable; in fact, they actually may reflect a minimal degree of stretch. When managers develop personal goals with little input from or review by other executives, the chances for misalignment and conflict increase greatly. To what extent does this process reinforce collaboration and teamwork? Given the history of performance, it seems clear that these incentives do little to drive rigorous levels of performance. The CEO's reviews, especially when he or she relies on his or her personal assessments (with little input from other executives) to modify the recommended payouts, may further undermine the pay and performance relationship.

Reliable—Does the Program Operate Consistently with Its Purpose and Objectives?

The system is easy to administer and is handled only once a year. The executives rarely discuss progress on the key objectives (i.e., feedback), and yet the plan has provided a payout in 9 of the last 10 years. It is interesting to note that the plan is not perceived as broken, yet does it truly drive desired performance? For the participants, this has become a standard element of their compensation. While it may be described as a pay-at-risk plan, the reality is that there is little, if any, actual risk. The only risk is that the executive may loose what he or she has grown to expect.

Timely—Does the Plan Operate to Encourage Real-Time Action to Achieve Results?

By providing reviews on an annual basis only, the plan is nonoperational for approximately three-quarters of the year. Serious attention to the objectives occurs only in the last quarter, after the executives determine whether or not the 95 percent profitability target will be met. The rest of the time there is little sense of urgency about the performance commitments of the plan. Thus, in terms of timeliness, the annual plan has little impact on performance.

The key issue in this discussion is not why the plan does not work, but rather whatever made us believe that it would work in the first place. Like many organizations, the company in the case study established its management bonus plan as a way of retaining market competitiveness for total compensation. However, the plan has evolved away from a process to reinforce the implementation of company goals or the accountabilities of executives. The plan is simple to understand but ultimately too simple to drive desired performance. The program has become a way to distribute bonus dollars. Simply stated, the company is not getting value from these expenditures. The task is not to eliminate the plan but to modify it, both in design and in how it operates.

Managers who have grown accustomed to the plan will experience a degree of risk if the plan is replaced or redesigned to link it with the core business goals. Managers who have confidence in their ability to achieve great results likely will leave the company because of the lack of real rewards. This is the challenge of designing reward systems that are genuinely oriented toward the economics and risks of the business. It is no wonder that executives are reluctant to extend incentives to other areas of the organization. The paradox is that they will not give up the comfortable features of their plan nor design a plan that would be effective in reinforcing the desired performance of others. This is a typical example of resistance to change.

Understanding the Value and Impact of Variable Pay Plans

One of the most interesting features of variable pay plans is the extent to which they vary from one company to another. Few companies do, or should, install the plans developed at other companies. Each situation is different, each strategy is different, and cultures reinforce behaviors that are different. Thus each plan *should* be different and reflect the *special* requirements of the organization.

A central issue in developing such programs is determining the fundamental purpose of the plan. Is the plan intended to reward individuals for their own achievements, or is it intended to motivate individuals to collaborate on improving team, unit, or organizational performance? Often we find that executives are attracted to incentive pay plans because they offer a method to reduce the fixed costs of compensation and make pay more variable. While this may serve the interest of managing costs and is often a benefit of such programs, the philosophy inherently may establish a win-lose philosophy for the plan. It is better to focus the plan on improving performance than on reducing compensation costs.

The plan needs to stimulate new actions by people so that the organization is more competitive and more successful. This approach will yield a true win-win arrangement in which the corporation becomes more successful and competitive and its employees benefit financially and feel more appreciated. It does require careful consideration of the philosophy and strategies of the organization. If people do not need to modify their actions, there is probably no need for a variable pay plan. Hence these programs should focus on encouraging and rewarding change, responsiveness, and achievement of challenging goals.

Organizations usually have a number of different plans, each uniquely suited to different employee groups. For example, it is common to have the sales staff on one type of incentive plan and the senior managers on another, operational employees on one plan and support staff on another. This portfolio approach to incentive plans enables the organization to target specific reward systems to the roles and tasks of specific employees consistent with its overall competitive strategies. A thoughtful reward strategy should provide a unique focus to each of these plans.

When considering a variable pay program, it is very important to determine which group or groups to include in the plan. These are known as the *target groups*. This means that plans should be organized around groups with common work processes, customers, and/or lines of business. The variable pay plan can then be focused on the unique performance requirements of each group.

Assessing the Readiness or Effectiveness of Variable Pay

Incentive pay plans are not for every organization. While many managers are interested in installing variable pay programs, there may be good reasons for caution.

Executives would be wise to assess the firm's readiness before proceeding to develop a new variable pay plan. The benefits of such programs must outweigh the costs and risks. Conditions do not need to be perfect, but there are certain factors that can support these programs.

Assessing the readiness or the effectiveness of existing plans serves several very important objectives. First, it indicates whether or not an incentive plan makes sense for the organization and the selected target groups. Does it support or disrupt what the organization is attempting to do? Second, if conditions are generally satisfactory but there are some concerns, the process can provide insights into what needs to be done to support the organization's changes as well as indicate critical design or implementation issues. Finally, the assessment can provide an understanding of what is possible for improvements in performance. Hence the readiness or effectiveness assessment is often a critical step for strong variable compensation plans.

Seven Key Factors for Assessment

While the importance of an assessment process is clear, what should one assess? What are the critical factors leading to a well-designed and implemented incentive program? Figure 9-1 shows seven key questions that can be used in the assessment. They are discussed in detail in the next few pages.

1. *To what extent does the target group control its performance?* If the target group has little control over the variables in its performance, the process is destined to fail or result in payouts that are

1. To what extent does the target group control its performance?
2. Have most of the major structural or system changes been completed?
3. Do clear, reliable measures exist for the unit?
4. Is the current compensation adequate from an internal equity and external competitiveness standpoint?
5. Are the managers of the unit generally effective in providing the leadership necessary for the group?
6. Is the culture of the organization characterized by trust, mutual respect, and a willingness of performers to work together for common goals?
7. Does the plan have a sponsor and a champion?

Figure 9-1 Assessing the readiness for variable compensation.

not justified by the actions of the target group. While no individual or group of employees has total control over their performance, it is important to determine the degree of impact they can and do have. A group that has a higher degree of control can have a higher risk-reward ratio. The target group for the incentive plan should have a high degree of influence over the big measures of its performance.

2. *Have most of the major structural or system changes been completed?* We live in a time of tremendous change. Organizations are frequently downsizing, restructuring, or reinventing themselves. If the target group is on the threshold of major changes or in the middle of such changes, an incentive plan may not be a good idea. The primary reason is that people in times of high-stress change seek clarity about their roles and security for their future. Further, the measures, historical baselines, and performance objectives may be unclear, and this may lead to setting incorrect goals. If the group is undergoing major change, it is best to either postpone the plan design process until the strategic and structural decisions have been made or use the process of developing the plan as a vehicle for gaining consensus on the work redesign decisions.

However, change should not be an excuse for forgoing effective reward systems. The organization may find that using a variable pay plan will enhance the change process in terms of speed or implementation effectiveness. For example, a large newspaper organization was planning on eliminating its evening edition and on selling higher-margin business. Introduction of a variable pay plan helped the transition because managers and employees could see personal economic benefit from effective implementation of this change.

3. *Do clear, reliable measures exist for the unit?* Performance measures are an essential element of variable pay plans. If measures do not exist, it will be very difficult to develop a sound variable pay plan. We have often used the design process as an opportunity to develop concrete, controllable performance measures. We have found that there is often a broader consensus on the performance measures after the design or redesign of an incentive plan.

4. *Is the current compensation adequate from an internal equity and external competitiveness standpoint?* A variable pay plan should be used to address performance issues and achieve its stated purpose rather than fix some existing pay problem. The primary task of the reward strategy is to define the purpose of the variable pay plan in business terms. If there are basic issues regarding the base pay system, either because of its inequities within the organization or because of its inadequacy in the external market, the variable pay program may become diverted from its original purpose. There are opportunities, however, in which the variable pay plan can enhance the organization's competitiveness from a total compensation perspective. While this can be a benefit of the plan, market competitiveness should not be a primary objective of the plan. This needs to be understood and stated as part of the objectives of the program prior to its design.

5. *Are the managers of the unit generally effective in providing the leadership necessary for the group?* This is a critical issue for the implementation and ongoing effectiveness of the program. Managers who wish to be effective at managing incentives should

- Provide an effective sense of purpose and direction based on the overall objectives of the unit and supported by the incentive plan.
- Use reliable, meaningful measures to track performance.
- Use ongoing, real-time, data-based feedback to the performers.

- Reinforce behaviors for progress and celebrate critical achievements.

There is often an unstated assumption or hope that if the incentive plan is well designed, it can replace many tasks of management. Nothing could be farther from the truth. In fact, incentive plans require more, not less, management involvement. However, the role of the manager changes to translating the performance measures into meaningful directions and actions for people, ensuring that people remain informed of how well they are doing (and in as timely a manner as possible), and providing coaching, encouragement, and reinforcement to people for desirable behaviors. The manager is often called on to listen to ideas for change and improvement in the work process and to take actions to address problems within or outside the group that are interfering with its ability to perform. With incentive plans, a manager's job becomes even more active, important, and rewarding.

6. *Is the culture of the organization characterized by trust, mutual respect, and a willingness to work together for common goals?* Few organizations would be able to say that they have a corporate culture characterized by high levels of trust, respect, and teamwork. The dimension to be examined here is more of degrees than absolutes. If the employees in the target group do not fundamentally trust what management has said or believe the measures and performance feedback, it will be difficult for the incentive program to have a positive impact. If there is general confidence in management's ability to make the right decisions and implement programs effectively, the incentive pay program probably will be viewed positively. If conditions are adequate but not desirable, the process should be used to strengthen trust and confidence. This can be done through a variety of strategies, such as involving employees directly in the design of the plan, communicating with employees often, and removing bottlenecks to their performance.

7. *Does the plan have a sponsor and a champion?* In any process of major organizational change, individuals need to serve important roles. The *sponsor* is the individual who sanctions the work, provides the resources, and creates the environment in which the plan can be assessed, revised, or developed and implemented.

The sponsor is critical to the development process because, without such support, the plan will not have sufficient commitment from senior management to gain approvals. The *champion*, on the other hand, is the one with the technical skills and drive to see that a new program is created or current programs are changed. The champion wants to see the program developed, revised, and implemented and will do practically anything within reason to make it successful. Without the contributions of a sponsor and a champion, the development of new variable pay plans or revisions to existing ones probably will never progress beyond the talking stage.

Asking and answering these seven questions will provide an effective framework for assessing the conditions necessary for a successful variable pay plan. As mentioned in connection with several of the questions, the issue is one of degree, not absolutes. After examining each of these seven areas, one of three possible conclusions can be reached:

Stop—wait for better days. In this situation, there are many reasons why the time is not appropriate for the variable pay plan. The assessment should identify areas that present the most critical barriers, and the choice should be to address the issue in new ways or take another course of action.

Proceed with caution—use the process strategically. This is the most common situation. There are important barriers, but they can be overcome as the plan is revised, constructed, and implemented. For example, if trust is a major concern, one can involve the opinion leaders of various constituencies in the development of a new plan. This will either create a plan that will be effective for everyone or clarify the primary areas for negotiation and compromise. In either case, the process will indicate whether further organizational work is appropriate.

Go for it—make the change happen. In this case, there are important indicators supporting the development or revision of the plan. Although one always must work to create a plan that reinforces the right conditions for performance improvement, the absence of major inhibiting factors indicates that there is real support and opportunity to realize success with the plan.

In Chapter 10 we will review a process for designing or assessing the critical factors in a variable pay program. This will involve using the guidelines and principles discussed here in specific elements of a variable pay plan. As stated earlier, each organization has unique characteristics and strategies, and the design or enhancements of a variable pay plan should reflect the specifications of the company. Chapter 10 will show how these requirements can become a reality.

Design Variable Pay Plans with a Difference

If you always do what you've always done,
you'll always get what you've always gotten.

Anonymous

O<small>NE SHOULD NOT EXPECT</small> that designing a variable pay plan is a neat, logical process. Each step, although logically leading to another, will need to be reviewed once subsequent decisions are made. It is often best to describe this process as a *spiraling activity*, one that backtracks at times to review and ensure a strong linkage of the plan's different elements. No decision should be complete until all decisions are complete.

There are several alternative strategies for assessing a current plan or developing a new one. First, an outsider can develop the plan whether he or she is from another area in the company or is an external consultant.

The advantage of this tactic is that the outsider tends to see critical issues from an objective or nonbiased perspective. The use of an outside expert who has experience with similar organizations also can speed up the development process because such experts have the tools, experience, and methodologies already developed. The disadvantages of this approach are that the person may need time to learn the business, may not fully understand the uniqueness of the business's culture or operations, and may not be around to build the internal capabilities to manage the plan. If the commitment of the performers is not achieved during the design process, it will need to be addressed during implementation and overall management of the program.

Another alternative approach is to use a management design team composed of the senior managers of the target group. This has the advantage of putting the managers in a situation in which they will be designing a rewards system to support their primary accountabilities. They will both understand the plan and have a high degree of ownership for its effective implementation. The disadvantages are that the design team may not look objectively at current activities or be creative in developing a new program. Further, the process may enhance the mistrust of management by employees. The workforce may be skeptical of the management design team's true intent and resist changing practices to achieve desired results.

The third alternative is to use a cross-functional design team composed of potential participants in the plan—managers, supervisors, operational employees, nonexempt clerical staff, and possibly internal customers of the target group. The advantage of this method is that it can create support for the plan and increase the capabilities for managing it. Often these representatives have a wide variety of perspectives that will enrich the program. The primary disadvantage is the time needed for the individuals to work well as a team and for the team to be educated on the strategic issues of the organization and variable pay plans in general. Furthermore, this approach may create expectations that design team members should "represent" their area or somehow be accountable to others in the company.

The approach selected must be considered carefully in relation to the primary objectives of the plan, the need for commitment and internal capabilities, and the time one has to prepare the plan for approval and implementation. The executives of the target group should determine who is best suited to help them build or dramatically improve the variable pay plan.

To assess or develop such a plan, several important steps need to be taken at the start. First, the design team (whether it is composed of an outside expert, a management team, or cross-functional representatives) should be given the authority and time to develop a plan that it believes will work for the organization. Often executives want to specify several limits on their considerations, such as types of measures, the need for the plan to be self-funded, the eligibility criteria, the timing or size of payouts, and so on. While these limits may be important to executives, they reflect a lack of trust and confidence in the design team itself. When this happens, the team members often question the true motive for their involvement and the level of commitment they should have for the task. Do senior managers want the team to create the optimal design, or are they just putting up a facade of participation and involvement?

The mission of the team is to design a plan that meets the needs of the organization. This means that the plan must be something management can support fully. The team needs to keep the executives informed at critical times during the development process so that the basic direction is not in conflict with the strategic requirements of the company. Executives ultimately will need to approve the plan. An important task of the design team is to use the knowledge, objectives, and experiences of both the executives and the target group.

Second, employees should be assured that they will not face layoffs if there are improvements in performance. Employees are also often concerned about what will happen to their pay if a new variable pay plan is put into effect. Depending on the purpose of the plan, the managers will need to make the appropriate assurances. Studies on variable pay plans indicated that 84 percent of the plans were add-ons to existing base pay plans, 10 percent reduced future pay increases, 2.4 percent reduced base pay, 2.4 percent replaced an existing incentive plan, and 1.2 percent replaced an existing recognition plan.[1] Thus, in most cases, the plans were in addition to existing pay plans and therefore focused on improving the performance of the organization, not reducing pay.

Finally, as the design team begins its work, it will quickly find that the task is very complex. There is often a need to simplify early on so that people can understand the plan. The risk here is that the resulting plan may be too simple to truly address the critical issues facing the business. It is very important that the plan be simple enough to understand but not simplistic in addressing the task of changing human behavior.

If the organization is reducing the historical pay increase levels, this should be done separately from the design of the variable pay program. This keeps the focus of variable pay on improving performance and does not allow it to become a mask for base pay reductions.

Developing a variable pay program will involve making over 100 decisions. To facilitate this process, these decisions are categorized into eight steps. They are shown as a design wheel in Figure 10-1. Each is described in detail on the following pages.

Step 1: The Purpose of the Program

The purpose statement of the plan should be to define why the plan exists and its three to five key objectives. Is it focused primarily on individual or group performance? Should the emphasis be on improving financial results or operational and value growth factors? How important should improving the external competitiveness of pay be in the

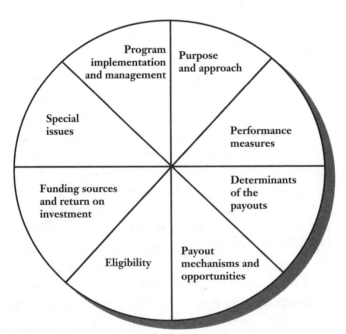

Figure 10-1 The variable pay program design wheel.

plan, and how much risk should there be in the plan? Do you want the plan to enhance the firm's ability to attract or retain talent, or is its focus primarily on existing staff? Finally, how should this program address the business's current challenges and the firm's strategy and values?

The purpose statement should include an overall statement and a set of principles or guidelines from which the design team will design the plan. The reward strategy outlined in Chapter 4 may provide additional information for the process of articulating the plan's purpose. An example of plan purpose statements is given in Figure 10-2.

Once the overall purpose has been determined, the next issue is to define the overall approach. Although this will be discussed in more detail when we examine payout mechanisms, the approach defines the nature of the incentive plan. For example:

- What will be the primary unit of focus? Will the plan be for a natural work group, such as a department, division, or section, or will it be for cross-functional task forces, project teams, or other temporary teams?
- Will the plan provide participants with a share in the economic benefit of improved results, or will it target a series of performance levels and provide payments when certain results are achieved?

The purpose of our performance-sharing program is to share with managers and employees the responsibilities, opportunities, and successes we achieve to create value for our customers, our shareholders, and our company.

The objectives of this program are to

1. Focus our efforts on those areas that define our key success factors, implement our strategic plans, and give us a competitive advantage.

2. Encourage collaboration across all areas of our company by working together to meet customer needs, grow our business, and utilize our resources in the most efficient manner possible.

3. Recognize and reward individuals, teams, and business units in how they contribute to making a difference in our company's performance.

4. Increase the responsiveness, sense of urgency, and flexibility to meet the ever-changing nature of our marketplace.

5. Reinforce a culture that is truly unique and valued by those who work with us.

Figure 10-2 Variable pay plan purpose statements.

- Will the plan be designed for a temporary period of time such as for a project, or is it intended to exist as long as it is effective for the business unit?

The answer to these questions will help define the purpose, approach, and specifications of the variable pay plan. This sets the stage for addressing other key decisions of the plan.

Step 2: Performance Measures

Perhaps the single most important and difficult issue in developing variable pay plans is selecting meaningful performance measures. Since the basis for the payout and the focus of the participants' attention will be on the measures, they should to be selected carefully. When companies start the design process with measures, they often first look at what is currently being measured. The inadequacy of current systems can become a controversial issue and may cause the design process to be slowed or stopped altogether. The alternative is to start with an understanding of the customers and their wants and establish measures that reflect these factors. A more thorough discussion of this process was presented in Chapter 5. Further, we reviewed four types of measures earlier:

- Financial measures
- Customer measures
- Operational measures
- Capability measures

In many situations, a combination of measures describes the strategic results needed by the organization. While the financial performance may define the size of the monetary award available, operational or customer measures may focus on the key drivers of financial results. Incentive plans should be limited to between three and five measures. This enables a number of complex issues to be addressed simultaneously with a clear focus on actions. Most functions and jobs are not so simple that a single measure will suffice.

By their very nature, effective variable pay plans create win-win situations for people and the organization. A single performance measure is often inappropriate because it does not fully account for the primary determinants of strategic performance. The exception may be when a single, common outcome reflects the desired actions of customers. This usually corresponds to a transaction-related customer relationship. Examples might include the following:

Residential mortgage company. Increasing the volume of mortgage applications per month

Distribution company. Increasing the number of deliveries per day

Trucking company. Increasing the number of shipments delivered on time

Telemarketing function. Increasing the number of calls made per hour or handled per hour

Each of these examples reflects a single priority function that is of primary importance to the customer or is a primary indicator of key success factors. In this case, the team collaborates on the actions necessary to achieve the common result.

Measures provide a mosaic of the factors that determine the success of the unit and define the balance of conflicting pressures or the trade-offs necessary to achieve desired results. For example, balance revenue growth with expense reduction and productivity improvement with quality and customer satisfaction. In the ideal world, measures will reflect different aspects of the organization's strategy, and the challenge will be to find the optimal balance. When measures are inherently in conflict, performers need to seek an appropriate balance between measures that address current situations and those that serve the needs of their customers. Finally, the variable pay plan should not attempt to capture all the critical factors of the business. There are other reward programs, such as base salaries, equity participation, and recognition programs to support the factors that are not captured in the variable pay plan.

To summarize briefly, the critical considerations regarding payout mechanisms and opportunity should include the following:

- The specificity of the performance measures
- The degree of control over the performance factors
- The availability of historical reference, peer comparison, or strategic factors for setting performance targets
- The reliability of the basis for establishing the performance levels or expectations

- The economic benefit provided to the organization from improvements in performance

Step 3: Payout Mechanisms

The next major step involves translating the performance measures into a mechanism that will reinforce the desired performance. This is the engine that will drive the incentive compensation plan and determine how payouts will be earned.

There are four key considerations for selecting the most appropriate mechanism for the variable pay program.

Line of Sight

For an incentive plan to work effectively, people need to understand the relationship between their efforts and the desired results. This is often referred to as the *line of sight*. While a direct relationship is most preferred—John does X and gets Y—this is not always feasible or appropriate given the many conflicting requirements for creating value and meeting customer needs: quality versus productivity, delivery versus cost, timeliness versus accuracy, and so on. While creative individuals will find avenues for achieving both (i.e., the optimal solution), there are situations in which true performance is a combination of complex factors. The measures identified in step 2 should direct the performers to high-priority tasks and provide guidance about how they should and should not do them.

This specificity is important for determining how much money (i.e., payout opportunity) will be available from the plan. If there are many variables outside the control of individuals, the amount of the target payout should be less so that the organization is not overpaying or underpaying for the performance.

Make the Goals Challenging and Achievable

David McClellan, former professor at Harvard University, demonstrated in his research that high achievers set goals that are challenging but achievable.[2] Achieving goals that are perceived to be too easy is not meaningful. Goals that are seen to be too difficult to achieve are not pursued. In this case, the performer initially may try hard but eventually may give up or make do, realizing that the rewards are not likely. Consequently, the best goals are not overly *stretch goals* (i.e., unachievable goals) but goals that generally are viewed as achievable with focused effort.

When a plan has a single goal associated with a measure, the performers usually work to achieve the goal by the deadline. The performer produces just enough to receive the payout. This is characteristic of the behavioral pattern associated with negative reinforcement. This means that performers do what is necessary to avoid a negative experience but do not do more because they will not receive additional gains if they excel. This is an important concept when it comes to constructing the levels of performance in an incentive plan.

When there is a range of targets, with a minimum and a maximum level of achievement, performers focus on what they believe is achievable and then keep raising the bar as they progress. This provides performers with a range of targets and reinforces continual performance improvements. This is inherently more motivating and likely to lead to higher levels of performance. Finally, the number of performance levels usually is associated with higher achievements; five to ten levels have been shown to be optimal in our experience and research.

Make It Timely to Reinforce the Focus

This factor relates to the frequency of the payout. Reliance on an annual payout cycle usually leads people to pay little attention to the incentive until the end date is in sight. People will tend to focus on immediate concerns regardless of the incentive plan measures. If there are few reviews of progress, the incentive plan is basically nonfunctional for most of the year. Depending on the sense of urgency required and the types of behaviors and results necessary for success, the timing of the payout can be a critical issue. A plan that pays out on a quarterly basis creates a high sense of urgency to achieve the quarterly results (note the example of executives held to quarterly earnings reports to investors). This has the advantage of creating more pressure for performance. The disadvantage is that this approach requires business cycles and performance measures that correspond to monthly or quarterly rhythms. For example, if most sales occur in the first quarter and most costs occur in the third quarter, plans that do not reflect this buy-and-sell pattern may distort the understanding of performance. This design decision needs to be considered carefully so that people do not adjust their performance in such a way as to maximize personal income at the expense of the organization's profitability.

Some companies have moved to monthly payout schedules in order to create a strong sense of urgency about achieving desired results. In behavioral terms, such an outcome is referred to as a *J curve*.[3] This means that performance/behaviors proceed along at a minimal pace for a period and then pick up in intensity as a deadline approaches. The challenge is to create reward systems that encourage results to be achieved earlier without sacrificing an optimal level of performance.

The conflict between schedule and quality is reflected in these comments by employees:

- "On Monday we ship quality. On Friday we ship quantity."—Supervisor
- "Poor products are often put back into the line for rework or shipment toward the end of the month so the supervisors can receive their bonuses."—Operational employee
- "The last two weeks of the quarter are always a challenge. I wish we could smooth out our production schedules to achieve more regular delivery performance. It costs us in overtime, product quality, and just pressure. But we've always made our targets."—Plant manager
- "We don't usually schedule any meetings during the last quarter of the year. That's when we make up for the year's slippage."—Functional director

Another example of a J curve can be seen in a chair manufacturing company's "healing wall." During the month, employees were empowered to remove any chair that they felt did not meet the customer's quality specifications. They placed defective chairs on a back wall of the plant for analyses and repair. This wall provided a visible measure of the quality in the plant. This process operated well until near the end of the month. If actual production was below quotas, the supervisor would go through the chairs that were stacked on the back wall and select ones to be put back into production. When asked about this, the supervisor said that the problem was not significant and could be repaired later in the manufacturing process or that the customer would never notice. This wall was referred to as the "healing wall" by production employees because it was where the chairs were "healed" during the production process.

These comments reflect this pattern of timing associated with rewards. If a strong sense of urgency and focus on critical issues is needed, a shorter time frame is desired. However, if the payout schedule needs to be linked to the company's fiscal year, a multiple set of reward systems may be used. For example, the payout may occur annually, but the company can provide recognition and spot bonuses as business units meet or exceed monthly, quarterly, or project objectives.

Work to Make It Work

The management and reliability of an incentive system have a direct impact on its effectiveness. First, a system that is so complicated that the performers must wait for a long time to get the results will have a less positive impact on performance. However, a program that is so simple that it reinforces the wrong behaviors is equally inappropriate. The design process needs to achieve the right degree of sophistication.

Figure 10-3 illustrates two dimensions of this concept: the degree of sophistication and the degree of impact on performance. For an organization to achieve a high impact on performance, it needs to find the right balance of sophistication and impact. A program that is too simple will not have the desired impact because it may set up conditions to reinforce wrong behaviors or have no impact at all. One that is too complicated will not achieve the desired impact because people will not understand what they need to do differently. The degree of sophistication is defined by the nature of the work, the frame of reference with such systems, and associated communication and education needs.

Effective incentive plans address a wide array of both business and behavioral issues. The ideal plan has something in common with an automobile. A car is a very complex and sophisticated piece of machinery. It has an onboard propulsion system, a guidance and steering system, a braking system, an environmental control system, an entertainment system, a safety system, and so on. Yet it can be operated by an individual with minimal formal education and little training. Similarly, an incentive system must be no more sophisticated than the target group can comprehend, but

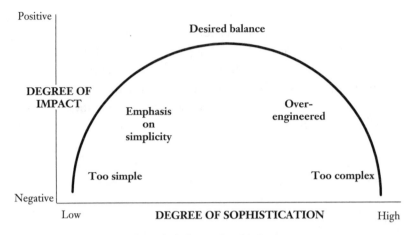

Figure 10-3 Achieving the right balance of sophistication.

it must not be so simplistic that it fails to encourage and reinforce desired behaviors effectively.

These considerations will determine how much money is appropriate for the incentive plan and what type of mechanism should be used. The nature of the performance measures often will determine the most obvious payout mechanism.

Although there are many variations, basically there are three different approaches to determining the payout of an incentive plan. These are

1. A formula or a percentage of the measure based on achievement (e.g., revenue growth, profitability, number of units, value added, productivity, etc.)
2. The measurement of specific objectives or goal achievements (e.g., management by objectives, performance to plan or budget, etc.)
3. A portfolio of measures with payouts associated with different levels of performance (e.g., on-time delivery, yield rates, error-free rates, new product launch, etc.)

Each of these is explained in more detail below:

1. *Formula-derived payout.* Most profit-sharing, sales commission, and gain-sharing plans use this approach to determine payouts.

Simply stated, when performance exceeds a historical or baseline level, a portion of the overage is provided to the performers. For example, if the operating margin for a unit exceeds 20 percent, the members of the unit split 50 percent of the excess margin with the company. Other examples might include cases in which the productivity of a unit exceeds a rate X, or in which a pool is generated based on the dollar value of this productivity increase (say $\$Y$ for each unit produced over the productivity threshold), or in which Z percent of the sales/profits over a threshold is provided to the performers (as in a sales commission plan). The formula should be derived from a few (one or two) performance measures, reflecting customer-focused achievements and true value creation for the corporation.

2. *Performance to objectives or goals.* Performance objectives or targets are useful when the nature of the work is task-oriented or has clear outcomes (such as implementing a new MIS system by April 1, launching a new product for the July 15 trade show, or resolving specific audit report discrepancies by January 1). Such projects have a finite dimension, and achieving them earlier or with a variety of quality levels is not essential. Most "management by objective" programs have these characteristics. As discussed earlier, objectives or goals are more effective where there are multiple levels of achievement, such as minimum, target, and maximum.

3. *Portfolio or multiple measures.* When a number of measures are needed to reflect desired performance, a matrix can serve a useful purpose. Figure 10-5 shows a matrix that will accommodate a variety of measures, enable the organization to weight them differently, and define a 10-level array of performance. As shown on the performance matrix, the target is set at 100. A minimum level of performance is set at 60, and a maximum level of performance is set at 150. In most circumstances, the historical performance or baseline comparator performance is set around the 60 to 80 level, meaning that performance needs to improve in order to achieve desirable payouts. Each measure is weighted based on a total 100 percent allocation. The performance score can be calculated easily by finding the level associated with actual performance (from 60 to 150), multiplying this number by the weight

assigned to that measure (such as 20 percent), and entering the score in the far right column. The scores for each measure are then added, and the total shows the performance score for the period. The final score can be applied to a payout table to indicate the actual payout participants will receive (as shown on Figure 10-4) or used as a percentage that is multiplied by a target payout (i.e., 110 percent × $10,000 payout target = $11,000 bonus). This variable pay plan tool is shown in Figure 10-4 with an illustration shown in Figure 10-5.

Having an array of performance levels is very important in behavioral terms. First, the wide range of possibilities gives performers an opportunity to find an achievement level within their grasp. Some plans fail to produce desired behavioral change because they use only a single goal that performers feel is beyond their reach. Second, being able to indicate even minor levels of improved performance enables an organization to reinforce actions that produce improvements even when the payout is not significant. Let's say, for example, that a team's performance improves from 75 to 90. Even though its current performance remains below target level, there is still reason to celebrate—and an opportunity for positive reinforcement to encourage continued improvement. Then people focus on what they need to do to get to 100 or better.

Third, the matrix enables the organization to display ongoing progress in performance. This is important in supporting the feedback necessary for behavioral change. Fourth the matrix also enables the organization to integrate a number of measures (some of which may in fact be conflicting), weight them according to their strategic importance, and coach employees on actions necessary to achieve higher performance. It allows measures to include corporate objectives, as well as department, unit, and individual objectives. The matrix, although complex at first glance, in our experience has proven to be a very simple and powerful tool in the design and management of incentive plans.

In summary, linking the performance measures to the payout mechanism creates the engine that drives incentive programs. They determine how much is to be paid out and for what. They give the performance measures special meaning. Finally, they are the primary focus of most participants' attention.

BUSINESS UNIT _____ PERFORMANCE PERIOD _____

MEASURES	X Weight	60	70	80	90	100	110	120	130	140	150	Points

TOTAL SCORE

Figure 10-4 The performance scorecard.

BUSINESS UNIT _____

PERFORMANCE PERIOD

MEASURES	X Weight	60	70	80	90	100	110	120	130	140	150	Points
Customer Satisfaction	20%	60	65	70	75	80	85	88	90	92	95	26
On-Time Delivery	20%	80%	85%	90%	92%	94%	95%	96%	97%	98%	99%	24
Net Revenue	15%	$900	$950	$1,000	$1,050	$1,100	$1,200	$1,300	$1,400	$1,500	$1,600	17
Product Quality	15%	5 pts	8 pts	11 pts	14 pts	17 pts	20 pts	24 pts	27 pts	30 pts	35 pts	14
Controllable Expense to Budget	30%	110%	105%	100%	98%	95%	93%	90%	88%	85%	83%	33

Payout Opportunity Table

Total Score	Payout
0 - 79	0
80 - 89	2%
90 - 99	3%
100 - 109	5%
110 - 119	7%
120 - 129	9%
130 - 139	12%
140 - 150	15%

TOTAL SCORE 114

Comments: _____

Approved _____ Approved _____

Figure 10-5 Illustrative performance scorecard.

Step 4: Payout Opportunity

There is a conventional wisdom in the professional field of compensation that unless an incentive offers between 10 and 15 percent of base pay, the performer will not be motivated to achieve the desired results.[4] This commonly held belief has not been substantiated by objective research. Research completed by A. Dickinson at Western Michigan University's Department of Psychology indicated that a 3 percent incentive yielded the same performance level as did rates of 13, 25, and 55 percent.[5] The performance was nearly doubled for those without incentives, but there was no significant difference among alternative payout levels. However, most compensation surveys show that payouts are exponentially related to salaries in the United States. See Figure 10-6 for a summary of average payouts associated with different salary levels from recent compensation surveys.

Other factors also influence the amount of payout necessary to motivate desired behaviors—the clarity of the task, the performer's ability to perform it, and the frequency and meaningfulness of feedback following the task. These factors can serve to decrease the amount of money needed for the payouts to be meaningful. This is so because the

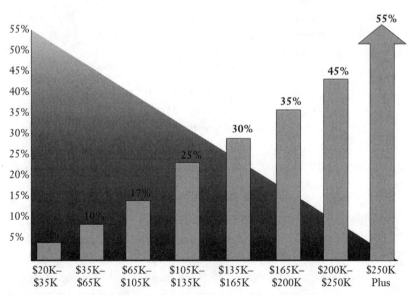

Figure 10-6   Average variable plan payout by income level. (*Source: World at Work, 2000-2001 Total Salary Increase Survey.*)

reinforcements that come from the work environment, the task itself, one's peers, one's superiors, and so on can be more immediate and personally meaningful than monetary rewards.

These other factors are not intended to diminish the importance of a high payout opportunity. Rather, the *meaningfulness* is defined by the performer, not the organization. A performer may be aware of comparable pay practices within the organization or within other organizations. A performer may translate the value generated to the payout he or she receives. For example, a salesperson who makes $1 million in sales that generate $180,000 in profits for the company may find a $3000 commission payout as unbalanced. When a team saves the company $3 million by developing and implementing a process and receives a $500 special award for each member, team members may see the reward as unworthy of their efforts. If this award were to be accompanied by a special celebration, other personalized awards, and meaningful discussions with top executives, the team might view the overall reward to be more in balance. The degree of meaningfulness of the payout can be measured by observing whether people talk positively about the reward, say they feel valued, and are willing to engage in similar activities in the future.

Once the target payout opportunity has been established, several critical factors determine how the payout should be made. This is obviously highly dependent on the mechanism used in the plan design. Among these are the following:

1. *Will the payout be paid as a percentage of the individual's current base salary, a target bonus, or a flat dollar amount to each participant?* This question is always one of great concern when the plans involve both management and nonmanagement people. If the payouts are a percentage of base salary, managers and senior managers will get more money because their salaries are usually higher. However, if the incentive is paid equally, then everyone will get the same amount, but it will be a lower percentage of pay for the higher-paid individuals. If the plan includes nonexempt employees (in the United States), the payouts need to be adjusted for overtime payments (see "Step 7 Special Issues" below). A target bonus sets up a clear payout expectation, and if people are paid less than this amount, the reasons need to be very clear. Finally,

equal payouts may not reflect the real differences in accountabilities and the impact that specific individuals have had on the organization's performance. In practice, most firms use a percentage of a worker's total earnings (salary plus overtime) for the performance period.

2. *Should there be a minimum threshold of performance before any payout is provided?* Most organizations maintain some form of minimum performance clause, meaning that if the financial performance of the company falls below a predetermined level, no payouts will be made. Some organizations require at least a baseline level of overall performance before the plan is activated. While this will protect certain costs associated with the program, it can have a negative impact if the threshold is not seen as clearly achievable. If the participants feel that the threshold is too high, they may disregard the opportunities of the plan and wait to see if the threshold is met before focusing on the plan's performance objectives.

3. *Should there be modifiers to the plan's payouts?* By *modifiers* we mean performance factors that should influence the plan's payouts. This may include such measures as employee safety, product quality, customer satisfaction, and corporate profitability. These are modifiers because they increase or decrease the payout after it has been calculated. For example, a large health care organization modified its incentive payouts to all its employees based on the results of patient-physician satisfaction surveys. A telecommunications company modified payouts based on specific community relations activities that enhanced the company's image in communities it served. Other companies have modified the payouts based on corporate profitability, return on assets, and absenteeism.

4. *Should there be caps on the payouts?* A *cap* means that there will be a maximum payout to the participants. These are used when the payout is based on a predetermined formula or commission-type structure. Caps are appropriate when the relationship between the payout and the performance maximums is not clear and excessive performance should not be attributed to the individual or group. If there is little historical data to support setting performance levels, the upside opportunity for improvements is

uncertain. In other circumstances, when the organization is continuing to make capital and/or process changes to increase the productivity of the unit, caps can prevent the organization from overpaying due to investments not reflected in the performance objectives. This can be especially important when the performance is a result of factors beyond the performers' control, such as pricing increases, a surge in market demand, or product design changes. Caps can have a negative impact on performers by restricting the payout opportunity, but there may be an appropriate justification. They should be sufficiently high so that most people do not see them as a deterrent to their performance.

5. *Should a portion of the payout be held in reserve?* When a plan is paid out more frequently than annually, there is often a question about whether any of it should be held back until the results of the annual performance are determined. This addresses the concern that the organization may pay out incentives during a first or second quarter only to have the entire year's performance fall below the threshold. In this case, the firm will have paid out funds with no annual gain in performance. The reserve fund is a common practice in many quarterly incentive plans. Studies report that the average holdback is 25 percent of the payout. The range is between 20 and 50 percent of the payout, and all or a portion of the reserve amount is paid out at year end based on overall performance.

   Two alternatives used by organizations are to make the performance cumulative for each period or to base a portion of the target payout on annual results. For example, if a target annual payout is 10 percent of salary, then 2 percent is the target on a quarterly basis and 2 percent is for the annual results; this makes the reserve equal to 20 percent of the total target payout. Each quarter is considered independent of the others, but there is a portion tied to the overall year. The final payout is based on the total annual results. Using this approach, the firm can increase the sense of urgency on a quarterly basis, focus its people in each quarter, and yet link each quarter's results to an annual payout.

6. *How often should the performance goals be raised?* The answer to this question establishes the policy for when and how the organization should change its performance requirements. From the

organization's perspective, this is important to do on an annual basis because it has paid for process changes or improvements in performance. As the firm invests in capital equipment, engineering designs, or new information systems, the baseline of performance needs to be modified accordingly. From the employees' perspective, this adjustment may seem unfair because the improvements in the economics of the business can be realized forever, while the payout is a one-time event only. The participants need to understand that changes in performance that are integrated into the operations of the unit may cause an adjustment in the payout opportunities and that continuous improvements are essential to the firm's competitiveness. Further, competitiveness in the marketplace involves a never-ending struggle to improve performance. An alternative may be to increase base pay or the incentive opportunities in relation to increasing the performance requirements.

7. *Should the payout be in cash or some other form of reward?* For many organizations, the answer to this question is quite simple—*cash*. However, in some organizations, the use of cash may have a negative impact on employee relations or may result in a negative public reaction. A large teaching hospital that had experienced significant downsizing and trouble with the local community wanted to implement a team incentive program to support the new direction of the organization. The use of cash would have caused significant conflicts. Consequently, the plan supported improvements in financial and service measures, but performance awards were funds each team could use to improve the quality of its working conditions or training for its members. The expenditures would be at the discretion of each team, with approval by senior executives. In another case, a large technology company used the points earned on a scorecard for awards certificates that members could "cash in" for items in a merchandise catalog. One large company used this type of payout until the program completed its pilot phase, and then it converted to payouts in cash. Another firm continues to use merchandise credits to award points earned through its plan.[6] Hence the inability to make cash payouts should not be a barrier to an effective incentive plan.

Step 5: Eligibility

Who should be included in the plan, and why? This decision has been delayed until this point in the assessment and design process because companies tend to include or exclude too many people in initial considerations of the plan. Although groups or individuals were identified during the purpose stage, the participants should be reexamined in light of the measures and payout mechanisms of the plan. It is necessary to determine which groups and/or individuals make direct contributions to the performance measures and therefore should be included in the plan. Once such groups or individuals are identified, several additional questions need to be answered:

1. How long should new employees have to work with the group before they become eligible to participate in the program?
2. How should payouts be handled for people who leave the target group during the performance period? Should they be excluded from the payout, receive a pro rata portion based on their time with the group, or receive a full share?
3. What if the person transfers to another area or is promoted and is no longer eligible for the program?
4. What if the person terminates employment? What if the termination occurred after the performance period ended but before the payouts were made?
5. How should the payouts be handled for employees who retire, have long-term disability, or experience short-term disability? If the payout is prorated, should there is a minimum time period during which they are eligible for a payout?
6. How should the payouts be handled for other interruptions in employment, such as jury duty, military service, special assignments, or participation in extended training programs outside the immediate area?
7. If terminations in the group affect its ability to achieve its goals, should the goals be adjusted?
8. If the plan involves a pool and individuals leave, should the share that would go to the previous employee be distributed to remaining members or be retained by the company? What message does this reinforce?

In most cases, employees are excluded from participating in the plan unless they are present during the performance period. Some firms require people to be employed when the payout is made, not just at the end of the performance period. Some state laws prohibit this policy. Companies often prorate payouts for employees who retire, experience any disability (excluding normal sick leave), or are on military service or jury duty. Whether an individual terminates employment for voluntary or involuntary reasons (except as noted above), they usually forfeit any rights to payouts in the incentive plan. Other special considerations concern employees who transfer from the unit or participate in some major project or outside activity that prohibits their full participation in the target group's performance. These employees will need to be considered in the context of the particular structure of the plan and its primary objectives.

Step 6: Funding Sources and Return on Investment

Incentive plans may require an increase in the costs of compensation. This is a *may* because if the results are not achieved, there should be no payouts. In many cases this is justified by improvements in performance, as in plans where the funding is created by the performance. Regardless of the structure of the plan, it is necessary to examine the potential costs of the plan at different payout levels with the associated performance achievements. This means that incentive plans need to be viewed from a total return-on-investment (ROI) perspective. This analysis is useful for anticipating the exposure to the company, to gain approval for the plan or its changes, and to compare actual ROI with planned ROI at a future point in time.

Furthermore, the plan participants often calculate their own ROI by comparing the payout opportunities with the amount of extra effort or change they will need to make. If the projection is positive, the new behaviors may result. If not, the plan will not be viewed as a positive and worthwhile venture. People will accept the payouts but not take ownership of the performance.

The same logic applies to executives who are considering whether to accept a new or revised plan. They want to understand the financial exposure of the plan as well as the return that will be realized from the performance. Baseline performance and historical performance are useful tools for determining the ROI. The measures need to support the firm's competitive pressures directly, and the payouts will not be made unless these results are achieved. Finally, executives need to see that the desired results are not likely to be achieved or sustained without implementation of such a plan.

A number of studies of group-based incentives have shown that the payouts generate a 3:1 to 5:1 ratio of gains in financial performance to individual payouts. The greatest gains—over 400 percent—were reported in plans that had a combination of financial and operational measures.[7]

Some organizations seek incentives to improve the competitiveness of their compensation with the outside marketplace and use this objective to justify the potential costs of the payouts. This is an important consideration if a priority issue for the firm is its ability to attract and retain key talent. This approach is also valuable when public scrutiny is an important factor in the design of the plan. When comparing executive compensation or compensation opportunities with those of other companies in one's marketplace for talent, the company needs to assess the total compensation levels from a competitive position and market strategy viewpoint. The objective is to establish a target level of pay relative to the outside marketplace or other comparable external groups.

To complete the task, one must compare the current level of compensation with that of a peer group (e.g., marketplace or internal unit), pinpoint relevant risk issues, and compare the total compensation at various performance levels (e.g., current, target, maximum, etc.) with a comparable set of data. Most compensation surveys at this time unfortunately do not link compensation data with organizational performance. Such data are becoming more available for executive compensation because of the 1992 Securities and Exchange Commission ruling on proxy statement requirements but are not available in most compensation surveys. The payout opportunities must be examined for whether or not the payout provisions will enable the firm to achieve its desired market position. Examining the ROI makes it possible to examine both the risks and the benefits to the organization and employees of supporting a particular plan. With this support, the primary challenge will be to achieve the performance goals and use the payouts to reinforce the celebration of achievements without reservation.

Step 7: Special Issues

At this point the basic plan has been assessed, designed, or modified. It is also always necessary to address how the plan fits within the fabric of the organization. Understanding and developing an appropriate response to this issue contributes directly to the effectiveness and credibility of the plan. This issue can include the following considerations:

1. *Should the incentive payouts be included as employee benefits?* Customarily, incentive payments are included in employee benefit provisions when they amount to more than 20 to 25 percent of the employee's salary. Depending on the amount of money that is related to the incentive, a portion or all of the incentive may be included in some benefit plans. For example, defined-benefit retirement plans may use total compensation for determining final years' average compensation (salary plus incentives).

2. *How should overtime be handled?* In the United States, the Fair Labor Standards Act requires that incentives awarded to employees who are considered nonexempt (the Fair Labor Standards Act provisions apply to them) should be considered as part of their base pay rates when calculating overtime pay. For example, if a participant is paid $300 per week and receives an incentive that is, in effect, $30 per week, the overtime pay should be $8.25 per hour ($300 + 30 = $330 ÷ 40 hours), not $7.50 ($300 ÷ 40 hours). The payments for overtime will need to incorporate the incentive payouts. A simple method to calculate this is to use payout as a percentage of total earnings (wages plus overtime) for the performance period. This approach also meets the requirements of the Fair Labor Standards Act.[8]

3. *Who determines the performance levels and the payouts?* The decision-making process in an incentive compensation plan is an important factor in credibility and ownership. When plans are developed by a design team, it is often useful to establish or continue some form of oversight committee to review the results and performance goals for subsequent years. This retains the spirit of involvement developed during the initial phases of plan development. However, performance measures and levels should be a management prerogative. In one large manufacturing organization, this

balance was achieved by management reviewing the performance requirements with a steering committee, discussing the rationale and competitive pressures. The steering committee made comments on improvements to plan operations, but management made all approval decisions.

If hourly or nonexempt employees are included in a committee to design or oversee an incentive plan, it is necessary to be aware of current case litigation and other rulings by the National Labor Relations Board (NLRB). The NLRB continues to review such cases but recently has encouraged companies to involve employees in decision making as long as it does not substitute for valid union activities.[9]

4. *How should the incentive plan be integrated with other plans?* An organization's ability to compete with speed and flexibility often lies in the alignment of the various reward systems. In operational areas, employees frequently are concerned that their managers' performance measures may conflict with or not support their own performance measures. In some organizations, employees are concerned that the performance requirements for staff (for revenues) are not consistent with those of other areas or departments (for costs).

One very innovative organization took an approach that integrated everyone into the core incentive plan of the company. Then special incentives were added onto the core plan for sales professionals, senior managers, and key operational project contributors so that an alignment of interests was achieved across all parties. Further, the performance measures were displayed publicly, discussed frequently in cross-functional meetings, and developed in combination with each unit's mission within the company. This enhanced the teamwork, collaboration, and focus on strategic goals and contributed directly to the organization's overall competitiveness.

5. *How should changes in competitive strategy, windfalls, and cave-ins be handled?* Every business faces a dynamic marketplace. Part of the purpose of incentive plans is to share the fortunes of the organization with those who make it happen. The traditional attempts by employers to protect their employees from changes in the marketplace lead to a widespread feeling of entitlement. Over

recent years, commitments to career-long employment have fallen by the wayside. The answer lies in sharing both the good times and the bad times with employees by engaging them in the business and making them partners with management. To accomplish this, employees need to understand the strategy of the business and the critical priorities that determine its competitiveness, as well as the realities of current challenges. Employees will be less concerned about any changes in performance measures or lack of payouts when they feel a direct connection to the operations of the business.

A *windfall* occurs when a unit achieves a dramatically high end result but did little, if anything, to make it happen. A *cave-in* occurs when the performance of a unit is hurt dramatically by a situation beyond its control. The important concept in handling these situations is to build contingency plans that reinforce the integrity of the rewards program. If people are to share in the downside risk, they also should share in the upside potential.

A large specialty chemical company faced a situation in which its incentive plan did not pay off because of a decline in its core business. The nonfinancial performance factors, such as quality management, on-time delivery, and reduction in waste, all were at superior levels, but due to the volume of business (i.e., the company's revenues declined but much less than its competitors), there was no payout. The question was, Should the organization pay out anyway? Although the answer was "no," funds were made available to every unit that achieved above-target performance (all were eligible) to use in celebrating their achievements, but there could not be any cash payments. Instead, the dollars could be used for improving the unit's work areas, holding a celebration event, or anything that would be meaningful and reinforcing to the team members. The company was able to achieve a dramatic return on its investment even though it was not able to make an actual payout.

6. *If the plan is not for the entire organization, how do you handle those who are not eligible?* The way an organization responds to this concern depends on its overall objective. If the firm ultimately wants to put everyone on some form of variable compensation, the response can be to say, "Be patient. We will get to your department as soon as possible." A key message is that if the department performs the

necessary business analysis and incentive design tasks, it can have an incentive plan. This balances the needs to have a plan with the responsibility to design one that meets the group's specifications and the firm's guidelines. A major Boston area medical center started with three pilot department plans the first year. Within 2 years, plans were adopted by 16 other departments using a similar process. If a department did not commit the time and resources to developing a sound plan, it could not have one. Other firms respond by indicating that such plans are not appropriate for all areas, and therefore, "If you want to work for incentives, transfer into work areas that offer them." Regardless of the overall objective, the important thing is to indicate that people will receive incentives when they earn them; incentives are not a form of additional compensation for working in a given department.

7. *If the plan is oriented primarily toward team or large-group performance, how will individual performance be rewarded?* A traditional-thinking paradigm creates a potential conflict between individual and team performance. The resolution is not in selecting one over the other but in achieving both. Total quality management (TQM) experts have taught us that productivity and quality are not opposite ends of a continuum but interdependent forces of success. Here too, individual performance needs to be reinforced by the team, and team performance needs to be celebrated by the individual members. Effective systems of rewards create conditions in which everyone at every level—employee, manager, shareholder, and customer—can win simultaneously. Only the competitors lose. Therefore, if the objective is to reward the team, then provisions must be made for reinforcing the individuals whose high performance contributes to the success of their team. Chapter 6 presented concepts relating to rewarding individuals through base pay, Chapter 11 will present concepts involved in recognition programs, and Chapter 12 will explore how stock options and other forms of equity ownership can be used for creating long-term value. Depending on the purpose and design of the plan, team-based plans can be modified to reward individual performance. Three ideas are to

- Allocate a portion of the team awards (10 to 25 percent) to individuals who provide the greatest contribution to performance.

- Modify the teams payout (±25 percent) based on individual performance.
- Incorporate individual-based measures into the plan.

Step 8: Program Implementation and Management

Once the plan has been assessed, developed, or redesigned, determine how it will be implemented and managed over time. This is one of the most critical steps of all. One can design an excellent system, but if it is not implemented and managed expertly, it will not yield the desired behavioral changes, performance results, or value creation.

A useful strategy prior to final approval is to test-market the plan with the participants: managers, supervisors, and employees. This can be done best through individual or focus-group discussions. Be sure that the executives clearly understand and support the new plan prior to discussing it with participants. The feedback may either enhance the design or build support for its implementation.

If a design team has been used to develop the plan, this review is particularly important. First, the task of going in front of one's peers creates a useful pressure to communicate the plan as simply and clearly as possible. Second, the discussion and reaction to the plan will tell the design team a great deal about what will make the plan successful. This process will determine how easily participants will understand the plan and what new actions they need to take. It will reveal whether the payout mechanism is truly workable from their perspective and whether the payout opportunities are meaningful, and it will identify outstanding issues to be resolved concerning eligibility, funding, and so on.

Once the revisions have been completed, the plan will need to be analyzed, finalized, and presented to executives for approval. The approval process must incorporate the design team's final recommendations for the best possible plan, based on its work, the feedback from participants, and reviews from managers. Executives will then have to decide whether this plan is worth the investment it requires and will achieve its purpose. Once the plan is approved, the implementation process will have three components:

1. *Communicate the plan to all participants.* The preapproval review sessions usually include only a small number of the actual plan participants. This implementation step should explain the plan in the most direct and meaningful manner possible to everyone involved. One rule of thumb is to communicate the program to small groups so that employees have a chance to discuss and ask questions. They also should be given a written document that conveys the details of the plan and why it is important to them as members of the organization. Managers should receive the document early in the process so that they can support the communication effort. One company established a hot line and an email address for employees to direct their questions regarding the plan. They were not used very often, but it symbolized the importance of building the employees' trust.

2. *Establish the necessary support systems.* Feedback on performance on a continual basis is essential to facilitating behavioral changes. Depending on the measures, information systems may need to be created or modified to communicate ongoing progress. Information systems need to provide performers with reliable, timely, and meaningful data on how they are doing and ideas for actions they could take. The decision-making process should be clear for assessing actual performance against the measures/objectives and determining the payout. Finally, the payout results will need to be communicated to people as soon as possible after the end of the performance period, with the actual incentive payout checks following soon thereafter.

3. *Use the system to its full potential.* To create and support an effective incentive program, the entire process of managing performance needs to come into play. Managers should become more involved, not less, and in a manner that strengthens the organization by facilitating communication, problem solving, and ongoing reinforcement of performance. This is the fundamental requirement for success.

The key managerial skills needed in this process are the ability to

- Translate the incentive plan measures into specific, meaningful, and targeted measures for small work teams or individuals.

- Provide frequent, real-time feedback to the performers of the unit so that they know how they are progressing.
- Use all forms of consequences but primarily positive reinforcement to encourage and reward behaviors that will lead to positive results.
- Work with teams to identify and resolve barriers to their performance. This can include work-process issues, supplies, communication with customers, support from other areas, or any aspect of the work environment that might inhibit a team from achieving its maximum potential.

The key objective is to achieve desired performance improvements and therefore make the incentive plan successful. If it has an effective implementation process, an incentive plan has a strong chance of success for both the participants and the organization. The employees win by receiving additional compensation as well as other rewards for achievements in performance, the organization wins by realizing improved results and a stronger competitive position, and shareholders win by seeing the value of their investments increasing. This is the ultimate win-win outcome and the fundamental purpose for engaging in a variable pay program.

Assess the Risks versus Rewards

Variable pay plans are by their very nature at risk. This means that the payout may not occur. People need to know and trust how the program works. The difference between risk and uncertainty lies in knowing what to do. Uncertainty occurs when one is not sure how to achieve or avoid a particular consequence. (Some people refer to this as *fear* or *resistance to change*.) Risk, on the other hand, indicates that one knows what to do, although the actions may not always produce the desired results.

Variable pay plans create for their participants a stake in the performance of the organization. While some refer to this as *pay at risk*, we view such plans as *opportunity pay*. If the firm can realize specific gains as a result of the combined efforts of its members, it can offer them the opportunity to share in the results. However, sharing the good times means sharing the declines as well. This is part of life. No one can be insulated from the risks and fortunes of a challenging marketplace (Figure 10-7).

- **S**pecific
- **M**eaningful
- **A**chievable
- **R**eliable
- **T**imely

Figure 10-7 Criteria for an effective variable compensation program.

Summary

Variable pay plans are not for everyone. Developing, implementing, and managing them requires thoughtful and deliberate actions. They are difficult to undo once implemented. However, they offer one of the most powerful systems of rewards available today.

The key challenge is to design, implement, and manage the variable pay program in a manner that focuses on drivers of strategic success and reinforces desired behaviors. Many incentive plans today either fail to reinforce desired behaviors or work against the principles of collaboration, flexibility, and competitive advantage. To develop a plan that successfully links results with behaviors and fosters win-win opportunities—both for the organization and for its members—requires the creation of conditions favorable to collaborative change. The SMART criteria offer useful guidelines for this goal (see Figure 10-7).

Variable pay programs offer a new force for change and an almost limitless reserve of strength for the organization. The process of developing variable pay plans is meaningful and rewarding, but it is only the beginning of what can be achieved by people who truly feel a part of the enterprise, share its goals, and take the initiative to do what has to be done.

11

Make Recognition Strategic and Special

We never get tired of receiving praise for the things we love to do.

John Williams, Conductor, Composer

T HERE IS PERHAPS no management process so obvious and yet so misunderstood and underused as the recognition process. Executives and managers either consider themselves as experts in the process or conclude that the process has little value or meaning. Yet virtually every high-performing company demonstrates how it uses recognition in significant ways—from Hewlett-Packard to Disney, from PepsiCo to CitiGroup. For many of these firms, recognition programs are used extensively. Whereas variable pay programs may be complex to design, they will virtually run themselves if the design and support systems are effective. Recognition programs, however, are relatively easy to design but very difficult to operate consistently and effectively. Fortunately, books by Bob Nelson (author of *1001 Ways to Reward Employees*[1] and several more recent titles), Herb Kelleher (chairman of Southwest Airlines[2]), and other leading authorities have clearly demonstrated that recognition programs are not "nice things to do" but in fact can create the culture needed to effectively implement a firm's strategy and achieve a sustainable competitive advantage. Let's look at a simple example that may help us to understand how these programs work.

Case Study: A Professional Services Firm

The Thoreau Consulting Group (TCG) is a consulting firm specializing in strategic alignment and people management systems. Unlike other professional service firms, when it comes to performance-based rewards, TCG employees do not become like the cobbler's children, who have no shoes. Integrity is one of the core values of the firm, and one of the ways in which it is demonstrated is by using the principles applied in consulting engagements when "back home at the ranch." Creating a workplace that is fun, balanced, and personally fulfilling is a deliberate part of the firm's everyday culture and is reflected and reinforced by informal recognition programs and practices. At the start of each fiscal year, budget dollars are allocated for recognition as a part of the strategic planning process. Given the company's relatively small size, all employees participate in the annual planning process; thus all employees have input into each year's strategic objectives and the resources allocated to different initiatives. The recognition program is intentionally informal, which maximizes spontaneity and creativity. While on vacation, TCG staff members frequently purchase gifts (Belgian chocolates, California cookbooks, etc.) or send postcards to other staff members to thank them for taking care of business during their absence. Birthdays and other landmark events are celebrated with enthusiasm—and are treated as an opportunity to acknowledge and celebrate the contributions of the individual(s) to the firm's success.

In professional service firms, a great deal of time is spent at client sites and focusing on client needs—TCG compensates for this by creating opportunities to acknowledge and appreciate others on an ongoing basis. When semiannual bonuses are distributed, the (sealed) checks are handed out randomly to other staff members so that each staff member may personally deliver a bonus check to another staff member—and offer thanks for specific contributions during the previous

6 months. On one stormy wintry day, one TCG staff member pur-chased "Island of Misfit Toy" stuffed animal from a drug store near the office for each staff member who braved the storm to get to the office and meet clients. Although these toys were presented almost 2 years ago on a whim (and on sale), they are still greatly valued by the staff members who received them, are displayed prominently on desks year round, and serve as a symbol of the spirit of TCG. The informal nature of recognition and the element of surprise allow for a great deal of fun for all, whereas the emphasis on contributions prevents the creation of any form of entitlement. Any TCG staff member may use the resources in the recognition fund, and all staff members are encouraged to recog-nize the contributions of others—which may include other staff mem-ber(s), a client, or a friend of TCG who refers a new prospect to the company. Over the past few years, this strategy has been so successful that TCG recently implemented a formal "thank you" program to bet-ter track recognition of the increasing number of clients and friends of TCG. It rewards individuals for using this process. Employee recogni-tion will continue to be informal—until the point in time when the organization grows too large to keep track of recognition on an infor-mal basis.

What Can Be Learned from This Story?

There are powerful lessons in this story about how to create a culture that brings out the best qualities and efforts of people. Compensation plans, by their very nature, are delayed in their ability to recognize and reinforce desired behaviors. Consequently, their impact on behavior may not be as great as an immediate comment or display of appreciation for an individual's performance. This chapter will examine the roles of managers and employees in reinforcing and encouraging desired behaviors in a timely, effective, and credible manner. Note that the actions of people create desired outcomes. Our focus will be on how to make recognition special by both making it meaningful and delivering it with the sincere appreciation that is typically lacking in most organi-zations. We will review the primary practices of effective recognition efforts, examine a variety of recognition programs, and conclude with a summary of the guiding principles that make them successful in support-ing the culture and strategic objectives of an organization.

Review of the Principles of Reinforcement

In Chapter 2 we examined the fundamentals of effective reward systems and began to explore the impact of consequences on human behavior. There are three forms that consequences may take: positive, negative, and extinction.

Positive consequences tend to *increase* the frequency of a behavior, whereas *negative consequences* tend to *decrease* the frequency of a behavior. Negative consequences work on the "do this or else" principle; either actually or by implication, performers are threatened with unpleasant consequences if they do not do something. This approach may be effective during short periods of crisis management but can be unpleasant for employees and may lead to high levels of attrition. Positive reinforcement involves the reward principle. Performers receive something they value—that is, they experience pleasant consequences—for something they do. If the reinforcer is effective and truly valued by the recipient, it will increase the probability of the desired behavior. *Extinction* is the absence of anticipated consequences. In other words, the person receives little feedback, affirmation, or criticism for his or her action. The person is simply left to wonder if anyone really cares about what he or she did.

In Chapter 2 we also examined four basic types of positive consequences that can be used to recognize desired results or behaviors:

> *Verbal/social.* Something is said or done that makes a group or individual feel valued or successful for some action. The challenge is to ensure that the recipient, not just the giver, recognizes the value or success of the contribution, so it is important to state clearly what an individual or group did that was of value when acknowledging the effort. Whether a simple "thank you" directed to an individual, a letter of appreciation sent to an employee's manager (with a copy to the employee), or a group celebration to more widely publicize a team's accomplishments, these are effective because of the speed, sincerity, and personal nature of the reinforcement. (A group celebration may involve a low-cost fooseball competition, a catered breakfast, or an elaborate cocktail reception.)
>
> *Tangible/symbolic.* These are awards that are given in recognition of an achievement or important contribution. Examples include a

certificate of achievement, a coupon for extra vacation time, a customized trophy, a commemorative pin, a sculptured piece reflecting the company's logo, tickets to a movie/theater/opera, a "purple heart," or points that can be accumulated and used to buy merchandise from a catalog. As more and more employees are expected to work long hours and weekends to meet customer timetables, an increasing number of organizations are providing weekends away with friends or family. Here, the challenge is to provide something that is meaningful to the recipient and not just the giver. When considering what to give to a recipient, it is very important to be sure that the symbolic and real values are consistent with the achievement. Further, if a company just underwent a massive layoff, extravagant gifts are very much out of place. Alternatively, if operational employees receive a certificate for a day off for working on a nonscheduled Sunday, a software developer may react negatively to receiving a $500 bonus for working weekends for several months.

Work-related. These are awards that are related to tasks, responsibilities, or quality of work life and given in appreciation for some achievement. Examples include a promotion, a title change, greater work autonomy, participation on committees with decision-making authority, work assignments that are of great interest to the individual/team, or the provision of resources or equipment desired by the recipients. Here, organizations must be careful not to simply reward good work with "more work" or make a fuss over providing equipment to an individual that many other workers already have—if so, employees may become frustrated or cynical.

Money-related. These are awards that have immediate or long-term financial value to employees and are given in appreciation of an achievement. (Examples include a promotional pay increase, a special spot bonus or additional incentive payout, stock options, and stock grants. These items are most commonly associated with formal total compensation programs. It is important to realize that each of these programs provides valuable opportunities to recognize and acknowledge the contributions of others, whether for the achievement of established goals and objectives or for truly outstanding or special contributions.

When organizations design and implement special recognition programs, there is a tendency to focus primarily on the use of tangible or monetary acknowledgments. Frequently, these are used as a substitute for more personal verbal/social forms of reinforcement. The risk in an overreliance on gift giving or cash-based rewards is in creating a transaction-oriented economy within the firm. People wait to take actions until they see the potential awards. Instead of enhancing value, self-worth, and self-confidence, the process may create an expectation that each desired action will result in a tangible reward.

Success Criteria for Recognition Management

As shown by the types of awards and the associated risks, recognition is not a simple process. There are characteristics that make recognition systems successful. In Chapter 2 we discuss the conditions or factors that make rewards effective in encouraging desired behaviors and results (STRIVE). When these general principles are applied to recognition programs specifically, new criteria emerge. The five factors can then help one understand why some recognition programs work and others do not (Figure 11-1).

These criteria are important principles, that need to be integrated into the design of new programs, to assess an existing one, or to train managers on how to use rewards programs effectively:

> *Sincere*. Rewards have to be given in a manner that is honest, appreciative, and from the heart. Employees can easily see through actions that are calculated, manipulative, or simply intended to meet some corporate requirement. Recognition that is given insincerely probably will do more damage than good.

- Sincere
- Timely
- Understood
- For the person
- Fun

Figure 11-1 Criteria for success.

Timely. Rewards should be provided as soon as possible following achievements or contributions. Waiting for approvals, deadlines, or completion of an end result often dramatically reduces the impact of the recognition effort. Timeliness also can dramatically underscore the specific and meaningful aspects of the contribution to the performer, thereby increasing the likelihood of repeated results.

Understood by the person. Employees need to understand why they received the reward. It is important to clearly articulate to the individual(s) why a reward is given and why the contribution is important to the organization. Although this may seem blatantly obvious, it is surprising how few organizations make it clear why rewards are given to recipients.

For the person. Rewards need to be meaningful to the performer. In order for a recognition effort to have the desired impact, it must be something the performer values. Mary Kay Ash, founder of Mary Kay Cosmetics, has been known to say, "There are two things people want more than sex and money: recognition and praise."[3] Although everyone wants recognition and praise, not everyone likes to receive them in the same manner. The type of reward and the method of delivery need to reflect the preferences of the individual(s). While some people crave public attention and praise, others cringe at the mere mention of it. Recognition and any associated rewards need to be earned so that people feel that they have truly achieved some action or result. Further, for recognition to be effective in encouraging desired actions, it is best for the reward to be personalized based on what was done.

Fun. Recognition should be fun so as to provide maximum impact and lasting value. Since the definition of fun varies tremendously among individuals and organizations, the best way to ensure that recognition is considered to be fun is to provide opportunities for different departments to customize their recognition efforts and to use employee input in the design of the program. Examples of employee input include focus groups, surveys of employees on recognition and reward preferences, or having employees on recognition design teams.

How items are delivered is more important than what is delivered. An important principle to remember is that the value received is not always the same as the value given. Special recognition efforts are best viewed as providing *acknowledgment and appreciation* for desired actions. They do not need to occur after every action; however, they should be sufficiently frequent that people relate the performance actions to the rewards. If you want people to take certain actions, they need to be able to know when they do it, understand why others appreciate specific actions, and recognize for themselves the value for doing them. Hence the STUFF criteria provide an important framework for implementing effective recognition rewards practices.

Recognition provides opportunities to generate excitement around the achievement of desired behaviors and results and thereby enhances the desired spirit of the organization. In this way, each organization can make recognition truly meaningful and effective—and special.

Types of Special Recognition

Many different recognition methods are practiced today. Few are viewed as being effective or helping to create and sustain competitive advantage. Too many have rules that stifle creativity or hinder the behaviors they hope to encourage. The reasons will become clear as we examine these approaches more closely using the STUFF criteria.

Within this context, there are four basic types of recognition initiatives (Figure 11-2). Each is discussed in detail below:

> *Employee recognition.* Employee recognition efforts are designed to acknowledge and encourage the contributions made by individuals and/or teams in the performance of their jobs. Examples include special employee programs, spot bonus plans, and employee appreciation events that may recognize and reward desired behaviors, specific results, or years of service with token or more significant monetary awards.
>
> *Team celebrations.* These events are designed to recognize the performance of a team or group. Examples include an on-the-spot ice cream social to celebrate a major new client or successful computer conversion, company meetings or global conference calls where people are recognized for their achievements, an afternoon at a local bowling alley or video arcade to celebrate the successful launch of a new product, and a holiday party to celebrate the

---

**A Systematic Way to Create Alignment and
Deliver Positive Consequences**

1. Employee Recognition Programs
   - Thank-you notes or notes of appreciation
   - Spot bonus programs (dollar awards)
   - Appreciation gifts (e.g., tickets, dinners, gift certificates)
2. Team Celebration Programs
   - Special award dinners
   - Spot celebrations
3. Achievement Clubs
   - President's club
   - Key contributors groups
4. Suggestion or New Idea Programs
   - Special suggestion programs
   - Quality improvement teams

Figure 11-2 Types of special recognition initiatives.

year's accomplishments and/or thank clients and friends. These programs are intended to celebrate the contributions of teams and their partners toward the achievement of company goals. The best team celebrations include groups and individuals outside the team who helped the team accomplish its objectives.

Achievement clubs. These clubs recognize top performers and key contributors for outstanding contributions to the organization. Examples include a "president's circle" or "chairman's club." Whereas in the past it was common to send a select few top salespeople that achieved "gold circle" levels of sales to an exotic location, resulting in few winners and many losers, today it is somewhat more common to create various levels of performance (e.g., silver, gold, and platinum), providing rewards that are commensurate with the level of performance. Silver-level employees may earn a night out on the town, whereas gold-level employees earn a weekend in the country and platinum-level employees may earn a week in the Caribbean. This approach tends to create more winners than losers.

Suggestion or *new idea programs.* While other recognition efforts may take the form of formal or informal programs with guidelines for managers, these efforts recognize individuals or teams who have generated solutions to problems or contributed ideas that improve the performance of an overall unit. Frequently they involve cash rewards based on the value of the idea—say, 10 percent of the money the employee's suggestion saved during the first year of its implementation. In organizations implementing total quality management efforts, special cross-functional teams are often used to form the new generation of suggestions to improve the productivity or quality performance of a unit. These programs are less common than they were in the past but continue today to be very successful in manufacturing and production environments.

Each type of recognition attempts to provide individuals with an acknowledgment of their contribution that is beyond their daily work—whether the task is outside job responsibilities or performed in a manner that clearly exceeds expectations. In practice, recognition within a particular company may use a variety of reinforcers—verbal, tangible, work-related, or financial—and span a wide variety of time frames and organizational levels. What differentiates one from another is how the recognition is delivered and what is being recognized and encouraged. Each of these recognition categories is discussed in greater depth in the following pages.

Employee Recognition

Employee recognition initiatives have a long history in American industry, and a great many of them have been created for special applications. Perhaps one of the most traditional types of special recognition is the employee-of-the-month plan. Although this type of initiative has fallen out of favor with many companies due to its relatively exclusionary membership (with only 12 winners per year), some companies successfully sponsor employee-of-the-month initiatives by making them part of a broader and much more inclusive overall recognition program. Other employee recognition initiatives may involve the use of on-the-spot awards or project-completion bonuses. Sales organizations have used short-term contests as a way of rewarding individuals for the highest new sales, the fastest growth in new business, or the most effective promotions of new products or services. Salespeople can earn points that can be redeemed for merchandise, special trips or weekend awards, or cash bonuses. Today it is not uncommon to see similar contests or games designed to engage and energize other types of employees in the attainment of business objectives. Some examples include contests rewarding call center employees for reducing costs per call or average call wait times and recognizing members of the scientific and research community for submitting articles for publication, applying or being accepted for patents/copyrights, or making presentations at major conferences. The following real-world case studies illustrate the design and impact of these initiatives.

Case Study: An Employee-of-the-Month Club

MyBank.com has an employee-of-the-month club. Each month managers and supervisors are asked to submit to the Human Resources Department a list of employees they feel are deserving of membership in the club. The senior management team reviews the names and selects the one individual who has best demonstrated superior performance. This individual is awarded a $100 check, presented by either the division executive or the employee's manager. The individual's picture is also published in the company newspaper and is displayed in a large frame in the employee cafeteria.

Over the last few years, the Human Resources Department has screened and recommended club members to senior management. It is always difficult to get nominations, especially when times are really busy. There have been suggestions to make the process quarterly or provide larger monthly awards. Other suggestions have been to use a company that provides merchandise awards so that people can receive a more "meaningful" reward.

Although there has been a desire to spread the awards around, certain individuals have been nominated again and again. At the end of the year, employees who have won the monthly awards are eligible to receive an employee-of-the-year award. This award includes a special article on the individual and his or her family in the company newspaper and a check for $1000. Eligibility for nomination is open to all employees, with the exception of the management team, but high-level nonexempt people and midlevel professionals win the awards most often. The executives have great fun handing out the awards and carefully rotate this responsibility to give all members of the management team a chance to do so.

The original purpose of the program was to recognize individuals who had clearly distinguished themselves among their peers.

A recent interview with a woman who has won several times revealed a mixed reaction to this recognition initiative. First, the award winner frequently did not really know why she had been selected for the award, although she had been praised frequently for her problem-solving ability and her knack for troubleshooting Web-based applications. Furthermore, she was embarrassed by the picture of herself displayed in the cafeteria and newspaper and found all sorts of excuses to work at home and schedule offsite meetings during her "month of glory." Moreover, while the money was nice, it was gone quickly. She enjoyed the interaction with the management team but was embarrassed when they repeatedly did not pronounce her name correctly. She felt that the program was more about the management team looking good by shining the spotlight on the "little people" than demonstrating appreciation for individual contributions.

In another instance, a man who had been nominated frequently for the award by senior managers was really not well regarded by his peers. It seemed that whenever a senior manager called for a special request, this employee went into action. He drove through all procedures, interrupted any priorities, and got the action sought by the executive in record time. However, when work was at a normal level, he did little to support the group. When he was nominated and eventually selected for a certain month, his peers knew that the system of recognition was flawed. They did not want to be selected because the award clearly was not based on fact but on the notions of the senior managers.

What's Wrong with This Process?

If we examine this system in relation to the STUFF criteria, we can easily discover several major weaknesses in it.

Is It Sincere?

Although the executives appear to be genuinely interested in handing out awards, by failing to make it clear why awards are granted, they are missing out on an opportunity to demonstrate sincere appreciation for real contributions by employees. As a result, employees do not feel that selection for the award reflects their performance. The executives continue to believe in the program; after all, they take time out of their busy schedule to be nice to the employee selected.

Is It Timely?

Monthly performance recognition of this nature is not likely to have much influence on the employees because it is not directly linked to any particular achievement of performance. The only groups that appear to be receiving positive reinforcement from this program on a timely basis are the executives who hand out the checks. They see the employee smile and say "Thank you." They believe that they are promoting excellence by recognizing top performers, and the program reinforces this perception. The award recipients continue to play the game with executives because the consequences for not doing so may be career-limiting.

Does the Person Understand What He or She Did?

The case clearly demonstrates the problem with many such programs—people simply do not understand what they did to deserve the award. To make matters worse, most of the individual's peers do not know either. This lack of communication and understanding creates conflicts, jealousy, and other negative consequences. Thus, while the program may have had noble intentions, the result is often the opposite or worse.

Are the Rewards Meaningful for the Person?

Employee-of-the-month clubs like the example in the case study that satisfy the needs of the givers (executives) typically fail to meet the needs of the recipients. The best recognition initiatives involve some empirical research to understand employee preferences and allow for some flexibility in the types of awards provided and the method of delivery that enable customization to individuals or teams.

While few people turn down the award, many do not feel that it is a meaningful reflection of their contribution. The issue is not only the amount of the award but also the method of delivery. One of the most important aspects of reinforcement is how the reward is delivered. Hence whether an award is delivered by a manager or handed out by a senior executive may or may not matter to the employee. The test for the value of the process is to examine what employees talk about after receiving the award. If they feel proud about the ceremony, it is likely to have been a memorable event. If they barely mention it, the process is likely to have had little personal value. Finally, some of the employees selected are actually embarrassed by being selected, whereas others do not want to be associated with those who have been selected. The overall meaning of the award actually may be more negative than positive.

Was It Fun?

Of all the success criteria, most employee-of-the-month clubs fail to meet this one. MyBank.com has over 1800 employees, yet only 12 people can be selected each year; this leaves 1788 people who are not recognized by the process. Hence the program is basically out of the reach of most employees and has no impact on their performance. In addition, the award ceremony is usually a 5- to 10-minute event between the employee and manager or division head. What is fun about that?

The best alternative to address the inherent problems with employee-of-the-month clubs is to *eliminate them*—unless they are a small part of a broader-based recognition initiative. Company time and resources would be better spent in trying to understand what people are really doing in their jobs. Further, programs of this nature tend to give managers a false sense of confidence that they are reinforcing desired performance. For too many organizations, the reality is that these programs are at best a waste of time and money and at worst a counterproductive force.

What else can a company do? Let's proceed with another example.

Spot Bonuses

Spot bonuses are a way to provide cash awards to individuals and/or teams for achieving some major milestone or level of performance. Such programs may work in one of three ways (or in a combination of the three). First, some spot bonuses are provided to individuals or teams when they accomplish an important project milestone or achieve some major result, such as acquiring a new major client. These bonuses are usually given immediately, at the time when the result or achievement occurs. The payouts may range from $1000 to several times this amount, depending on the overall budget and the value or importance of the achievement to the organization. In some organizations, the decision process involves a review by several levels of management, which may slow the granting of the award.

A second type of spot bonus is much smaller in scale and is usually undertaken directly by a manager or supervisor with little upper-management involvement. These awards are given "on the spot" and are usually for important tasks, such as completing a crucial project, negotiating a successful deal, or filling in for a coworker. The amounts tend to be less than $500; they usually range from $25 to $100. While the awards may be in cash, they also may be in the form of dinner or ticket certificates worth an equivalent amount of money.

The third type of spot bonus goes to the other extreme and usually reflects a major accomplishment by an individual or team. Such awards are limited to very few company employees and are given only after much review and assessment by senior management. Examples of the kinds of major achievements warranting this type of spot bonus include getting a plant up and running under budget and ahead of schedule or developing a new process or technology with significant impact on the company's competitiveness. The dollar size for these awards can range from $5000 to $20,000. IBM and other major corporations have given awards up to $100,000. Needless to say, such awards are very infrequent and limited to a very few people. Their power, however, lies in their size and the notoriety that often goes along with the cash. Hence they can be very meaningful to recipients. Because of the small number of individuals who are truly eligible, however, they provide little motivation to most employees, except those in highly technical or strategic roles within the organization. It is ironic that some recognition recipients are told not to tell anyone outside their immediate family about the award. Therefore, these awards may become something to be embarrassed or secretive about in the presence of one's peers.

Spot bonuses of the first type also have their limitations. Their effectiveness depends on specifying the achievements that qualify employees for them, but since companies tend to present these awards to member(s) of special teams (such as new product development or project management units), they offer little opportunity for those whose primary focus is to maintain ongoing operations. Such awards are effective rewards only for those involved in a special undertaking of the corporation. They are usually provided in conjunction with some ceremony, which gives them the potential for having a significant immediate impact on the recipients. The potential impact on other employees lies in the hope and expectation of achieving the award if they achieve certain levels of performance. The performance requirements need to be very clear, however. This clarity can come from communicating the requirements or by applying selection criteria that are consistent and well understood by everyone concerned. In this way, such programs can be effective rewards for participants working to achieve a special level of performance.

Perhaps the most frequently used and abused program of spot bonuses is the second type, in which managers give out "spot awards" of relatively small sums. Such awards derive their potential impact from the timing of the cash presentation and the relationship it has to the desired behaviors. For example, a division of a large multinational company presented crisp, new $50 bills to unit members when units achieved specific on-time performance standards and sustained their level of performance for an entire quarter. A $50 bill was given when the unit first achieved the standard and again when the team continued the practice for an entire 3-month period (not necessarily related to the company's fiscal quarters). The power of these rewards was their timeliness and symbolism.

This kind of program can be abused, however, unless the company is absolutely clear about what the individual or team has accomplished. Recipients have been known to falsify records, take inappropriate shortcuts, and fail to support other teams in order to receive their prizes. In addition, managers have been known to use such programs for manipulating others to perform a task that may be inappropriate or unsafe or to favor their friends. For example, in one company, all the executives participated in a sales organization's special trip to an exotic location but spent little time with the salespeople. It did not take long for the organization's members to know about this breach of trust and confidence in the program. Objective data and a public display of the award recipient usually will to prevent these systems from being misused.

Nonetheless, depending on the leverage factor—sincere, timely, understood by the person (or team), for the person (or team), or fun— spot awards can be effective in supplementing an array of informal practices to reinforce behaviors that achieve desired results.

In an environment where winning is reinforced often, winning becomes a habit.

This means that people become excited about winning—not for personal gain but for what the gain means to their company, their work team, their peers, and themselves. This keeps people focused on the critical factors of success and allows them to become self-motivated because of the environment. The practices were created by these organizations and continue to serve them well despite growing competitive pressures.

According to many quality and team management experts, an individual makes very little difference to the performance of organizations. These experts demonstrate through their research and illustrations that performance is driven by collaborative efforts and that it is through collective efforts that organizations flourish and are able to retain the spirit of success in all kinds of economic or market conditions.

However, in the American business culture, the efforts of individuals are held in high esteem, and we often create heroes out of leaders or individuals who go well beyond their expected role and responsibilities. When employees see a great reliance on teams within an organization, they may fear that their own particular uniqueness or their own particular contribution will not be noticed. This is not surprising when you consider that although an organization may focus on overall team performance, performance appraisals still focus on individual employees. If we recall the impact of the extinction consequence (i.e., individuals slowly stop doing something for which they no longer receive the reinforcement they want or expect), we know that performance will decline in such situations. Therefore, whatever philosophy is used in an organization, it needs to account for the contributions of the individual as well as the combined efforts of teams, groups, and the enterprise.

Finally, it is important to remember that a team does not experience reinforcement. It is the individuals who make up a team who feel the value of recognition and rewards. The peers on one's team can enhance or minimize the value of a reward given to the team for some achievement. A team that is exceptionally productive provides its members with a high degree of positive, personal, immediate, and meaningful reinforcement. A team that relies primarily on negative reinforcement (i.e., the fear that team members will experience unpleasant consequences if they do not act in a certain way) may be productive in the short term but soon lose its members' commitment. To be truly effective, reward systems need to be applied in creative ways to recognize, reinforce, and reward the contributions of individuals according to their levels of effort, commitment, and talent.[4] Furthermore, high-performance teams reinforce in their members the behaviors that contribute to success of the team or business. Thus the question is not to reward the team versus the individual, or vice versa, but to reward *both*.

Team Celebrations

At a recent special recognition dinner hosted by a large medical products firm, attendees were heard saying:

> "I wonder when this will be over."
> "I wonder when he will stop talking."
> "She doesn't really understand what we did. Notice how she got the facts mixed up. She even mispronounced the project leader's name."
> "I wonder where they got this food?"
> "This is the seventh dinner we've been to, in the same hotel, this year."
> "We have a lot left to do to live up to what they say we've accomplished."
> "I wonder when this whole charade will be over."

Throwing splashy, expensive recognition dinners and similar team celebrations does not necessarily mean that the people being recognized really feel valued for their accomplishments. While the objective is usually well intentioned, the delivery often leaves much to be desired. Event planners tend to focus on the satisfaction of the executives funding the event rather than on the people for whom the celebration is intended.

To illustrate, let's examine a true story. Kelly, Susan, and Ned, all highly skilled technicians at a medical electronics firm, were considered instrumental in exceeding their team's objectives last year. Among those being honored at the company's annual awards dinner, they were asked to sit at the head table with the firm's top executives. They were driven to and from the event in the company limo. During the postdinner ceremony, they were presented with a large Lucite sculpture of the company's logo. What were the results? The next day they all called in sick.

Examples of Effective Team Celebrations

A team of employees at a division of a large international corporation staged a theatrical presentation about how they achieved improvements in their workflow process. Their skit was called "Murphy's Law" and depicted the before and after flow of their work. Each team member represented a certain task within the system and contributed to a very humorous and instructive presentation. The skit taught them as much as it did their audience, and everyone enjoyed it. In fact, it was talked about for months afterwards.

A new product team from joint-venture financial products and pharmaceutical companies developed a video on the history of the development of one of their major products. They interviewed people as the new product was being created, filmed the special events and milestones, and showed the new product performing its function at the customer's site. The video created an opportunity to relive how the product was created and how each person played an essential part in developing this important new product that saved the lives of many people.

A division of a long-established manufacturing company brought all its employees together for an ice cream sundae social served by the managers and supervisors when the division accomplished a major breakthrough in its on-time delivery. Charts and graphs of each unit were on display in the cafeteria, and people were asked to tell how they made improvements in their work process that lead to improved delivery performance. It was both a meaningful experience and an opportunity to press for even greater delivery performance.

A small division of a medical device company conducts weekly meetings with all its employees to review two critical variables in the business of the division: new orders and shipments. The division general manager stands in front of two thermometer-type charts and discusses the week's key events. He tells the group the results and then selects a member from a department that did a special activity during the week. The activities mentioned include handling a high volume, overcoming a problem, helping another department, or demonstrating significant performance improvements. The representative of the department then colors in one of the two charts for the week's performance. Two departments are singled out each week. The entire process takes less than 20 minutes, and people often talk about the meeting all week long.

Team celebrations offer an important opportunity for organizations to recognize the performance and achievements of many people. To take full advantage of the opportunity, the celebration needs to be founded on the principles discussed above and tailored to the person or groups being honored. A quality manager at a large chemical company often says, "Reliving an experience is often more meaningful than living an experience."

Case Study: A High-Impact Achievement Club—The Top Gun

A trucking company that delivers automobiles from factories and train depots to dealer showrooms has a unique recognition club program. Whenever a nick, scratch, or break is encountered en route, the cost is significant in terms of both repairs and the cost of inventory that is not immediately available to customers. Although this company's performance was for a long time comparable with that of the industry in general, this level of performance was not giving the company an advantage in this intensely competitive marketplace.

The top executives decided to develop and implement a program to recognize drivers who were able to deliver automobiles with minimal defects. They entitled the program the "Top Gun Club" (a name suggested by one of the drivers). When management analyzed driver defect records (lists indicating the number of times there was a difference between the pickup inspection and the delivery inspection), about 10 percent of the company's drivers could boast a 99 percent damage-free record for 12 consecutive months. The challenge was to bring 90 percent of the drivers to the same level as the top 10 percent.

When a driver was able to achieve this 99 percent damage-free performance for a month, he or she became a member of the Top Gun Club. At the time of initiation, he or she received a special hat with the Top Gun logo. As drivers sustained this status for longer periods of time—quarterly, annually, and so on—they received Top Gun pins, patches, license plates, and other symbolic trophies of club membership. Over a 3-year period, the damage-free standard rose from 99 percent to 99.7 percent, and the percentage of drivers in the club grew from 10 percent to over 60 percent.

The chief executive says, "One thing we've learned is that programs don't have to be expensive. What this has done is develop a culture in the company where people want to perform properly. We provide the tools to improve and recognize that performance. The pride aspect is really what works the most."

This program has several very important features. First, the measures are specific and can be measured reliably by the performers themselves. Thus feedback can be almost instantaneous. Second, by setting a performance level that some people had already achieved, managers were communicating that the requirements were achievable, a fact underscored by their gradually raising the standard as more and more people achieved the level. Third, there was no zero-sum game; no one won at the expense of someone else. In fact, it was in everyone's interest to get as many people into the club as possible. Increased performance lead to better competitiveness for the company, and this enhanced everyone's job security. Fourth, performance was summarized on a monthly basis but measured daily. Awards were announced monthly by publishing the list, and people were encouraged to keep their names on the list for long periods of time. Finally, the rewards were meaningful for the status they conferred.

The company initially had tried using tangible rewards such as VCRs, radios, and so on, but they had little impact on performance. The club concept was used because many of the drivers already belonged to clubs or community groups in their off-work time. By observing what people did when they had choices, the executives were able to identify high-value rewards. By making membership in the club a measure of status and using tangible symbols and celebrations, the company was further able to create meaningful rewards associated with performance. They found drivers and supervisors frequently helping other drivers to achieve membership in the club by sharing skills and tricks of the trade. The essence of this achievement club was fundamentally a win-win situation for all parties.

Suggestion Systems

One of the oldest forms of employee involvement is the suggestion system. Started in the early 1900s, suggestion systems sought to encourage employees to contribute ideas that would improve productivity, working conditions, or the quality of a firm's products. The concept was simple: Place little red boxes throughout a plant facility and encourage people to write down their suggestions and put them in the box for consideration by management.

Needless to say, the results of such practices were less than overwhelming. When management began offering to share as much as 10 percent of its first year's savings from a good idea with the employee or team who contributed it, there was a significant increase in the number of suggestions, but many proved impractical. In some cases, ideas were actually stolen from employees, and awards were given to the wrong person or group. Periodically, the major media publish stories about an employee who receives a very large sum of money for a major suggestion, but like winning the lottery, this happens too infrequently to have much impact.

In the 1970s American companies imported an idea from Japan called *quality circles*. These were meetings at which employees were trained and encouraged to develop ideas that would improve the business. Employees tolerated the process; after all, it was better than working at a hot or noisy machine. From time to time good ideas arose from these quality circles, but they usually meant more work for the supervisors and engineers, who then had to do the documentation and justification for the change, in addition to their normal responsibilities. The reward, if not 10 percent of annual projected savings, was usually a thank you from the plant manager, along with a comment that the idea was either too expensive or would involve too much effort to be implemented.

With interest in total quality management, employee empowerment, and the self-managed workforce going in and out of style, firms periodically become interested in suggestion systems.

In 1986, Modern Management Co., Ltd., conducted a study that compared the suggestion systems in American firms with those in Japanese firms.[5] The executive director of Modern Management, Hiroshi Yamada, reported some very interesting findings. The primary points are shown in Figure 11-3.

To summarize the study's key points, Japanese companies generate a significantly greater number of suggestions from their employees than do U.S. companies. The participation rate is higher, the number of suggestions per employee is higher, the percentage of suggestions implemented is higher, and the overall savings are 13.5 times greater. While American firms were able to achieve a higher saving for a given suggestion ($5554 versus $141), the suggestions implemented were so few as to have little real impact on the firms.

In behavioral terms, one can see that the act of making suggestions is more reinforced in Japanese firms than in U.S. firms. In fact, Japanese

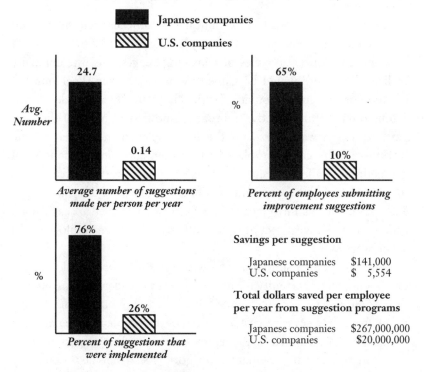

Figure 11-3 Comparison of suggestion systems in the United States and Japan.

employees receive significant social recognition for any suggestion, regardless of how small or insignificant it appears on the surface. Japanese managers are rewarded (in a nonmonetary fashion) when their people are able to find solutions to problems in products, work processes, or equipment. They are also accountable for the speed at which they get back to the employee with a response to their ideas. American managers are seldom recognized for encouraging suggestions, nor do they recognize their employees for such actions. In most American firms, more suggestions just mean more work for the supervisor and engineering departments. The reverse is true in Japanese firms.

In the United States we continue to expect that special suggestion programs will help to produce useful ideas. In reality, the most value comes from these initiatives when the process is considered a normal part of doing business.

Case Study: An Employee Suggestion System

A Canadian division of a large chemical company changed the method by which it solicits and handles employee suggestions. After comparing Japanese and American styles of managing suggestions, the company realized that more would be gained by increasing the sheer number of ideas than by simply looking for the "big win." Hence it developed a simple but highly effective approach. The first element of the suggestion system was to explain the importance of new ideas to the workforce. The company placed the presentation in the context of competitive challenges and the need to make certain changes to improve the quality, speed, and use of resources within the plant. Then a simple form was introduced. The form was provided to each work center and was the subject of weekly meetings between employees and supervisors.

The form had a simple point system. A suggestion would receive one point if an opportunity for improvement were identified. A suggestion would receive another point if there were supporting data related to the frequency, severity, cost, or extent of the problem. The nature of the data was determined by the nature of the problem. Supervisors did not want to make this element too rigorous lest they discourage any new ideas. A suggestion would receive two more points if specific actions were identified to address the problem. Or if a problem had been handled in an innovative way, the person whose suggestion it was would note the actions taken. Supervisors and employees would examine the impact and note any significant change. Finally, after the idea had been implemented for some period of time, the suggestion would receive another point if the results were documented. The suggested savings also were noted as a way of reflecting the positive impact of the suggestion on the work group or company.

The point system was designed to do several things. First, it provided a way to track the number of suggestions and the progress of those suggestions within the work center. Charts were displayed in various work areas showing the number of points generated by that department on a weekly basis. Second, every step along the suggestion's path was reinforced. No suggestion was too small; no amount of involvement was too restricted for inclusion. Third, the focus was not on the individual or team developing a suggestion but rather on the overall suggestion-generating process. People from across the entire plant were involved in suggestions, and everyone was encouraged to generate, support, and find creative ways to implement the changes.

Supervisors and managers conducted the actual scoring of suggestions and created charts for their work areas. The suggestions were discussed in weekly work center staff meetings and in the manager/supervisor meetings within the plant. Everyone was involved, and actions supporting this process were reinforced continuously.

The results are quite impressive. Some of them are as follows:

- Seventy-five percent of employees were involved in making suggestions.
- Seventy-seven percent of the suggestions were implemented.
- The average savings per suggestion was approximately $150.
- The cumulative savings were over $30,000 per month in the first year.

The reinforcement came in a variety of forms. When people handed a suggestion to a supervisor, the supervisor took time *at that moment* to read it and comment positively on it. He or she scored the items and provided a weekly feedback on the work centers' total points. As ideas were implemented and savings were documented, the supervisor noted them for each department as well. People received special recognition for their ideas in weekly staff meetings, as well as in plantwide meetings. People saw their ideas being implemented quickly, or, if the ideas were not approved, had the reasons explained to them within a week. Positive comments by various departments were written on the suggestion forms and given back to the employees. Finally, to get the program started with a bang, supervisors gave 50 cents per point. The awards were minor in relation to the impact of the suggestions, but the power of the reinforcement encouraged the desired behaviors.

What's Right with This Picture?

Analyzing this program using the STUFF criteria, we can quickly understand why this suggestion process was so successful.

Sincere

Although the employees received financial rewards (50 cents per point), they were minor in comparison with the personal recognition and appreciation they received. Their ideas were discussed in open forums, in staff meetings, in plantwide meetings, and through various other communications. Sometimes employee names were associated with the idea, and sometimes an original idea was built on by many others and took a new form. People knew that their ideas were being valued, and this was the part that was meaningful.

Timely

This is perhaps the most important element of this program: The feedback was immediate. The supervisor reviewed the suggestion *on the spot*. There were weekly reviews about point levels and specific suggestions that were in process. Employees were reinforced as they contributed their ideas to the overall effort of building the company into a more competitive organization.

Understanding by the Person (or Team)

Employees knew why suggestions were important and what to do to receive the rewards. They were reinforced for any actions leading to identifying, researching, solving, and providing follow-up to their suggestions.

For the Person (or Team)

The process involved the supervisors and work teams. People received frequent and meaningful praise by supervisors, peers, and upper management. People often took great pride in seeing their ideas implemented. They appreciated how their suggestions were talked about, charted, displayed, and implemented. Occasionally, the plant manager and other members of upper management reviewed the results with the departments. They were looking for ways to encourage more ideas and support the improvements; they were not looking for cheaters. Cheating is a problem only when more value is received by an individual for fabricating the information than for doing it right.

Fun

Little effort was needed to enhance the recognition of this process. As ideas were being generated, employees began to set their own limits as to what was a reasonable suggestion. More reinforcement was given to those with ideas that would have a substantial impact on the company. And people enjoyed doing it.

The process became a way of doing business. It moved from being a program to becoming a process. Initially, suggestions included generic complaints and meaningless ideas. They were scored and valued, but ideas that made more sense to the business got a lot of public attention. Hence the actions of making more and better suggestions, seeing to their implementation, and measuring their cost savings were encouraged. The suggestion process continued because people found very creative ways to address the complex challenges of the firm. Employees were reinforced when they made suggestions and when they saw their ideas, sometimes enhanced by others, becoming a reality. It did not take long to do this, but it did take a recognition that there is a better way than a suggestion box. The suggestion process had become part of the culture and the company's way of doing business.

The Guiding Principles for Making Recognition Special

Whenever one develops a recognition initiative that is associated with a point system, it is critical to ensure that the purpose is reinforced—improve the productivity and competitiveness of the company. If the focus shifts to earning points, it is very easy to get trapped in a transactional, entitlement-based relationship. Here employees will do things beyond the most minimal aspects of their job only if they can earn points.

This chapter has provided an overview of many techniques to reward and reinforce individuals and teams for their performance. Special recognition techniques have certain advantages over salary and variable pay plans. They can be more timely, more personalized, and more contingent on the process of achieving a specific result, and as a result, they become more fun! As stated earlier, there is no single right way to recognize contributions. We can draw some very important conclusions about how to create, develop, and manage such special recognition programs (see Figure 11-4).

1. Keep the Focus on What Is Valuable to the Organization

Special recognition programs are targeted toward reinforcing individuals for doing something the organization needs, which may change over time. In most cases, these are actions that are outside the scope of employees' normal daily activities or represent a major achievement within such activities. Whether the group involves technical researchers, teams of engineers and marketeers, operational employees, support staff, sales staff, or managers, it needs to be clearly identified. It is imperative to know *who* you want to do what.

2. Make the Reward/Recognition Contingent on What You Want People to Do

Some programs are used to recognize people who generate new ideas, regardless of the size or impact of the idea. Others are used to recognize a team that has developed some new applications of existing technology. Still others are used to recognize individuals who go well beyond their current job responsibilities and make important contributions to the work of others. By segmenting the populations (i.e., the organization), the program can be designed around what action or behavior best reflects what is desired.

3. If It's Worth Doing, It's Worth Measuring

Measuring actions or outcomes is essential if rewards are to have any meaning and credibility. Whether or not the measurement process is used to select recipients (teams or individuals), it is essential to use it in deciding to grant awards. Measurement helps make the basis on which the reward is given more specific and thereby more clearly in the performer's line of sight. Finally, measurement reveals whether the performer actually has accomplished what you wanted. It is an essential element of the process of reinforcement and feedback. It defines the difference between an "attaboy" or "attagirl" and true positive rewards.

4. Make It Personal and Meaningful to the Performer

While money may be the universal reinforcer, it is not universally applicable. When one is starting out with a new form of recognition, it is often best not to start with money. It is always relatively easy to progress to using money, but it is very difficult to go back without making employees feel that something had been taken away, even though the substitute award may be of the same financial value. Further, if you want to see what is meaningful to an individual, note what he or she does when there are choices. Look for things that people do on their own time that create naturally reinforcing conditions, and you will find the kinds of rewards they see as positive and meaningful (Figure 11-4).

5. Make It Timely

Perhaps the reason that special recognition has more impact on performance than do compensation systems is its immediacy. Pay systems have an inherent limitation to them: The recipient has to wait until the annual performance review, the final accounting of the firm's numbers, or changes in the marketplace. Base pay is often in the future, and variable pay is usually uncertain. However, special recognition can be given *at the time* when the desired event or behavior occurs. If an employee

---

**A Systematic Way to Create Alignment and
Deliver Positive Consequences**

1. Keep the focus on what is valuable to the organization.
2. Make the reward/recognition contingent on what you want people to do.
3. If it's worth doing, it's worth measuring.
4. Make it personal and meaningful to the performer.
5. Make it timely.
6. Make sure everyone can win.
7. Remember: You are competing with other consequences.
8. Reinforce the reinforcers.

Figure 11-4   Guiding principles of special recognition.

achieves a desired result, it can be recognized immediately and with certainty. This requires an identification process that is clear and very easy to handle. Above all, it requires that supervisors, managers, or others be aware of and attentive to rewarding the desired actions.

6. Make Sure Everyone Can Win

As illustrated by several of the case studies, associate the value of the award with what was achieved and not with who was excluded. Effective recognition programs do not use a ranking process or set up any other form of internal competition in order to achieve a desired result. People work hard when they know that they will be rewarded for it and that the reward will not be at the expense of others. Competition inherently creates winners and losers. Special recognition, when it operates at its maximum potential, has only winners and those who have not made the effort. If people do not accomplish something desired, they are not recognized; those who do *are* recognized. Since everyone has the same opportunity, there is a level playing field. The best situation is one in which everyone can get over the goal line by winning his or her own individual race.

7. Remember, You Are Competing with Other Consequences

The workplace has numerous conflicting pressures. People are affected by many personal situations that require or attract their attention. Peers have a major impact on one's performance. Management does not always understand, realize, or address the other factors influencing what employees do. Hence it is important to realize that recognition systems are in competition with other consequences that have an impact on individuals. In order to win more often and enable employees to feel valued and rewarded for achieving the results needed by the organization, a company's recognition systems need to be more attractive to its employees than the other consequences in their environment.

8. Reinforce the Reinforcers

Many special recognition systems are meant for employees, not supervisors or managers, on the principle that supervisors and managers are recognized as a normal part of their job. However, as most individuals in first-line and middle-management positions will indicate, they are often the most left out, ignored, and underdeveloped resource within the organization. This is especially unfortunate because a special recognition initiative will not work without managers and supervisors who are also rewarded and skilled at using the process effectively. If an organization wants its managers to recognize its supervisors and its supervisors to recognize the staff below them, its managers and supervisors must be recognized themselves. Otherwise the system will just be seen as yet another burden that top management is "laying on" the organization.

Many organizations have established reward and recognition committees, task forces, or special councils that flounder around searching for some way to help increase the amount or effectiveness of recognition practices. In our opinion, their task can be made much easier simply by finding ways to increase the rate and effectiveness of recognition within the organization. *Recognition* as a word simply does not fully convey the nature of the effort required to support the changes needed in today's organizations. Recognition is really about sincere appreciation and acknowledgment, multiple rewards, and meaningful reinforcement.

Summary

This chapter has explored multiple facets of the recognition process. It has attempted to expose the fallacies inherent in some current practices and to provide an understanding of why some approaches do not work.

Further, it has attempted to show what can be done when one takes a behavior-based approach, understanding that the nature of the task is to reinforce desired behaviors with sincere appreciation that is meaningful to the recipient.

By understanding that the meaningfulness and effectiveness of recognition are defined by the recipient(s), we can make special recognition truly effective. When it *is* effective—keyed to what is positive and meaningful to the individual—the results will be clear and impressive. Recognition is an essential part of the process of change within an organization. Change—especially change involving increased collaboration—means that people need to do some things differently. Special recognition practices can create the context in which these new behaviors flourish. They become the process *between* the paychecks, whether base or variable. By taking this approach, we can create a more competitive organization and foster a process that is more clearly able to achieve a win-win for all members concerned.

Take Stock of Your Options with Equity

It's ours now, let's work smarter.

> Sign put up by an airline
> worker inside the
> maintenance base

T HROUGH THE 1990s and early 2000s we have seen a dramatic change in the importance of equity compensation as an element in the total rewards mix. Technology companies in particular initially led the way. What started as an "equity revolution" in one industry has become even greater, more widespread, and more issue-laden than was conceived initially by executives and regulatory officials.

Companies as diverse as Internet startups and major banks granted stock options to all employees. In the 1990s, new millionaires were as likely to be age 25 as age 65. Senior executive's wealth skyrocketed even more. The bigger story at the dawn of the new century was how ordinary employees were attaining "seven-digit-income nirvana."

Chief executive officers (CEOs) and compensation directors who provided equity plans to all employees became as popular as investment bankers. Four percent salary increases suddenly were not an issue for the new engine of wealth creation. It was the "stake in the company" that put many employees in the same boat as owners and offered an opportunity to finally achieve the American dream.

Then the bubble burst. In early 2000 and 2001, the promised profits did not materialize. The Nasdaq and New York Stock Exchange plunged. Sophisticated investors sold shares rapidly, while "employee-investors" saw their wealth vanish. Then came the bankruptcies of Polaroid, Enron, Kmart, and other well-known companies. General investors lost confidence in equity-participation programs and saw their real incomes decline.

What went wrong? Some in the financial press blame stock options as the cause of this situation. They argue that stock options caused everyone to focus too much on raising the stock price. Some argue that stock options are "bad for shareholders" because there is no accounting charge related to the income growth executives and employees received from their companies. Stock options are "bad" because shareholders pay through a dilution of their ownership while executives undertake no real risk and receive all the gain!

These points have merit and no doubt will fuel the debate and lead to regulatory changes. However, stock options have dramatically changed the relationship between employees and employers and have created new meaning for the concepts of risk and opportunity, both short and long term, for a company and its shareholders.

This chapter provides an overview of the different types of equity plans and useful case studies. However, its best used to provide guidance to companies deciding if (or how) equity compensation truly fits as part of their reward strategy. We have put together a short "quiz" as an initial starting point to help evaluate an organization's equity program. Then we will describe some of the basic legal, tax, and accounting requirements and explore alternatives to creating a long-term stake in a company.

Assess the Alignment of Equity-Participation Plans

The following is a list of questions that highlights the issues involved in using stock or other forms of equity compensation as part of a company's total reward strategy. If the answer is yes to all these questions, then it is likely one has process for using equity effectively. If one answer is no, then care should be taken in relying too heavily on these programs to drive organizational and customer value.

1. Is there a clearly articulated philosophy describing the role of equity in the total rewards strategy mix (i.e., what are we trying to achieve)?
2. Is the total rewards "portfolio" diversified enough (i.e., does the company rely on a variety of reward programs with comparable risks and opportunities value)?
3. Has a thorough market study been conducted to compare market prevalence, dilution, and value delivered?
4. Is adequate governance in place to oversee the operation of the plan (i.e., compensation and audit committees of the board of directors with objective viewpoints)?
5. Have employees been communicated to thoroughly so that everyone clearly understands the plan's objectives as well as the possible risks and rewards?
6. Is resource support for personal financial planning available to employees?
7. Does the company understand where it is in its industry and whether it is in a growth cyclic, or in decline? Assuming the company understands its position, what does the company expect as potential gains from its stock plans?
8. Have the accounting, tax, and regulatory requirements been fully researched, understood, and complied with?
9. Does the company's short-term incentive/bonus plan use different performance measures from the long-term equity plan?
10. Are salary and bonus levels adequate to cover employee/executive annual living expenses, and are they appropriately competitive with the market?
11. Are vesting and equity-retention requirements fair between executives and other employees?
12. Do shareholders support the use of equity for executives and key contributors that is competitive with or greater than for their peer group?

Background on Equity Compensation

The application of equity-based programs has long been the domain of executives and their consultants. The increasing rancor about equity compensation has led many in the media, in organizations, and on boards of directors to question the return on investment of these programs. Yet we believe that stock-related programs will continue not only in small startup companies in the technology and biotechnology fields but also in major corporations. They offer meaningful and effective ways for companies to attract, engage, and retain top talent because people are still looking for a stake in the business. The "new news" for many companies is that equity plans need to be designed in the context of a business and rewards strategy to be successful.

In a study conducted in 2000 by Rutgers University, the research team examined the relationship between equity ownership, primarily through employee stock ownership plans, and corporate performance. They found that in companies where employees were significant owners of equity in the company, sales were 2.3 to 2.4 percent greater than in companies where the ownership was more limited. This is corroborated by other research that demonstrates the importance of equity ownership and organization success.[1]

This chapter addresses a wide range of ideas for developing innovative reward systems tied to the equity or ownership process of the organization. The principle underlying these systems is the use of rewards to create a shared sense of identity, a shared commitment, and shared goals for the organization among employees and management alike. While not attempting to address all current controversies about executive compensation or trying to explain the full tax and accounting implications of each option, this chapter seeks to provide ideas and stimulate creative thinking about equity-based programs.

Readers should be aware that many of the provisions for stock-related programs may be changed by congressional tax legislation, rulings by the Securities and Exchange Commission (SEC), rulings by the Financial Accounting Standards Board (FASB), and loopholes found by executive compensation and legal experts. Therefore, before taking any action, one should seek the counsel of those who have expertise in these areas and can address the particular circumstances of the company involved.

As discussed in Chapter 9, group-oriented incentive plans such as gain sharing, goal sharing, and project incentives provide cash awards to people based on the performance of their team, department, division, and so on. By their very design, profit-sharing plans offer employees a stake in the profits of a business when those profits exceed a certain level. Properly designed equity-related programs, the next logical step, offer employees a stake in the ownership of the business and thereby in the long-term viability of the organization. There are differences in risks and opportunities in both types of programs, as well as differences in timing, restrictions, and tax implications.

The point of all cash compensation plans is that they emphasize current operating issues and encourage people to take actions that benefit them immediately. Long-term wealth, however, whether it is for the organization or for individuals, cannot be achieved by maximizing immediate short-term cash. Therefore, structuring reward systems to encourage a dynamic balance between cash flow and value growth is necessary for a healthy organization.

The principal objective behind the use of stock-related compensation programs is to create a true alignment of interests between shareholders and those accountable for the organization's success. Some major corporations require executives to buy and own shares in the company in amounts relative to their total cash compensation, usually between 5 to 10 times their annual salary. Whether the shares are purchased directly, bought through loan provisions, or granted through performance-based programs, the objective is to reinforce executives as true stakeholders. This means that the personal net worth of the executives will be tied in some measure to the fortunes of the company.

Overview of the Key Terms and Basic Types of Equity Programs

Within this context, it is important to define a few terms. These are highly abbreviated, and the provisions are subject to change based on the actions of Congress and other regulatory agencies.

Stock options These are rights granted by a corporation to its executives and/or employees that enable them to buy shares in the company at a predetermined price at some future point in time (usually between 5 and 10 years hence). For example, a stock option at $30 per share could be used to buy a share in the company in the future. Thus, if the price went to $35, the owner would realize a gain of $5 per share when the option was exercised (one used the option to buy the share at $30).

Exercise price This is the price at which the owner of an option can buy a share of stock. This is usually the same as the market value of the stock on the date of the grant, but not always (see *Discounted, Premium,* and *Indexed Options* below). A stock is regarded as "in the money" when the exercise price is below the market value when the person can exercise the option; and it is "underwater" when the exercise price is greater than the current market value of the stock.

Vesting period This is the period of time in which the individual cannot exercise his or her stock options. The time period is usually 4 to 5 years, but it may be longer. The vesting period may be graduated (25 percent of shares "vest" each year) or cliff (100 percent of the shares "vest" after 4 years). Also, the vesting period may be based on the time the person is employed with the company (usually unvested options are forfeited if the individual terminates employment) or varies based on performance (as with accelerated vested stock options).

Incentive stock option (ISO) These are stock options that meet the requirements established by Section 422 of the Internal Revenue Code. The Internal Revenue Service (IRS) requires that ISOs be granted to company employees through a plan that has been approved by the shareholders. The term is set at 10 years, and the option price must equal the fair market value of the stock on the grant date. The gain is not taxable until the stock is sold, and the gains are not tax deductible by the corporation. If the individual holds the stock option for at least 2 years from the date of the grant or 1 year from the exercise of the option to stock, any appreciation is taxed at the capital gains rate. This is a particularly attractive feature when the individual's ordinary income tax rate is higher than the current capital gains rate (currently 8 to 20 percent). There are some limits on the value of the ISOs that can be awarded each year to an executive (currently $100,000).

Nonqualified stock option (NQSO) These stock options do not qualify for the tax-favored treatment (capital gains) the way ISOs do. However, they offer more flexibility. The option price can be set equal to, above, or below the fair market price. The option becomes taxable when the individual exercises the option and receives the stock, regardless of when the individual sells the stock. Short-term capital gains tax rates (which are currently the same as ordinary income tax rates) apply for any gain realized between the exercise price and the fair market value of the shares on the day of the exercise. If an individual holds the stock for 1 year, then long-term capital gains rates would apply to any gain in realized value when the stock is sold.

Stock appreciation rights (SARs) These are compensation provisions that are similar to stock options except that they do not require a person to take ownership of stock. Instead, he or she is paid the gain between the exercise price and the market price at the time of exercise. For example, if a person has 1000 SARs and the stock price increases by $5 per share, he or she is awarded $5000 in cash (or in equivalent shares of stock). The company charges this as a compensation expense, and the individual is taxed at ordinary income tax rates. SARs are sometimes granted as a companion to stock options in order to pay the tax liabil-ity of the option gain or used for subsidizing independent business units where a value of the business (a simulated market price) can be retained.

Phantom stock This is used when a company's stock is not available (as is the case with privately held companies) or when an attractive alternative becomes possible (e.g., when a company wants to establish an equity simulator program for a division or subsidiary). Phantom stock operates like SARs, but the focus is on the value growth as deter-mined by a formula, such as a multiple of earnings, book value of the unit, or an economic value-added model. The individual receives sym-bolic shares, which are valued at the date of grant and revalued at some future point in time. The value of the gain on the shares determines the award. The awards are treated like a bonus program for tax and accounting purposes, but the payout is made over a long-term period.

Performance share plan This is a program that provides stock (or stock options) to an individual for achieving specified performance goals, usually for a multiyear period (3 to 5 years). The performance determines the number of units one earns, but the stock price of the company at the end of the period determines the value of each unit at payout. When the payout is made in cash, such programs are usually called *performance unit plans*.

Restricted stock These are stock programs that award actual shares (net options) based on performance or contingent on future perfor-mance. Some companies use continued employment with the company as the contingency for securing stock awards. This is usually for a 3- to 5-year period. Other firms use financial performance as the contin-gency factor—the growth of the company's stock, achievement of a cer-tain amount of financial growth, improvement in the firm's profitability, return on asset/equity ratios, and so on.

Discounted or premium stock options These are rights that place the option price at a rate lower than the market price of the stock (dis-counted) or higher than the market price (premium) at the time the option is granted. For example, if the stock is trading at $30 per share, a discounted option may have an exercise price of $25 per share. Thus, when the person exercises and sells the stock at $35 per share, the gain is $10. The company expenses the per-share difference, and the individual realizes the gain at $10 per share. Premium options work similarly, only in reverse. The exercise price is set at $35, and only until the stock price exceeds this amount is the stock "in the money." This is available for nonqualified stock options only.

Indexed stock options Similar to discounted or premium stock options, this form of option does not have an exercise price that is the same as the market price on the date of the grant. Instead, the price is indexed to either an industry index (such as Nasdaq computer companies) or to a peer group of companies. If the index goes up, the exercise price goes up in relation to the index, but the gain in the option comes after the company's actual price exceeds the exercise price. Indexed options minimize the pressure to reprice stock options, but they carry a charge to earnings that is different from that of standard stock options.

Reload options This is a program where new options are granted on the exercise of existing options using actual shares. This enables the participants to realize all the future upside potential inherent in the original option grant and ensures that the participant continues to have options available. This program is sometimes called *accelerated ownership, restoration options*, or *stock-for-stock exchange.*

Employee stock purchase plans (ESPPs) These are programs where individuals can buy shares in their company often at a discount of the going rate. An employee can have a portion of his or her regular paychecks withheld, and at a certain point, shares are purchased in his or her name. There may be some vesting or other restrictions on selling these shares, but they are purchased with the employee's money.

Employee stock ownership program (ESOP) This is a program where a trust is established and a portion of the ownership of the company is acquired by the trust for the benefit of the trustees, who are the employees of the company. While there are some tax advantages to this kind of program, as well as features to protect a company from a hostile acquisition, it is used primarily for private companies that want to transfer ownership from the founders to the employees.[2]

Case Study: A Management Stock Bonus Plan

The CATE Energy Company (an actual company, but a fictitious name) has a long-term executive incentive program. The purpose of the program is to provide senior managers with ownership in the company consistent with their performance. The plan extends down to department managers. The plan is intended to create a sense of common interest among the executives, managers, and shareholders. The stock options are nonqualified stock options and have a restriction that requires them to vest over a 5-year period, or 20 percent per year from the date of grant. When managers cease to be employed by the company, they lose all rights to those shares not vested and must exercise any vested options within 3 months of termination. There is a simultaneous purchase and sale of the options that enables managers to exercise the options with the sale of other options at the same time. This enables participants to acquire shares from the proceeds of exercising and selling options or pay taxes on the gain.

CATE is a publicly traded company, and stock performance has been on par with the general stock market and industry. This performance has not made any executive wealthy, but the stock ownership plan is an important part of the total executive compensation package.

Each year, after the close of the fiscal year and the awarding of the executive and management bonuses, CATE executives engage in an allocation process for the stock program. The compensation committee of the board of directors and the CEO determine the amount of stock options available and how many each executive and manager will receive. Of the total number of options available, 40 percent go to the CEO. The remaining 60 percent is spread among the senior executives and lower-level managers. The CEO allocates 30 percent to senior executives based on her judgment of their individual performance.

The remaining 30 percent of shares is allocated on the basis of the perceived performance of the managers as recommended by each functional executive. Once all the recommendations have been submitted, the CEO, the vice president for human resources, and the chief financial officer (CFO) meet to discuss the recommendations and make final decisions. When a final allocation is made, the CEO sends a personalized letter to each recipient telling him or her the amount of the award and the exercise price.

Receipt of the options letter is always an important event. In approximately 90 percent of cases, the allocation awarded is similar to that in the preceding year. Those who received 200 shares last year probably will get between 175 and 225 shares this year, for example, depending on individual performance and the performance of the company. Approximately 70 percent of the shares that become vested are exercised each year—that is, the managers exercise the options and sell a large portion of their stock as soon as it is available. This program has become a significant element in the total compensation package of the managers, and receiving the stock options has become an important sign of recognition to CATE's managers, who regard it as an indication of their perceived value.

What's Wrong with This Process?

The original intent of the CATE stock ownership plan was to align the interests of the executives and managers with those of the shareholders. The underlying idea was that executives would take actions and make decisions consistent with building long-term asset value for all stakeholders. The program also was intended to recognize individual performance more cost-effectively than cash payments would. The idea was to emphasize the long-term interests of the company and balance these with the immediate profitability pressures of the management bonus program.

The problem is that CATE's stock option plan is not working as intended. Let's examine the various features of the program in relation to the principles of effective reward systems that we have discussed in this book.

To have an impact on behavior, rewards must be clearly linked to desired behaviors or results. CATE's plan has several limitations in this regard. First, the CEO and compensation committee of the board determine the number of options each person will receive often with little input from other executives. Most participants are unaware of any criteria and may see little line of sight between their results and their awards. In CATE's case, most of the managers tend to treat their options awards as a reflection of their perceived worth by the CEO, not as an indication of their impact on the company's performance. Further, since the pool is fixed, when some managers get more shares, others automatically get fewer. Hence the behaviors being subtly reinforced are those related to serving top management, not serving customers, implementing the firm's strategy, or working collaboratively.

The value of the stock option rewards is determined by a combination of factors. First, the gain is realized when the share price exceeds the exercise price. Because CATE is in a large, global industry, the company does little to sway investor confidence in the industry. The company's earnings are also highly influenced by the price of energy.

Consequently, the company's performance is not always reflected in its share price.

The number of the shares a manager receives is based on what is competitive with other companies or internally equitable. The number reflects the perceived importance of retaining the executive rather than a reward for his or her contributions to the company's long-term value. The participants often have different interpretations of the award's significance because the criteria for awarding the options are unclear and at times inconsistent. Awards are more for looking good than doing good.

Third, wealth is created by accumulating shares over time and building a "nest egg" of company stock that is proportional to one's individual investment philosophy and goals. When most of the managers sell the shares soon after the lapse of the vesting schedule, it is clear that the option program is treated as just another means of cash compensation. The time restriction transforms the "stake in the company's future" program into a deferred-compensation program. The real meaning of CATE's program is as a measure of perceived esteem, not true performance or creation of personal net worth.

In CATE's case, the basis on which the stock is awarded is unclear and at the discretion of the senior executives. The value of the shares is determined more by the marketplace than by the performance of the individual, unit, or team. The managers have little or no ability to take corrective actions when the market price changes. Finally, there is almost no alignment between what is earned and what is received. The value of the options and the subsequent stock ownership or option gains may be very important to the individual but are not having any direct effect on his or her consideration of what is best for shareholders.

We can conclude that CATE's senior executives need to redesign their plan to make it more effective in directing and reinforcing desired performance. But how? The answer to this question can be quite complex because stock-related programs are usually a very sensitive issue for executives and shareholders alike. No single design can be constructed to yield the desired behaviors in all cases. However, there are some identifiable conditions that can be used to create more real value in the program. To this end, the following pages provide a series of case studies in which stock-related programs have been used effectively to address complex business and human issues.

The Case of the New CEO

The Grigsby Company is a small, privately held, and generally profitable company (an actual company, but a fictitious name). It has a variety of business divisions with products that serve a range of markets from aerospace to telecommunications to construction. The company has existed for quite some time and had the same CEO for 12 years. Then the CEO died suddenly, and the board decided to recruit someone from the outside.

The candidate chosen had been a very successful executive at a very large industrial company. All the terms of his employment contract had been agreed on except the provision for stock in the company. In order for the board to determine the right mix of compensation, it needed to answer a fundamental question: Is the new CEO a hired gun or an adopted son? The answer to this question would determine how the stock arrangement should be structured. If a CEO is a *hired gun*, he or she is brought in to make improvements in the performance of the company or to take it to a new position of leadership within its markets. Then, when these objectives are accomplished, the CEO moves on to another company. The compensation plan in this situation emphasizes cash—large amounts of cash for significant improvements in the company's performance.

An *adopted son* (or *daughter*), on the other hand, shares the fortunes of the other shareholders or, in this case, the interests of the family that owns the company. At Grigsby Company, the CEO would be expected to make decisions that would support the family's short- and long-term interests. This would entail balancing the need to provide family members with adequate dividends from the company with the need to address the investment interests of the company. The CEO's own interests would have to be long term in building personal wealth through building growth in the asset value and profitability of the company.

To this end, the board chose the adopted son role for the CEO. Thus the stock-related program involved providing the executive a megagrant (1 million shares) over a 5-year period based on the performance of the company. The performance was to be judged on the basis of growth in the share price, which was determined primarily through a formula of book value, cash flow, and revenue growth. Were performance to exceed expectations, more shares would be awarded to the CEO.

If performance fell short of the plan, the number of shares would be reduced. Further, a stock appreciation rights (SAR) program was developed as a companion to the stock plan to cover the tax liability of the shares at the point of exercise. The objective was to encourage the CEO to own stock that was five times his annual total compensation after the first 5 years of employment. Depending on performance, this plan would be renewed after the initial period of the plan.

The Case of the New Products

WILCO Company (an actual company, but a fictitious name) desperately needed to introduce new products into its current line in order to retain its market leadership. Many new, primarily foreign competitors had entered its markets with products that were similar to WILCO's. While it retained a strong market reputation, the products of new competitors had attracted the attention of many of WILCO's key customers.

WILCO had been working on developing enhancements to its new products and other breakthrough technologies for several years. It had organized special product teams that included engineering, manufacturing, and marketing representatives to shift from a hands-off process to a design-for-manufacturing one. Despite this new structure, the teams still tended to work in functional subgroups with little true integration of the process.

While the concepts and prototypes were very strong and offered significant potential revenues, WILCO had been unable to get these products commercialized. They seemed to be caught in endless redesign cycles, and manufacturing appeared unwilling or unable to address the production requirements. The marketing function was strongly interested in using the advanced capabilities of these products, but the beta tests and other trials were slow and difficult to establish. At the same time, WILCO's engineers were continuing to create even greater enhancements to the products, giving the company the potential for even greater market leadership. The problem was that the products had yet to enter the market and be truly tested by customers.

The solution (in addition to leadership and other organizational change) was to develop a phantom share plan for each of the product teams. The program provided an opportunity for the participants to accumulate "shares" in their product. The value of these shares was to be based on the earnings the product generated for the corporation. The payout would be a function of the number of shares an individual received and of the economic value of those shares.

WILCO established a pool of shares that reflected a portion of the future profitability to be allocated to the team. The awards would be based on the product team's meeting or exceeding its product development milestones and project budget. The team could exceed its dates or budgets if it believed such actions would enhance the economic contribution of the new products once they were released to the market. The number of shares might be lower, but the value could be higher. The shares awarded at the critical design stages provided a symbolic piece of the action of the new products. Each member received a certificate with his or her number of shares and the product's name prominently displayed.

Once the new products were released, the value of the shares was established on the basis of the projected revenues and return on investment. The total potential income at the target level of performance was between 50 and 200 percent of a team member's annual salary, depending on the number of shares received. Over the 3 years following product release, the value of the shares was recalibrated every 6 months according to actual results. At that time, the product team members could cash in their shares according to a 3-year vesting schedule (one-third was available each year). The team members could retain the shares in the expectation that the share value would increase over the period. If they terminated employment, they would forfeit all rights to future earnings from the shares.

The results were dramatic. There was an increase in emphasis on bringing new products to market and on making the products excel in their performance with customers. During the early stages of the products' life cycle, the team members worked with marketing, sales, and customers to gain maximum value from the products. The share price of most of the products exceeded expectations, and the company was able to grow its market share despite the efforts of major competitors. The program provided a variety of both immediate psychic and symbolic rewards and a real tangible value as the earnings from the products were realized by the company and team members.

The Case of the New Executive Team

Pratt Industries is a large, diversified office equipment corporation (an actual company, but a fictitious name). The company has successfully rebounded from a grueling battle for survival with its competitors. In the course of the struggle, the company implemented numerous cost-reduction efforts, sold off divisions that were not related to its core business, and reinvested in technology enhancements to its major product lines. The company hired a new CEO, and she brought in or promoted several new executives who infused new leadership spirit into the organization.

Pratt implemented a new organizing concept around primary customers/markets and focused its people and investments on achieving and retaining a leadership position in these markets. Some of the markets were geographic, whereas others were industry-oriented. Pratt also focused several of its primary service and technology functions on supporting the market divisions, with minimal corporate staff, except where investments required cross-divisional support.

The challenge facing Pratt's CEO was both to focus the efforts of the senior executives on the performance of their divisions and to motivate them to optimize those areas where synergistic opportunities could be realized. For example, some of the major accounts crossed geographic and industry boundaries. The need was to maximize both divisional and company performance.

The solution was to create a stock-based incentive program in which the number of shares was used as the reward and the basis for the award was a combination of divisional and total company performance. Based on the achievement of a range of company financial performance and divisional performance levels, the company would give to each executive a number of restricted shares of stock and stock options. This was determined by using a matrix grid (Figure 12-1).

The vertical axis of the grid provided a range of performance for the division. This performance determined the number of units available to the executive from that division. The value of those units was based on the performance of the company, as shown on the horizontal axis in Figure 12-1. For example, if divisional performance and company target performance were achieved, the executive would receive 1000 units at a value of $200 each. This would result in a stock fund of $200,000

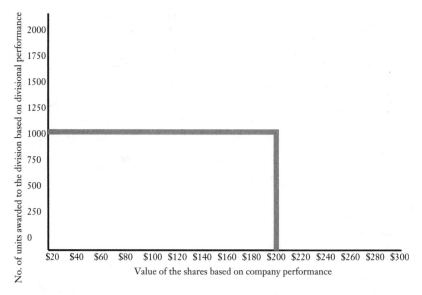

Figure 12-1 Senior management equity plan, Pratt Industries.

for the executive and would be used to purchase stock in the company. The stock awards would be restricted for a 3-year period. The purchase price was at the date of grant, but the shares would not become owned by the executive until the restriction had lapsed. The executive would be able to take advantage of certain tax code provisions to employ long-term capital gains rates.

There were two reasons for the restriction. First, the company wanted to create a significant share of the executive's net worth to ensure mutual interests with major shareholders. It was felt that providing options annually might not create a large enough stake. Although restricted shares have a major expense associated with them, the company determined that they would create a strong return on investment. Second, the company wanted to retain its top executives or make it very expensive for a competitor to attract them away from the firm.

The impact of this program was both dramatic and subtle. The focus on performance of each division was of critical importance to the executives. However, they sought ways to maximize the performance of the entire company, making necessary tradeoff decisions in order to increase the company's performance and hence the value of the units. Finally, as the program progressed over the years, the executives easily took on the perspective of the shareholders, looking for balancing annual operating results with long-term growth of the firm's shareholder value. The same model was then applied to key leaders and professionals within the divisions, but stock options were used for the award.

The Case of the Company in Transition

Transition Technologies (TTI) (a fictitious name, but an actual company) had passed through its startup phase and was gaining a reputation for highly customized, expertly crafted, factory automation-control products. The firm had begun as a spinoff of a larger technology company, with several key engineering and marketing people involved in the original venture. Although it had successfully introduced an initial public offering (IPO) to the market 2 years before, initial investors still maintained a sizable portion of the company's stock.

The company was looking to grow and develop into a larger company while retaining its entrepreneurial qualities for involvement, sharing risks, and fast action. The firm needed a way to attract talented new managers to bring leadership into the firm, highly trained technical professionals to strengthen its technical prowess, and employees (or associates, as they were known) who would willingly participate actively in growing the company. Since the company was still in the developing, emerging stage, revenues and costs fluctuated greatly. Cash flow was needed to build and support the operations of the company. The company could not afford to pay the big salaries of the large companies, but it needed highly skilled of talent.

The solution came in the form of a stock-related incentive plan to provide an attractive program for recruiting the necessary talent, creating the incentives for staff to assist in growing the company, and building a shared-fate philosophy in the future of the company.

TTI considered many options. First, it looked at the idea of creating an employee stock purchase plan. While this would not have had a negative impact on the firm's cash flow, it was believed that the plan would have few participants. Although the firm could discount the share price, many employees felt risking personal capital when the stock price fluctuated greatly and the future was highly uncertain was too great. Second, the firm explored establishing an employee stock ownership program (ESOP). This kind of plan has many attractive features for tax optimization and building retirement accounts, but TTI felt that an ESOP would have minimal meaning to its relatively young employees. Finally, the firm decided to provide stock options widely within the company based on two factors: overall company performance and individual or team contributions. Company performance would be judged on the basis of growth of revenues and profit before taxes (for a growing company, this is needed to increase its profitability).

On an annual basis, the company would establish 6-month and annual performance objectives. If these targets were achieved, a pool of stock options would be made available for distribution. If the performance fell short, no shares would be made available for the performance period, although they could be made up on a biannual basis (i.e., every 2 years). It was hoped that this plan would encourage not only a short-term emphasis on performance but also a view on the part of employees that short-term gains could be invested to achieve long-term (2-year and beyond) results. If the company exceeded the targets, the pool would be increased on the basis of a predetermined formula. Thus the number of options awarded would be linked to company performance, and the value of the options would be driven by the investor market.

For distribution, each department would be awarded a number of options that could be increased or decreased by 25 percent based on performance. Once the number of options was determined, they were awarded by divisional management for associates, by senior management for middle managers, and by the CEO and board for executives. The number of options available to any division was based on the percentage of payroll reflected in the total wages and salaries of the unit. The award guidelines were based on different tiers reflecting a person's role in, impact on, and value to the company's long-term growth.

The shares were awarded on a semiannual basis, and there was a big celebration when the number of available shares was determined. Further, because the stock was traded publicly, the company offered a simultaneous purchase and sale provision for the plan so that employees could exercise the number of shares they needed to buy the options awarded.

Senior managers closely monitored the number of shares sold by employees as a measure of the plan's reinforcement value. It was felt that if associates or managers sold the stock options when they became available, the purpose of the plan—that is, creating a sense of common fate—would not be achieved and that the plan then would have to be adjusted. The impact of the potential dilution of the shares was perceived as an issue by some of the major shareholders. However, the direct performance connection of the plan eased many of their concerns. If the plan were to be successful, the gain in the market value of the company would more than offset the potential dilution from new shares. The plan offered a way to create a real sense of ownership in the company for employees (a sense of ownership, moreover, that they themselves had earned).

The greatest future risk of this plan may be with the FASB (Financial Accounting and Standards Board) rulings on how firms must account for expenses related to stock options. At TTI, the company will wait and see, but today the company is enjoying the extra advantage of a turned-on workforce.

The Lessons to Be Learned from Using Equity

The preceding discussion and illustrative case studies provide an opportunity for learning how to use stock-related programs as part of a total reward system. Peter Drucker, a noted author and professor of management, indicates that in many companies the use of stock options and other equity-related award programs encourages executives to be more concerned about the closing price of the stock than the right decisions that create value for shareholders and other stakeholders.[3] In many cases the root cause of this lies in the lack of a line of sight between the value of the reward and the actions necessary to achieve it. Another potential problem lies in assuming that what is meaningful to top executives is also meaningful to all employees. While few employees will deny a stock option award, they indicate the value of the option when the restrictions on its use are removed. People often "vote with their investment decisions."

Summary

Equity-related programs offer both an exciting and a risky opportunity for rewards. They create a chance to recognize individual performance in relation to team and corporate performance. Using equity-type plans as symbolic rewards and as a real stake in the business can have a truly positive impact on commitment and involvement. In many cases, expert counsel is needed, but in all cases, expert management is essential. For some executives, the blessing and the curse of making all employees feel like owners of the business is that they will start acting like them. The answer is often found in understanding what best creates the culture and behavior needed by the organization to sustain a competitive advantage.

Putting Rewards into Practice

R EWARDS ARE NOT just compensation or a trophy for performance. Instead, they are a series of interdependent programs that encourage and reinforce behaviors that people believe are desirable. The greater the degree to which there is alignment between strategy and action, between the measures of performance and the indicators of behaviors, the more likely the organization will be to see the results it desires. And its employees will be more likely feel valued and important to the organization.

This final section of the book integrates the various programs into a system of rewards. This takes the organization from having just a "total reward system" to one that is integrated. Each program has certain inherent strengths and limitations. If these can be woven into a purposeful system, each program using its strengths to offset the weaknesses of other programs, the organization can realize real value from these investments. These chapters offer suggestions on how to accomplish this goal for different situations and for specific programs, so that they truly build toward success.

Organizations, like people, go through various stages of development. Chapter 13 will examine the characteristics of each of these stages and present the type of reward systems that are likely to have the greatest value. You will see also how reward systems can evolve and adapt to changes the organization goes through as it addresses a changing marketplace.

Throughout this book and in much of the literature about leadership, high-performing companies, and organizational change, organizations face the conflicts of a culture that becomes inconsistent with what the organization needs to be successful. An organization's culture does not just happen. As we have seen, cultures often evolve from consequences to individuals over time. In fact, to understand the forces that shape the culture of an organization, ask its employees what they get rewarded for and what they get punished for. The culture of an organization can be witnessed by observing what employees do when "no one is around."

Chapter 14 addresses the issues of culture from the perspective of entitlement and achievements and the challenges that face leaders who attempt to change the organization. We examine how rewards can, and at times should, be applied to support the process of change as well as what is needed to understand when to implement changes in the reward systems. This chapter summarizes the top 10 principles to be considered when implementing changes in the reward systems of an organization.

Throughout this book, there have been many suggestions and ideas. Hopefully, the content has served as a catalyst for many more new and innovative ideas. Chapter 15 summarizes the most important dos and don'ts regarding reward systems. The importance of these principles can be fully understood only if one knows the principles from which they are derived and the characteristics of the organization in which new reward systems will be applied.

The success of an organization is never permanent. Even high-performance, enduring organizations have times when what they are is no longer relevant to the marketplace they serve. Obviously, the focus, measurement systems, competencies, and systems of rewards need to change as well. This process of change and renewal often deals with forces that cannot be seen or touched, but they are very real. In Chapter 16, we examine the fundamental purpose of reward systems and review the principles that make them work. Since rewards influence the actions of people, in often unseen and unintended ways, the organization has a choice: to utilize rewards in a strategic manner or to treat them as infrastructure, with little understanding of their impact. This chapter reminds you of what is important and why. For if reward systems are not part of the solution, they will indeed be part of the problem.

How to Use the Right Rewards for the Firm's Stage of Development

There is nothing more difficult to take in hand, more perilous to conduct, or more uncertain in its success than to take the lead in the introduction of a new order of things.

Niccolo Machiavelli, *The Prince*

ORGANIZATIONS ARE FACING unprecedented complex competitive situations. As discussed at several points throughout this book, the global market and demographic and legal forces are driving these pressures. Startup companies have access to capital and technology, but they need to prove their business models to a skeptical marketplace. The Internet and other expansive communication technologies enable individuals and small companies to provide many of the services that once required the resources of large organizations. Large companies face the challenges of multidimensional competition and greater leadership agility and credibility. Regardless of its size or particular industry, a company must find ways to promote growth while reducing costs.

Success is temporary at best. Companies that once were champions of their industries either have been acquired and integrated into other companies or have divested major elements of their organizations and no longer command the market value they once held. New companies now take their positions as market leaders, if only for a short while. Success is sometimes due to luck, but most times it is due to the effective implementation of a well-conceived strategy. A great strategy, access to capital, proprietary technology, terrific people, and superior leadership will not guarantee success. However, they will increase the probability.

This chapter focuses on how to use reward systems to strengthen the capabilities of an organization at different stages of development. We will examine seven different situations—from getting a startup company going to driving the transformation of a major corporation. Then we will identify the common principles that have lead companies to be successful in facing their own unique challenges. These situations are derived from both the experience and research of hundreds of companies and the science that underlies the dynamics of organizational and individual behavior. (Readers should review the Bibliography of this book for additional references.)

"Let's Make a Deal" for Rewards in a Startup Company

Organizations form when three forces converge at the same time:

1. Someone has an idea for a product or service that will meet the needs of someone else who is willing to pay for this product or service. This idea may come from research or experience with a customer or from seeing a need in the community that has not been met. Some of the greatest entrepreneurs had a vision about a technology or service where there wasn't an expressed need. Once the idea was introduced, they created a market—for example, Henry

Ford of Ford Motor Co., Tom Monaghan of Domino's Pizza, Fred Smith of Federal Express, and Bill Gates of Microsoft.

2. The entrepreneur is able to translate the idea into a something real. This requires a combination of capital, materials, equipment, contracts, and people.
3. A customer appears who understands the value of the proposition and has the desire, resources, and ability to make the purchase.

Then a transaction occurs. At this stage the founder or founders do everything—provide the vision, the technical know-how, the energy, the capital, the housekeeping, the accounting, and the sales. The company is built on the talents of the owner and is often a manifestation of his or her personality. If customers purchase and continue to purchase, the owner hires people, and an organization is formed. He or she is a doer-manager.

The challenge at this stage is to obtain customers and maintain sufficient cash flow from operations to cover expenses. The focus is often on making what one delivers and keeping expenses to a minimum. The customers' impact is supreme, and all members of the organization know the importance of each customer.

In these organizations, systems to manage the business are informal or nonexistent. Planning is focused on ensuring that there is adequate inventory to meet customer orders and managing cash flow to cover operating expenses. Budgeting is also basically nonexistent because the firm needs to remain opportunistic about the situations it faces; it cannot be held to a budget. The structure is informal; almost everyone reports directly to the owner. New hires usually are known by the owner or by other members of the organization.

The spirit of these companies is fast-paced, action-oriented, and "living on the edge." People tend to move faster, stay task-focused, and feel the emotional ups and downs of the organization. There is little time for internal politics. Teamwork and commitment to common goals by all the firm's members are essential to success. The feedback is often quickly felt. The consequences usually are clearly derived from the customer and the affected manager. These firms offer an environment in which people can have a direct impact on the performance of the organization. In fact, it is often the frequency and amount of positive feedback that bring people into small organizations. These environments have many characteristics that their larger counterparts envy.

Compensation is based on "Let's make a deal." There are often few formal guidelines for decisions about compensation or other rewards. Pay is usually lower than that in larger companies. The draw for most people is a combination of a "livable" salary and the opportunity to share in the significant growth of the company.

Executives or senior professional contributors often receive a salary that is likely to be a lot less than they could receive if they worked for large, established companies. They are likely to receive significant cash bonuses or a percentage of the ownership. The bonuses are likely to be cash profit sharing, a share of personal sales or new business, or discretionary bonuses. If the company is cash-poor or has significant pressures on cash flow, bonuses are likely to be minor. Instead, the owner offers a stake in the company through restricted stock, stock options, phantom shares, deferred compensation accounts, percentage interest in the company, or partnership shares. For many people, this arrangement represents the tradeoff risk one takes to work for a startup company—lower salary in exchange for variable compensation or share of ownership.

Companies tend to offer either large cash opportunities or ownership but seldom both unless warranted by the person's background, role, or value to the company.

The key issues for reward systems at this stage therefore include

1. Salary or other fixed compensation costs that depend on a strong positive cash flow
2. Variable compensation that is clearly linked to the short-term performance and financial results of the company and tied directly to what the individual produces
3. Share of ownership that reflects the role and contribution of the individual to the long-term success of the company without diluting the investors' expected rate of return or shares for future leaders or investors in the company

Further, any long-term investment must provide an opportunity for the individual to realize gains (i.e., liquidity) and an ability to appropriately diversify his or her risks.

Rewards That Accelerate the Growth of Emerging Companies

In this stage of development, companies experience a major transition. They go from being a small, informal, "on the edge" company to one that requires professional leadership, functional strengths, and basic systems. Now the company has clearly demonstrated its business model, but it needs to expand market awareness of its products or services and build the foundation on which it can grow.

The primary challenge for companies at this stage is one of fulfilling new customer needs, building the desired brand image, and creating demand or establishing a clear competitive advantage for its products or services. They need to ensure that there is adequate cash to grow the firm and meet the investment needs for upgrading equipment and facilities, launching marketing programs, and hiring critical talent. Companies at this stage usually acquire venture-capital funding to support these investments unless growth can be capitalized from cash flow or through creative debt financing. The company may shift from "angel funding" to professional investment funding.

If the company acquires significant external financing, the ownership structure frequently changes. At this point, a new executive team may be hired to provide the professional business, marketing, and leadership skills the organization needs. Where the founder may have owned as much as 40 to 100 percent of the original startup company, his or her stake may drop to 10 or 20 percent, but the value is significantly greater—the company will be larger, more profitable, and more established. And if a new chief executive officer (CEO) is hired, he or she may be offered 5 to 10 percent of the company, with a comparable amount going to the senior management team. The founder's role may shift to chief technologist, chief marketer, or strategic guidance (not operational control).

Issues emerge when the new people do not fully understand or share the vision of the founder and may have values that dramatically change the culture of the company. For some firms, this change is essential to survival; for other, this change undermines the original concept, technology, and customer relationships. Firms that achieve this level create structures and define work responsibilities into roles that are usually organized around some functional or geographic areas.

Reward systems at this stage need to take a more strategic, systematic approach. "Deals" need to be understood, approved, and documented. If there is sufficient cash flow, salaries can be increased to reflect the role of the individual. However, sales, service, and management may continue to rely heavily on incentives. Certain support function employees can have base salaries, but linking these individuals with the profitability of the company reinforces a "common fate" philosophy. The incentives should be short term (e.g., quarterly or when dollars are available), and individuals take on more specialized roles because the work requires in-depth expertise.

At this stage the firm is likely to experience several primary issues. First, the "special treatment" for individuals with new roles within the firm will need explanation and strong support from the owner/founder. These roles will need to be documented and start setting a precedent for how the organization will be structured and managed. It is important not to pursue traditional job descriptions that focus on command-and-control characteristics of large companies. Rather, role descriptions should serve as a means to provide clarity of direction for serving the customer (see Chapter 6). Second, as the demands of the firm become more complex, there is often a mismatch between performance requirements and the capabilities of individuals. While many people will be able to rise to new challenges, not everyone will be suited for what the organization now requires. Therefore, the executives will need to increase the talent of the organization through selective hiring, promotions, development, and rewards. In addition, management must address the problem of very loyal people who are no longer suited for the job they hold. This often presents a major personal challenge to the founder.

Finally, the measures that determine the rewards need to be focused on factors that enable the firm to transition to the next level. Long-term considerations can be provided through equity-based programs, such as stock options, partnership shares, or deferred capital accumulation accounts. If too much emphasis is placed on short-term issues, decisions may fail to make the investments needed to capture emerging market opportunities. If there is too little emphasis on profitability, the firm may not survive unless it is highly capitalized.

There is frequently no reliable historical information on which to base performance objectives. In this case, incentive plans that use a range of measures are better than absolute objectives, or the objectives reflect critical milestones needed for the business to build the capabilities and market dominance it needs rather than an arbitrary objective. Then flexibility and integrity need to be balanced so that rewards are truly associated with performance.

Rewards That Sustain Market Leadership

If an organization is successful at creating or capturing market leadership, establishing a reputation consistent with its strategy, and building a strong, effective organization, it likely will experience great success. This is what most people and organizations seek. The challenge will be to renew and retain this position.

At this stage, key executives are often highly concerned with balancing cash needs to support growth and investment needs to keep the business growing. Firms need to sustain (or improve) the profitability of the core business and use this capital to finance growth, acquisitions, or expansion into new markets. The company may have gone public by this time and replaced venture or other forms of external financing with institutional or general investors. This changes the accountability and nature of shareholder value.

The market leadership strategy may take a number of directions. First, the firm can seek expansion of its current core technologies into new marketplaces. (A U.S. domestic firm might open operations in Asia or Europe, for example.) Second, the firm can capitalize on its existing customer base and expand product lines to better serve a current market. These strategies can be achieved either through acquisitions or through application of the firm's own internal skills and resources. Some firms try to do both, only to find themselves short of resources or looking for creative financing strategies. Key performance indicators in this overall growth strategy should relate the revenue increases to the achievement of strategic marketing objectives, such as milestones of a new product launch, achievement of market share, or expanding account penetration.

Implementing changes in the organization and reward systems often is ignored in companies that are feeling successful. This can have serious long-term implications for retaining performance-focused people. People come to expect their rewards because they have experienced several periods of high achievement. They grow to live on their total compensation, not just their salaries. They expect the value of their stock options to grow because it always has. Performance problems are often not addressed because having someone who at least can do some of the work is better than having extra pressure on existing staff. Often conflicts of internal equity start to emerge as the organization seeks to reinforce its culture of collaboration. Subtle or deep problems may start weakening the organization.

First, the culture of the organization shifts from being oriented toward achievement to being oriented toward entitlement. People come to expect—and in fact feel they deserve—what they have always gotten. Second, managers or functional heads may create systems that serve their own need for control rather than what is good for the company. They want discretionary variable pay or recognition programs in order to reinforce their roles within the company, while on the surface they are legitimately seeking to reward performance that current systems cannot effectively support. Distributing accountability for reward programs is often desired, but these programs must reinforce the strategy and core values of the organization. Companies frequently seek outside help to professionalize their systems by using consultants or by hiring highly experienced people. Finally, management may become overconfident and arrogant, unwilling to listen to other voices within or outside the organization. Executives may come to believe they are the true models of leadership—after all, didn't they grow the company to its present size? They can become used to hearing only what they want to hear—things that reinforce their preferred perceptions of reality. This process was very evident throughout high-technology industries in the 1980s.

A root cause of these problems is how people are influenced by success. While success is always desired, it also can narrow an individual's perceptions. Managers who are reinforced for what they *have* done lose sight of the importance of continuous improvement. They believe that they can control the organization's destiny. A paradigm is created. As long as the actions fit the needs of the environment, the executive will feel successful. When the market changes and the paradigm does not, major troubles emerge. The risks to survival for firms at this stage in their growth are often more subtle, more perceptual, harder to pinpoint, and more potentially destructive than the simple loss of a customer.

Organizations (or executives) that do not succeed may never really understand why.

Reward systems need to be based on a strategy that reinforces actions that support the firm's key success factors and its core competencies as they apply to its customers and markets. At this stage, the firm has the ability to introduce a wide range of reward systems. It should guard against plans that become disassociated from the real drivers of performance. Everyone should have equal opportunities, but the system should maintain an achievement orientation rather than become an entitlement because of the fear of conflict.

For example, a midsized health maintenance organization implemented significant base pay increases when it discovered that it had fallen seriously behind the market. Employees were told that these increases would enable the firm to be more competitive in terms of salaries. Senior management then expected that people would perform at a higher level because of the higher levels of pay. This is a "management by guilt" philosophy. While the employees were very appreciative of the pay increases, they kept doing what they always had. There was little need to change. Ultimately, senior management felt betrayed by the employees and attempted to remedy the situation with salary freezes and control-oriented incentive plans. These actions had the effect of making the firm less able to attract and retain desired talent, and it became less competitive.

In terms of reward strategies, this is often an excellent time to differentiate the company with its total employment value proposition by establishing new, more creative, or more meaningful reward systems. These firms should make extensive use of variable compensation plans tailored to unique roles or functions within the competitive strategy. The measures should reinforce actions and results that are consistent with the business strategy. Firms need to keep fixed costs at a minimum and reinforce a sense of urgency. They also should adjust long-term incentive programs to be based on growing the value of the company. They should calibrate pay levels and total compensation in terms of the marketplace for people but keep the focus on reinforcing the drivers of the business strategy.

Firms at this stage can offer creative career opportunities as rewards as well. Because the organization is still growing, it offers increasing job challenges, expanding roles for project and functional or team management, and global growth opportunities. When these are integrated with attractive reward systems, the organization has an important competitive advantage in attracting and retaining people.

What is needed is a dynamic balance between rewarding the contributions of individuals and rewarding the contributions of the team, division, or company. The focus must be on investing in efforts that yield immediate growth, managing cash to sustain the growth, and building long-term value for the company. Hence this sustaining growth stage offers significant opportunities for creative, high-potential reward programs, which in turn may enable the company to attract, retain, and motivate talent critical to sustaining this growth. The essential demands on the leadership are to build market share with a core technology, to work together with common values, and to remain committed to the firm's customers and strategy.

A reward strategy that supports organizations at this stage should

- Include salary plans that reflect responsibilities and emphasize the development of people. The base salary should be viewed as an investment in talent, and, as the talent increases in value to the organization, salaries should increase. Also, the pay levels and increase guidelines may be above market level, reflecting the performance of individuals and the company.
- Expand, formalize, and decentralize incentive plans tied to strategic performance measures of units or teams in order to strengthen the line of sight and reinforce collaboration on resource utilization, customer retention, and growing market value.
- Create and use funds to promote celebrations for teams, individuals, and the entire company for achieving important results.
- Create retention awards—cash or stock paid out over time based on sustained employment and performance—for individuals who are clearly at risk of going over to the competition and who are important to the firm's continued success.
- Use stock options or other long-term equity/ownership plans strategically. This may include either expanding the use to include more people or expanding the amount top performers receive. Depending on the company's ownership structure and equity philosophy, this is an ideal time to reinforce commitment to the organization's long-term success.

Firms at this stage can institute a portfolio of reward systems that create a large number of opportunities for recognizing individual and team contributions. The systems should be tailored to fit each particular business unit so that behaviors important to the unit's success can be reinforced. While there will be fundamental differences, everyone can participate in several programs. This can and should produce a sense of excitement about achieving results. The measures should be related to the key success factors of the firm and the overall reward strategy. This strengthens the alignment of strategy to measures of behaviors. In this way, the firm builds the capabilities and culture to sustain its growth and strengthens the commitment of its members.

Renewing and Transforming the Organization in Crisis

Firms in this situation see a decline in their growth rate, and expenses significantly exceed their revenues. They have reached a saturation point in their markets, are challenged by new competitors, or are facing a major decline in the demand for their products or services. This could be caused by a general economic recession or extraordinary events that hit their marketplace. Companies at this stage probably have seen the value of their stock drop dramatically, and their current stock options have little, if not negative, value. They may have an established customer base or a set of resources that enables them to withstand short-term pressures on profits. However, if the core issues are not addressed, there may be fundamental threats to the survival of the organization. The company may be able to continue its "slow flight" mode or will need to implement major cost reductions, acquisitions, recapitalization, technological breakthroughs, or new marketing initiatives.

From within the company, people may see the following regarding their own personal circumstances:

1. Their basic job may be at risk as well as their continued employment.
2. There are few or no payouts on their bonuses.
3. Base salaries may be frozen or reduced.
4. Salary increases may be reduced, postponed, or limited to only the top performers.

5. There are fewer or limited promotional opportunities.
6. The workload increases for those who have survived an organizational "downsizing" or other major restructuring effort.
7. Training and other development investments are eliminated.
8. Companywide events and fun activities (e.g., game rooms, pizza parties, etc.) are eliminated or significantly curtailed.
9. Employee benefits and services are eliminated or reduced, and their costs are shifted to employees.

Thus, in a declining, struggling organization with few, if any, tangible awards, the pressure on everyone intensifies. If there are other opportunities in the marketplace, why should any highly talented individual remain with the company? If top performers leave the company, then the company loses critical capabilities and high productivity, which, in turns, pulls the organization further down a difficult spiral.

There is perhaps no challenge so broad in its impact as that of changing an established organization. Rosabeth Moss Kanter, who wrote *When Giants Learn to Dance: Mastering the Challenges of Strategy, Management, and Careers in the 1990s,*[1] *Evolve: Succeeding in the Digital Culture of Tomorrow,*[2] and the Foreword to this book, Michael Beer,[3] Richard Beckhard,[4] and many others have discussed the dangers and opportunities of creating change. The complexity is immense. The task is monumental. The opportunities are enormous. And time is critical.

From a strategic perspective, companies are able to survive these challenges by focusing on both their core business strategy and their values. Different levels of urgency to change are depicted in Figure 13-1, which displays various levels of the need for change based on the degree of fit between the organization's capabilities and the needs of the marketplace.

Depending on the degree of risk to survival, companies at this stage tend to focus their change efforts on one or more of the following factors:

- *Cost reductions.* How do we provide a price for products or services that is better than that of competitors when measured in terms the customers value?
- *Quality improvement.* How do we increase the confidence of our customers in the reliability, convenience, and value of our products and services?

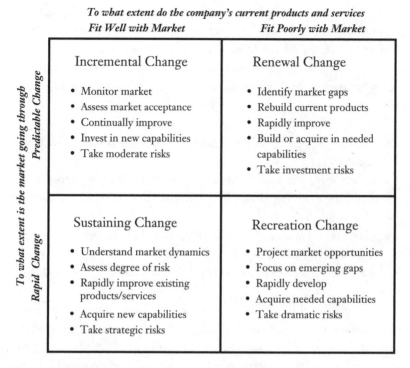

To what extent do the company's current products and services
Fit Well with Market **Fit Poorly with Market**

Incremental Change

- Monitor market
- Assess market acceptance
- Continually improve
- Invest in new capabilities
- Take moderate risks

Renewal Change

- Identify market gaps
- Rebuild current products
- Rapidly improve
- Build or acquire in needed capabilities
- Take investment risks

Sustaining Change

- Understand market dynamics
- Assess degree of risk
- Rapidly improve existing products/services
- Acquire new capabilities
- Take strategic risks

Recreation Change

- Project market opportunities
- Focus on emerging gaps
- Rapidly develop
- Acquire needed capabilities
- Take dramatic risks

To what extent is the market going through Predictable Change

Rapid Change

Figure 13-1   Four-box model on the urgency for change.

- *Service expansion.* How do we increase the level of innovation, responsiveness, and customized products and services we offer to our customers?
- *Time reductions.* How do we decrease the time to market for our products and services and make sure that customers receive what they want when they want it?

If an organization is not able to differentiate itself sufficiently in these factors that are worth the additional price to the customer, then cost will be the determining buying criterion. In many industries, quality or service is less a differentiating factor in the eyes of customers than is price regardless of what the organization believes the customer should value.

Once the organization has determined its strategy for regaining growth momentum, the key task will be implementation. Many traditional efforts involve reengineering work, restructuring reporting relationships (i.e., removing layers within an organization), training, communication campaigns, and setting up special task forces to find solutions to the problems (e.g., General Electric's workout sessions). Every strategy involves people taking some actions that are different from what they have done in the past. To get people to change their actions, the organization has three choices:

- *Change the people.* Terminate those you don't want, and hire those you do want.
- *Inform and train people to do what you want.* With the expectation that the gap can be closed when people know what and how to do what is needed.
- *Create an environment in which people take the initiative to be engaged in the desired changes.* Because the organization connects people to the achievement of desired progress and results.

Although the third strategy is obviously the preferred one, most organizations place only superficial emphasis on creating this environment. Instead, it is often easier either to replace people or to provide communication on what needs to change. Such companies rely on internal leaders to handle the workplace environment. While the ultimate objective is to create an environment in which people naturally achieve desired outcomes, the realization of this goal usually requires taking bold action that most established companies are reluctant to take.

What are the actions that involve rewards systems, and how can they be made to support the transformation process? Building on the organizational and human behavior concepts presented earlier in this book, as well as on the many types of programs and designs for reward, the following set of actions should refocus reward systems so that they have the desired impact on an organization undergoing change:

1. *Reinforce a sense of urgency and commitment to change by identifying which reward programs need to change and how they need to change.* For example, when the time frame for incentives or recognition programs is very short (e.g., on the spot, monthly, or quarterly), there is a greater sense of urgency. Programs that have a long time duration have less of an immediate impact on current

behavior. Identify which programs can increase the urgency and focus.

2. *Translate strategic and competitive plans into measures that mean something to every individual and to his or her role (his or her work) in the organization.* This cascading process should be driven down to a point where each person sees that he or she is no more than one or two levels from making a major impact on important results.

3. *Find a balance between the need for immediate action and the creation of permanent changes.* All major change initiatives should carry with them a clear threat ("do this or else"), and people need to realize the importance of making the necessary changes to programs, systems, behaviors, and results. However, positive consequences, as demonstrated in rewards and recognition programs, will have a more sustaining effect in reinforcing permanent change.

4. *Limit the growth in base salaries unless there is a clear demonstration of increases in capabilities or productivity.* When salaries are generally on par with those in the external market, the emphasis should shift to other key elements. When this is done well, the chances of loosing superior talent to other organizations is minimized.

5. *Create or redesign variable pay programs so that they support the strategic initiatives of the organization.* In addition to the cascading measures, variable pay plans can have an impact on key milestones and critical results. The organization also should consider whether to reduce the time frame for the awards from annual to semiannual or quarterly. The variable pay program may be used to stimulate attention to the key measures.

6. *Use recognition programs to reinforce progress and the contribution people made to "how" things are done.* Often recognition is associated with the good times or general "feel good" parameters. In times of crisis, there should be clear statements that as the organization makes important achievements, it will provide meaningful rewards to its people. A well-conceived action plan should have many easily identifiable points at which progress can be assessed and recognition provided.

7. *Reinforce confidence in the long-term growth of the organization.* Giving stock options, even options that currently have little to

negative value, can still be perceived as a meaningful reward. The organization can examine whether repricing, replacing, or indexing stock options is an attractive alternative (see Chapter 12) or whether using restricted stock or outright grants is more effective. The organization also should examine whether it can provide an increased number of options to people while the price is relatively low in historical terms or provide an increased number to individuals considered critical to the organization's future. If stock options are not available, the organization can develop a phantom share plan in which individuals earn "units" based on personal or team performance, and the value of the units is based on the success of the division or company. The value is created over the long term and should be used in combination with well-conceived short-term variable pay plans.

8. *Career development and promotional opportunities should shift their emphasis.* The problem the organization is facing is immediate; consequently, long-term rewards such as career and promotional opportunities are less relevant. However, in this time of crisis, people often value new challenges and new opportunities to develop and demonstrate their capabilities and exercise personal initiative. These actions should be encouraged in a manner that relates to the personal career aspirations of employees and the future needs of the organization. Consequently, the organization takes the situation of low opportunities for formal career progression and turns it into an opportunity for people to be challenged with more complex responsibilities and to have their initiative welcomed and highly rewarded.

One way to demonstrate the linkage between these programs is to focus on whether and how incentives should be given to task forces that identify and recommend changes. When the task force's suggestions are implemented, its members might be awarded a percentage of the first year's savings. However, issues will emerge because the work groups who are actually responsible for implementing the ideas would receive few, if any, awards.

In most circumstances, a better use of incentives would be to reward the work groups that implement changes. They must integrate the ideas of the task forces into their daily operations. They have to assess the impact of the change and determine whether it is feasible. This assessment must be made in light of possible rewards for performance improvements rather than with the idea of getting reinforcement for continuing past habits and practices. Those involved in task forces to identify and recommend changes should be heavily reinforced and honored but not compensated for their contributions. Team celebrations, special equity or similar awards, and visibility in other areas of the organization are often appropriate types of reinforcement. Further, the work group that may have contributed someone to serve on the task forces should be recognized for its ability to achieve results with one less staff member. This combination of reinforcement and rewards is essential for creating a strategic total rewards or reinforcement-enriched workplace environment.

One can tell if the process is effective when analyses of situations and implementations of change are undertaken with enthusiasm. The primary aim is to keep the focus on improving capabilities and results, not on analyzing problems and developing creative solutions. If the development process is not supported and reinforced effectively, it will not remain a priority focus of the organization. In the ideal model, those involved in identifying the changes needed also participate fully with those involved in implementing the changes in a total rewards environment.

An executive at a large telecommunications company complained that the problem with its reengineering efforts was that more attention was being focused on making changes than on achieving results. Managers who were successful in creating change were transferred to other areas only to be replaced by people who "undid" many of their changes in their own efforts to create change. The problem with managers as "change agents" is that creating chaos is so enticing. The risk inherent in more and more change efforts is that the actual process of improvement slows down.

In such a company, the challenge is to regain the "share of mind" in the marketplace and the confidence of the workforce. The marketplace needs to view this organization as focused on its needs and able to offer an increasingly attractive array of products and services. The firm needs to be viewed as strong and successful—a survivor and a winner. The firm's workforce should believe the same thing. This goal can be achieved by producing results in a way that builds strength and confidence. The road to this commitment and confidence can be paved with the multi-level rewards of the organization's practices.

Rewards for Organizations Seeking Continual Change

In a firm that is doing fine today but is facing increased competition and threats, what kinds of reward systems are right? The risks exist, but they are not threatening the immediate survival of the firm. There is no need for drastic action, but there is a need for continual action.

In many ways, this organization is facing more difficult challenges than the firm addressing re-creative change. It is often more difficult to express credible dissatisfaction when the status quo is generally successful. Most organizations are more likely to reward people for handling a crisis than for preventing one. However, if the executives and employees come to believe themselves invincible, they soon will not be. Therefore, the primary challenge of this organization is to promote continuous improvements at *a rate that is faster and better* than its competitors.

In terms of strategy for change, imagine a senior leadership team that senses declining market trends. Individual units may be facing competitive struggles, but resources are available to assist their efforts. Employees and managers may feel somewhat reassured that the firm is not yet facing the kind of survival struggles described in the public media, but they are probably worried about the possibility that the tide may turn on them. They are confident and hopeful that senior management is watching the situation, and they wonder what they can do to prosper in this organization. A strategy with these three basic elements needs to be employed:

- An understanding of the dynamics in the marketplace and the actions of the competitors and the ability to take preemptive actions.
- Monitoring of the changing needs of the customers and implementation of actions that enhance relationships with them.
- Continually encouraging quick action, avoiding unnecessary costs, and making improvements to processes and products and services.

They focus on their customers by removing barriers, increasing the number of contacts, and responding to their needs in an effective manner. Everyone in such an organization can serve an important role in the firm's strategy, which should include the following actions:

- Senior managers should meet frequently with customers and sponsor events between the organization and its customers.
- Functional/business-unit managers should meet frequently with their specific customers to promote contact between their staff and customers (including visits by operator/support personnel), make investment decisions in collaboration, and implement process improvements that can be linked to customer needs.
- Operational employees should meet with customer representatives to discuss issues, examine how products are developed or used, and build relationships of mutual support and respect.
- Support employees should meet with customers to better understand how the organization serves them and examine ways in which services and communication can be enhanced with and across their firms.

The basic strategy behind these actions is to create a closer working relationship between the firm and its customers. While many of these activities relate only to the firm's key accounts, they set a model of working relationships that should apply in some manner to all customers. Furthermore, they set in motion a process by which employees of the organization see themselves as members of a firm that is closely wedded to its customers. Retention of both customers and employees will be an important benefit from this strategy.

In terms of reward systems, the basic strategy is one that focuses on continuous improvement. Because there is little need for a sense of crisis, the reward systems can serve to build a workplace environment that is attractive for recruiting and developing desired talent. Being competitive in the marketplace will be important, but this can be accomplished by creating a reinforcement-enriched environment rather than by leading the market in pay levels. The reward systems will need to perform the following functions:

- Focus efforts on the customers' success and on taking actions that enhance the firm's ability to acquire, serve, and retain customers.

- Translate the requirements of customers into performance measures that are specific, meaningful, and important to all areas of the organization.
- Reinforce actions that continually increase the speed of improvements, fully use the resources of the firm, and enhance the competencies of the firm.

As in the case of a firm facing re-creative change, the role of the compensation function is to support the process of change within the organization. This is done by fashioning pay strategies and reinforcement practices that enhance service to customers, both internal and external. This will involve working with managers to set the right performance measures, providing customized reward programs, and increasing the ability of the managers and teams to reinforce desired actions.

From a line-management perspective, the focus must be on serving customers and on celebrating the achievements of people within the unit in the three areas noted earlier: customers, measures, and action. This means that managers must use the reward systems to their fullest potential. Waste in products or processes, in people or money, in time or effort are the devils to be rooted out of the organization.

In this context, base pay can perform several roles. In areas of the firm where it needs to create new competencies, a pay-for-competencies-employed type of program may be appropriate (see Chapter 7). This depends on the business reasons for hiring advanced or more flexible (i.e., cross-trained) talent. The process may entail paying people an increased level of compensation for acquiring and using the abilities needed by the firm. If the work is not available or the firm is not able to capitalize on this new talent to improve productivity, such a plan will only increase costs with little true benefit.

Base pay can be oriented toward reinforcing career progressions in management information systems, engineering, research and development, and other highly technical areas. In this case, the organization can offer career paths for people that are consistent with the human resource requirements for its future. As people progress in their chosen fields, there should be associated pay opportunities commensurate with the value-added nature of their work.

Pay levels should be externally focused in areas where the firm needs to acquire a number of people. These pay levels should be based on an analysis of the flow of people through the organization—identifying the entry, the "leakage" or turnover points, and the progression of people within the firm. The strategy for the base pay system needs to be based on the strategic requirements for human resources within the organization today and in the future. In this way, base pay can be used to make the necessary investments in building human resources capabilities for the future.

In terms of incentives, the use of team or unit plans can offer a powerful reward program for achievements. The measures need to be grounded in the requirements of the customers (see Chapter 5). They need to support continuous improvement of the unit's competitiveness and the use of its resources and encourage ways to improve the speed and value-added nature of work. The emphasis must be on people working smarter and harder.

The best form of special recognition is one that is as personalized and as close to the achievement as possible. This means that managers and employees alike need measures that create opportunities for reinforcement, team celebrations, for example, that are really focused on rewarding individuals for their contributions to the team's success. The corporation can support special recognition by encouraging such celebrations (it is important to measure this), by involving senior-level people in the events (to listen, not to talk), and by providing the funding for these programs.

Performance appraisals can shift from being judgment-based (or merely mechanisms to determine ratings) to reviewing performance factors, learning about what went well and what did not, and building relationships within the firm. The form is not as important as the process, which should be based on collaboration and reflection. Collaboration can involve managers and employees, peers and working partners, and customers and others within the firm. It is an opportunity to summarize all the data for a performance period and examine them with an eye to primary themes, threats to future performance, and priorities for the next period. The timing should reflect the natural cycles of the business, such as quarterly results and project milestones. In most cases, annual reviews are simply not frequent enough to do any good.

In companies facing this situation, the priorities are to strengthen leadership in the marketplace by building strong relationships with customers. This process brings every member of the organization into the act. Rather than looking upward within the firm for guidance, members should talk with their customers. Rather than limiting costs to create bigger profits for someone else, they should look for ways to enhance the value of each expenditure, increase savings, and share in the successes that are achieved. Rather than blaming others for not pulling their weight, they should integrate feedback and reinforcement in ways that improve performance.

These companies have a competitive advantage because of the way they operate. Customers are valued by the organization, and so are its employees. Resources are used wisely, even though there are mistakes. A crisis is viewed as a sign of weakness; both preventing problems and making continual improvements are valued. Both people and the firm progress because of what they are able to achieve and how they achieved it. This is a balanced organization, one that is able to be highly competitive in turbulent times because of its coordination, capabilities, and commitments. For those who find themselves on this path, there is an unprecedented opportunity for sustaining competitive advantage.

Building a Culture That Thrives on Change

This chapter has explored the world of organizations undergoing change. We have seen how different pressures are faced by organizations at different stages of development and in different market conditions. Some are driven by survival imperatives, and others face growing challenges to leadership. Tools and techniques to analyze such organizations abound. The challenge is to create an environment in which people take the initiative to use these processes and improve the value and competitiveness of the organization.

There is never a good time to implement needed changes. People wait until senior managers provide the leadership they are seldom capable of displaying. Senior managers try one set of initiatives only to become impatient with the results or frustrated by the costs. They introduce new initiatives or restructure the organization. Employees see programs come and go and wonder if there will ever be a time when they will not need to do something differently. Simply stated, they have created a "change gridlock" in which change is desperately needed but seldom sustained.

This chapter has offered reward strategies for organizations facing either a crisis or a challenge. We have explored how to drive the themes of renewed competitiveness throughout the organization and provide people with an opportunity to participate. If managers and employees alike redirect their efforts in ways that enhance the firm's capabilities to compete, the only variable will be the effectiveness of the strategy itself. The emphasis is on implementing change and reinforcing individuals for taking the actions needed by the firm now. Collaboration is not just about peers working together in teams; it is about building an environment in which the organization and all its various parts work closely with its customers to enhance value. When a customer receives greater value from its suppliers, it can create greater value for its customers in turn. This creates a chain of win-win situations not only at the individual and organizational levels but also throughout the interdependencies of industries as well.

Transform Rewards from Entitlement to Achievement

Never doubt that a group of thoughtful, committed citizens can change the world; indeed it's the only thing that ever has.

Margaret Mead

T HE SUCCESS of an organization is based on many variables. Academics, consultants, and executives continue to search for the winning combination of factors. Companies often know how to acquire facilities, equipment, and capital. They can assess the marketplace opportunities for their products and services and study customer preferences. Often they spend millions of dollars on these activities and use the information to build a more competitive organization. However, one thing that all success formulas have in common is that people need to act consistently with the requirements for success. Consider this illustrative story:

> Imagine that a ship from another planet came to earth and hovered over all the places where your organization works. It projects a ray that causes every person to stop all actions. However, the equipment operates perfectly, and other people can contact you. How long would it take before your customers started to experience something different about your company? How long would it take before the situation became serious?

This story illustrations one critical point: The performance of all organizations depends on the actions of people. Companies that understand this principle and then identify what actions are needed to support their strategy and how those actions will be encouraged and rewarded will always be at a competitive advantage.

To what extent do companies place a comparable emphasis on understanding what actions are needed to support their strategy? Do they hire and develop people to have the capabilities to implement their plans? Do their performance measures and reward system encourage the desired actions?

Throughout this book we have examined the many factors that influence human behavior. Given the dynamics of a rapidly changing marketplace, the strategy needs to define the business model and key success factors but leave significant room for individual initiative and creativity. Leadership is critical to the implementation of a successful strategy (see Chapters 2 and 3).

As we've discussed, performance measures provide the milestones and indicators that a company is performing as desired. Measures are then used as systems to provide information and feedback to guide the directions of people. Further, as organizations create or acquire the capabilities to respond to their customers, they develop the resources to win.

However, if people do not understand or feel personally engaged to achieve the same goals as the organization, the competitive advantage is limited. Herein lies the art involved in reward systems. Facilities, equipment, information systems, and capital are frequently similar among competitor organizations. However, their processes for focusing and rewarding performance are almost always different. No single reward system will work for every situation. In fact, many systems need to change over time to respond to changes in the firm's strategy and situation. Consequently, reward systems need to be creatively developed and applied to provide a company with a competitive advantage.

This chapter describes how to develop a strategy for achieving change. No idea, however brilliant and needed by an organization, will succeed if it is not integrated into an effective process for change, and being right does not mean being effective. Creating conditions that will minimize resistance and maximize acceptance of new ideas is a central challenge for an agent of change. The art of reward systems lies in applying the science of human behavior to real-world situations so that the organization and its members are truly valued for what they contribute.

Implementing a New Reward Strategy—How to Make It Work

When one examines the strategies of most organizational change efforts, there is often little mention of reward systems. Is this because rewards do not really influence human behavior? Or is it because if a significant reward system is changed, the process cannot be reversed without significant "damage control?" However, such companies as Sears, General Electric, Allied Signal, AT&T, Wells Fargo, Corning, and IBM would not have been successful with their transformation efforts without the strategic use of rewards. Further, such companies as Cisco Systems, Starbucks, Saturn, Southwest Airlines, Disney, Federal Express, Microsoft, and Home Depot would not have achieved their growth, market leadership, and financial success without the support and alignment of their reward systems.[1] Thus the question to the executive team that is facing the daunting task of strategic, fundamental change is, "How well do your current reward systems support the implementation of your strategy?" Changing an organization's reward system should be based on a clear and present need. This is best accomplished through an assessment of the effectiveness of existing programs and practices in relation to the firm's current strategy. Further, if an organization's executives have the mindset that compensation programs should perform like a basic infrastructure of the company, they will not likely see any gap as serious. On the other hand, executives who know the strategic importance of effective reward systems can use an assessment to establish priorities and allocate resources to strengthen the organization. Some of the indications that there may be a problem include

- Excessive employee turnover
- Excessive costs in relation to what the organization can afford
- A change in the firm's strategy with little or no change to the reward programs
- Employee complaints or grievances about the current reward programs
- Little effect on people or performance when moderate changes are made to existing plans

It is commonly understood that problems that seem to be a result of compensation plans frequently are caused by other factors (e.g., management practices, lack of communication, promises made but not kept, etc.). One needs to examine both the symptoms and the root causes of the problems and develop strategies to address the real issues. Frequently, reward programs can provide creative solutions, should support other goals, or be changed.

When introducing changes in a reward system, as in any change effort, certain factors will enhance the process of change. These can be expressed in a formula:

Success = dissatisfaction with the status quo × vision of how things could be × plan of action × capabilities to make it happen

Note that each factor is multiplied by each other. Thus, if one factor is 0, then there is no readiness for change; if one factor is 1, then value is not added by that factor. Each of these factors will be discussed below.

Dissatisfaction with the Status Quo

People must understand that a problem exists and have some appreciation of the underlying reasons. The information needs to come from a reliable source and be backed up with facts. Data are essential to establish the credibility of any concern about the current situation. If people do not accept that there is a problem, they will be unlikely to support a change. This is particularly true of executives, who usually have to sponsor and/or approve changes to reward systems. They will give only marginal support to a suggested change unless they see exactly how it can solve a very real and important problem.

A sense of dissatisfaction with the status quo also can develop as a result of a crisis or deterioration of a firm's ability to retain talent. The crisis can be regarded as a fight in the war for talent. In this situation, the continued prosperity of the company is at risk. The risks are very real and very great. Actions need to be swift, bold, and targeted at key people.

The degree of dissatisfaction with the status quo has a major impact on the nature of the change required. Obviously, major change needs to be addressed by a major level of support, whereas incremental change can be addressed through enhancements to existing programs and practices.

The issues at stake are more compelling if they are recent and derived from sources external to the organization. When the pressures for change are related to past organizational practices, members of the organization are likely to be defensive and treat the information skeptically. People generally do not like being punished, especially for something that occurred in the distant past. For example, a chief executive officer (CEO) of a large health maintenance organization wanted to spur action to increase productivity and attention to customers by the physicians. He hired a consulting firm to conduct a benchmark study comparing the organization with others in the industry and used the data to demonstrate the organization's poor performance. Instead of getting the desired response, he encountered tremendous resistance to change, and the process of improvement was set back for several years. Had he discussed how the market characteristics had changed and how the organization needed to adapt to remain competitive, the outcome would have been very different.

Dissatisfaction with the status quo needs to be expressed in terms that are important to the listener. If the audience is made up of direct labor, one might stress the risk to job security. If the audience is made up of executives, one might stress the costs associated with current practices or increasing the chances of survival, competitiveness, and continuity for the organization. In sales or marketing, the emphasis might be on competitive pressures, loss of market share, or a change in the strategy linked to a changing marketplace. In engineering, the emphasis might be on the loss of technical leadership.

Finally, the degree of change needs to be commensurate with the level of dissatisfaction. If there are few risks to survival, the change needs to focus on incremental improvements. If the risk occurs primarily in the future, the change needs to focus on increasing the capacity to respond to emerging threats. If the risk is the core survival of the firm, the change needs to involve an "all hands on deck" strategy with a strong and firmly directed campaign.

A Vision of How Things Could Be

The primary value of a vision or mission is that it draws people to it. Unlike dissatisfaction with the status quo, which is essentially negative, a vision of the future can present an attractive alternative or end result. The vision creates in the minds of the target group a view of how things can operate, should operate, and will operate if certain changes are made. It needs to relate to the values and concerns of the organization. Therefore, what may be attractive to an executive group may not be attractive to an operational group. The vision needs to inspire, attract, and offer a meaningful opportunity for reinforcement. In other words, "We are not bricklayers. We are builders of cathedrals."

Much has been written about the value of vision and leadership. In terms of our focus on reward systems, the vision can describe a process that will enable the organization to improve its competitiveness and work life. Then the changes in the reward systems will provide a means to that end. In selling such changes, the task is to demonstrate how the new program will produce a strong return on investment in terms of costs (to executives) and work effort (to participants).

A Plan of Action

This element of the change process involves developing a clear, specific set of recommendations that provide solutions to the problems. Once people understand the risks to the status of quo and share a vision about how things could be, they must have a solution, plan, design, or modification of existing programs that will close the gap. The specific elements of this task were covered in previous chapters. Once the modification or design of a new plan has been accepted, the implementation must include

- What needs to be done or changed
- How will it be done
- Who will do it
- What and when they need to do it
- What it will cost, in what time frame, and with what return on investment

The action plan provides the roadmap for taking action and defines the short- and long-term steps necessary for the program to be successful. It needs to define accountabilities as well as identify the resources necessary to achieve success. Further, it defines a way to measure progress and reinforce the improvements desired. Finally, for an action plan to be truly meaningful, it needs to define the specific steps necessary to start the process going.

Capabilities to Make It Happen

A plan without the capabilities to make it happen is at best a good idea. The capabilities will depend on what you are attempting to change. The assessment process can provide both advanced warning of what will be required and data for implementation planning. The capabilities may include the following:

- Expertise that is not currently available in the organization
- Financial resources
- Information systems
- Communications programs
- Training programs
- Administrative systems

Thus, in developing a program that involves new or significant changes in current procedures, practices, or work process, the organization needs to have a clear, compelling reason—a vision of what will be accomplished, a clear plan to address the issues and a plan for implementation, and the capabilities to be successful. Then all it takes is to do what has been committed to.

Implementing Change So That Results Are Achieved

Virtually every industry, and therefore every organization, is experiencing increased pressure to change. Whether the change involves focusing on customers, increasing services, introducing new products, reducing costs, reducing cycle times, improving delivery performance, building alliances, or eliminating waste, people need to do things differently. In traditional hierarchical organizations, change usually means a fundamental shift in the way business is conducted and behaviors are managed.

In her book, *Danger in the Comfort Zone*,[2] J. M. Bardwick provides an insightful description of the challenge of change. In traditional organizations, employees traded loyalty for job security. Workers were told what to do and where to work (which sometimes included moving to a different city), and they were expected not to question the decisions of those in authority. Employees were expected to perform according to the accepted norms and practices of the firm. In return, they received a job for life, protection from fluctuations in the marketplace, and regular pay raises that kept pace with inflation. Although operational employees sometimes were laid off, they were expected to return to work when needed as part of their employment contract. This sense of entitlement worked both ways—the organization and its employees each got what they expected.

As Bardwick points out, people do not appreciate what they have when they are enjoying an entitlement environment. Their advantages are expected, taken for granted. The irony is that they want more. They feel that they deserve more. They expect the organization to protect, provide for, and promote them.

A sense of entitlement is created when people receive something without having to do anything special for it. For example, in many companies people receive regular pay increases, managers receive annual bonus and stock option awards, and employees participate in the annual company dinners or events. People may view the company as being good to its employees, but there is little connection between pay and performance. The only requirement to receive the annual reward is to be employed by the organization. Such noncontingent awards create an organizational culture that is characterized by attitudes of entitlement.

In contrast, in an achievement-oriented environment, people are rewarded for achievements and feel that they have earned what they receive. In these organizations, people feel confident and empowered for taking risks and succeeding. Empowerment occurs when people have the opportunity to take risks—to fail or to succeed—and *want* to take the necessary actions. If they fail, they may be very disappointed, but they also seek to learn why and how to prevent such failure in the future. If they succeed, they feel confident, powerful, and valued.

Success builds confidence in the individual. If a person is called on regularly to make presentations and receives a number of positive comments every time, he or she will gain confidence. This does not mean that this person should not be coached on ways to improve his or her performance, but such coaching is placed in the context of continuous improvement. The root of success and confidence, therefore, is positive rewards.

In contrast, when people do not receive encouragement or positive feedback, they come to believe that they are not good at what they do. Experiences that are not associated with positive responses are regarded as either not good enough or negative. If there are no measures associated with their work, there are few frameworks against which they can assess their activities—positive or negative. If the members of this organization still receive regular pay increases, bonus awards, and so on, they will see little connection between their activities and the rewards given by the organization.

In an achievement-oriented organization, the loss of a merit increase, bonus award, or stock-option package with no value will be perceived as a problem. Members of the organization will know why these awards did not materialize. While they may be disappointed or frustrated, their commitment to the organization usually remains high. In fact, loss of the awards reinforces the key principle that they are in fact contingent on performance achievements.

Fundamental to this process is the creation of a "stake in the business" for employees. Creating a stake means sharing the risks of failure and the rewards of success with the employees rather than protecting them from the forces of the business environment. Nothing is certain in an environment where people share the risks of the firm. This means that rewards are based on individual, team, and organizational achievements.

The significance of this concept is essential to the development of a strategy for implementing new reward systems. People who are used to an entitlement environment are likely to expect an incentive payout. If they receive a payout regardless of how well or badly they do, the entitlement mentality is reinforced. If, on the other hand, they believe that they may not receive the payout unless they take certain actions, the organization begins to operate on the basis of contingency.

Creating a stake in the business or performance of the unit means sharing in the risks inherent in what the organization does. Measurement and real-time feedback are part of the process of managing performance. Further, as shown in Chapter 8, desired behaviors are encouraged when performers believe that there is a reasonable opportunity for achievement.

In many organizations, the stated policy of "pay at risk" or "pay for performance" is actually misleading, particularly when the determination of pay is based on the subjective assessments of managers using little precise performance measurement. In this situation, the "risk" is viewed as depending on how a manager evaluates an employee's performance, not on how the marketplace (internal or external) values that employee's actions. This means control, not contingency. As shown in Chapter 12, few managers have the ability to judge performance accurately without precise measures. Therefore, judgment-based assessments of performance quite often are ineffective despite being called "pay at risk" or "pay for performance."

Rewards that are contingent have a clear element of risk associated with them. If the risk is too great, a performer will not put forth the effort because the rewards will not be seen as achievable. Workers often describe such rewards as not being meaningful. However, if the risks are perceived as acceptable, the desired actions are likely. In an *entitlement environment*, people simply expect that they will receive the rewards because senior management will find a way to adjust the measures to justify the payout. In a *compliance environment*, people receive little reinforcement for their efforts, but the negative responses to problems or failures to meet certain goals are well known. However, in an *achievement environment*, people perceive the risks and opportunities as doable, and they engage in the tasks of the organization because they feel that they (and themselves) are important (Table 14-1).

Measurement and feedback are the tools that enable rewards to be associated with achievement and demonstrate that they are contingent on performance. A lack of clear measures is associated with an entitle-

Table 14-1 Rewards in the Entitlement versus Achievement Environment

Description of the Culture	How Rewards Reflect the Root Causes
Entitlement	• Increases in pay or delivery of rewards is based on tenure/seniority.
• People expect to be protected, provided for, and promoted.	• There is little clarity or communication about what determines the awards until after the period is over.
• They want more and feel that they deserve more.	• There is little feedback on performance until near the end of the year or after the performance cycle is completed.
• They focus on the threats to their stability and security.	
Compliance	• Increase in pay or receiving awards is based primarily on personal goals.
• They do what is expected and seek clarity of goals and tasks.	• There is little communication about what is desired until someone does something wrong.
• There is limited desire to take risks or do anything differently.	• Decisions are based on limited input, usually made by a single individual, with little communication.
• They focus attention on the leader.	
Achievement	• Measures and data are used to determine who gets what, when, and how.
• They do what is necessary to acheive desired results.	• Feedback is frequent and welcomed because it is used to support improvements in performance.
• They challenge conventional practices unless they work.	• Rewards and celebrations are focused on clear criteria that are well known and happen very often.
• They focus on the tasks to be done and communicate freely.	

ment culture (no one knows or cares). In a compliance culture, the measures may be very clear, but everyone knows the negative response they will likely experience if they either fail to meet certain standards or violate a particular policy or procedure.

Furthermore, the balance between risk and security is related to opportunity for success or failure. Risks will be taken when people feel there is a reasonable probability of success. Security will be sought when the forces that determine success are perceived as outside the control of the performers. The probability of success or failure is what defines the extent of the risk. In the pure entitlement environment, people never experience failure, nor do they experience the joys of success. Success means accomplishing something that was not certain— that was a risk—but was earned. The positive aspects of an achievement environment are that successes are met with enthusiasm and failures are met with disappointment and a commitment to work to do better. In a compliance environment, little is said if one achieves what was desired, but a lot is said if one does not.

The task of achieving change through alternative reward systems usually very much depends on the historical role of consequences within the organization. If consequences are basically noncontingent, the organization is functioning in an environment of entitlement. If consequences entail being ignored (extinction) or punished for not achieving specific standards or working outside prescribed patterns, the organization is functioning in an environment of compliance. If consequences involve rewards and reinforcements for accomplishing desired results, the organization is functioning in an environment of achievement.

Illustrations of Changing Reward Systems

To illustrate the concepts of entitlement versus achievement, risk and risk taking, and making programs more contingent-based, we now examine three case studies. These are actual companies, but their names have been changed.

Case Study: Shifting from Piece-Rate to Team Incentives

The Robert Johnson Manufacturing Company (RJM) was facing increased competitive pressures as patents on its key products began to lapse. In order to survive this threat, the company needed to reduce manufacturing costs—primarily materials usage and scraps rates—introduce new products, and improve its product delivery performance. RJM had a piece-rate incentive system that basically paid workers additional money when the number of units they produced exceeded a weekly standard. Many regarded this program as a major contributor to the firm's productivity. However, the piece-rate incentive plan was presenting major barriers to the organizational changes needed for the company to regain its competitiveness.

First, the company's scrap rate was three times that of other companies in their industry. Since over 65 percent of the manufacturing costs were in the materials, this "waste" resulted in weak profit margins. Second, a number of organizational changes in processes, procedures, and equipment were delayed or abandoned because of the impact they would have on the income of the piece-rate workers. Employees were earning highly competitive incomes through this plan because they were highly productive. Third, the firm was late on its shipments between 10 and 15 percent of the time. Finally, the piece-rate incentive plan served as a surrogate for management. Supervisors basically felt incapable of managing performance because of the restraints of the incentive plan.

The senior executives decided that to address the changes needed in the manufacturing area, they would eliminate the piece-rate incentive system and establish a team-oriented, goal-sharing program. In short, they developed and used a companywide performance scorecard (see Chapter 10) that included measures for revenue growth, on-time delivery, materials usage, and customer satisfaction/quality. The program replaced the piece-rate incentive system.

The process of change involved several important elements. First, senior executives began holding meetings with all employees on the current status and future of the business. They discussed specifics and displayed data indicating that the market environment was changing rapidly and that if the firm did not respond effectively, it would face certain decline. Second, they decided and informed employees that the piece-rate system would be terminated at the end of the current fiscal year. The reasons, they explained, were because the measures and characteristics of the system were no longer compatible with the firm's competitive response. They indicated that while there was a need to decrease costs, they sought to do this through materials and not labor costs. For example, management would guarantee a portion of the workers' incentive pay (i.e., add it to a base rate), another portion would be guaranteed for 1 to 3 years (declining over time), and another portion would need to be earned through a team-based, gain-sharing plan.

As expected, there was a significant negative reaction, particularly from the high earners in the incentive system. They expressed denial and anger and a number of times tried to negotiate the plan. Senior managers understood their concerns and met with many of them individually. These meetings sought to explore the potential impact on the individuals' earnings and show how they could earn comparable levels through the new plan. However, there were no side agreements, and elimination of the piece-rate incentive plan occurred as scheduled.

It was important in the communication between management and workers for management to explain the pressures for change in terms of external factors and to focus attention on the need to respond to a major crisis. It also was important to reassure people about what was not going to change and to indicate that change would follow a clear roadmap. Much of the communication was done in small groups in which the executives would meet and discuss issues face to face with their employees.

The process of developing the new goal-sharing plan involved a task force of operational, management, and technical professionals. The measures were tied directly to the competitive strategy, and progress was reported on frequently. As the firm implemented the new pay system and performance in the key areas improved, there were celebrations, at which people discussed how they took certain actions to retain customers, increase savings, cross-train others, improve the process, and strengthen the firm's competitiveness. The very real threat to the company's survival was translated into a spirit of change that was truly remarkable. The profitability of the company exceeded previous targets by five times, scrap rates were reduced dramatically, and employees cross-trained one another so that the staff could correspond to the workload.

Case Study: Implementing Team Incentives in a Low-Trust Environment

Murray Electric Glass Company manufactured glass panels used in television sets and computer terminals. The quality of its products and the products' specific features, such as weight, durability, and so on, were essential elements of Murray's competitive strategy. While the demand for its products remained strong, it faced significant internal issues. The firm was unable to effectively implement changes in the manufacturing process because of certain traditional management practices and pay systems. Murray Glass had major barriers between departments within the manufacturing site.

The senior managers wanted to change the culture of the firm to enhance teamwork, communication, and responsiveness across departments. The goals were to decrease all costs, increase productivity, retain competitiveness, and attract new customer orders. While a team-incentive plan works well in a high-trust environment, could it work to create trust in this setting?

With an understanding of this organizational context, the design process and plans were focused on improving teamwork within the firm. While employees were very excited by the prospects of greater teamwork, managers and supervisors felt very concerned. Their job had been based on how well they managed their own units. They feared a significant loss of control, authority, and status. They were unclear about what they needed to do differently or how to increase teamwork while still meeting their production goals. They were skeptical that a team-oriented process would enable them to achieve their business goals. They not only needed to be convinced, but they also needed greater confidence that this process was not just another fad.

The new incentive plan design process included a cross-functional team of managers, operators, and functional specialists (finance, marketing, engineering, human resources, etc.). Team members met periodically with the senior management team (a new expression within this environment) to review their progress. The senior managers expressed their complete support for the team and sought to reinforce each member for his or her contribution throughout the design process.

As the plan was being finalized, the design team met with senior managers, supervisors, and employees in focus-group settings. They presented the plan and discussed how to change the process of working together. They sought reactions and answers to specific questions from each focus group. The data from these meetings were then summarized and integrated into the final design plan and implementation strategy.

One of the key components that lead to the success of this plan was the feedback obtained on results at division and unit levels. The weekly results were communicated in a large display for all members to see. Each department had its own charts and graphs in its work area that tied directly to one or more of the key measures for the entire division. The plan paid out on entire divisional results, but significant reinforcement and celebrations involved the work of each team. There were frequent surprise visits by senior managers to each work area to discuss the ways in which goals were achieved. For example, one group developed a very creative solution to the hand-off process between shifts. The idea was then communicated to other teams, many of which found that it solved some key issues for them, and they quickly implemented the new process. This was an unheard-of event in the old organization.

The results included improvements in productivity and quality and reductions in costs. Employee grievances went down by 50 percent, and employee safety problems were virtually eliminated. The firm was able to reduce its costs, but, more important, it improved the quality and safety of the workplace through the effective implementation of a number of initiatives. The process built confidence and trust in both management and employees.

Case Study: Implementing Team Incentives with a Skeptical Management Commitment

Malanowski Medical Center is a major teaching hospital, and, like many of its counterparts in the health care industry, it is faced with increasing competitive and financial pressures. It had implemented numerous actions to reduce head count, delay pay increases, and minimize purchases. The results were always productive initially, but the cost pressures soon returned. The vice president of human resources felt that implementing team incentives at the departmental level would provide a much needed push to reduce costs and enhance the quality of services. However, the CEO and several other senior executives were concerned that such programs might create undesired disruptions in the organization. They were concerned about increasing costs or conflict within the medical center.

The strategy therefore was to develop pilot or demonstration sites that would be meaningful to the organization and yet not commit it to an undertaking it could not manage. Three departments were selected because they represented a variety of different operations—clinical, administrative, and operational. Further, the supervisors in all three departments were quite strong and highly committed to this effort.

The design process focused on three principal areas. First, sound and effective plans had to be developed for each department. Second, the plans needed to be compatible with other areas of the hospital that did not have similar plans and might be interested in developing similar plans in the future. Finally, the process had to increase Malanowski Medical Center's internal capacity to design, implement, and manage such programs. An important learning process was required from both a content and an experiential point of view.

To accomplish this, there was a steering council made up of representatives from each of the three pilot groups as well as several of their key customers—the nursing and finance departments in particular. After training in the design of incentive plans, the council broke into three design teams. Each team was composed of the manager of the target group, a primary customer, and an independent third party (i.e., human resources). The steering council met periodically to review status reports from each of the design teams. There were important reinforcement meetings because of the effort involved. The meetings also ensured that organizationwide design issues could be addressed effectively. The steering council presented the final plan recommendations to the hospital's senior management and the compensation committee of the board of trustees.

The results were very impressive. Not only did each plan yield a significant return on investment for the medical center, but employees in the pilot groups felt very special. They were members of the cutting edge, and they received significant attention for their efforts to improve the quality of their functions and services to customers. Finally, the pilot projects were expanded to many areas throughout the organization, and the new areas, too, achieved remarkable improvements in their performance.

Lessons to Be Learned from Successful Change Efforts

These three case studies illustrate 10 key principles for implementing successful change:

1. *Focus on the vital few.* Change efforts that are not clearly focused on addressing specific issues are seldom successful. The need for change has to be explained, as does what can be expected in the way of results. People need to understand what needs to be different in a manner that does not blame them for the problem.

2. *Tie changes in the reward systems to the needs of the business.* While this may seem obvious, it is essential that people see that the reason the changes are being introduced is to support the needed changes in the organization. We often say to executives, "If you can achieve the same results in the same time frame without changing the reward systems, do it." Reward systems simply offer a better way to achieve certain objectives than do current methods of management. Furthermore, they may serve as a catalyst to other changes needed within the organization—in systems, management practices, and working relationships.

3. *Clearly communicate what will be done and why.* The program, whether focused on changing the organization or on implementing new reward systems, should state the purpose clearly. It often needs to be presented within the context of broader change efforts. Examples help people translate the imperatives into personal action. The sponsors need to be visible about their commitment to and involvement in the change process. This will tell people that the new initiative is going to happen and that there is no turning back.

4. *If you don't have the support you want, find the support you need.* Executives often hold strong opinions about reward systems and how they should be designed and used. They also often need to respond to shareholder and board concerns about the company that are not understood by employees. If a new idea for a reward system emerges from within the organization but is resisted by some of the senior executives, a useful approach is to develop pilot or demonstration sites where the issues can be identified and resolved without full company involvement. Then, as results are achieved, this evidence can create a compelling story to gain broader or higher-level sponsorship.

5. *If appropriate, involve the target group in the design process.* Each of the three preceding case studies involved plan participants in the design process. The value of this is threefold:

- It increases the chance that there will be support for the changes by the target group.
- It increases the probability that the plan will be effective, relevant, and understood by the participants.
- It enhances the level of confidence and trust in the new system.

However, not every situation requires target group involvement. For example, the decision to eliminate the piece-rate incentive system was not accomplished through a consensus decision-making process. Decisions that are right for the business are sometimes best made in an executive fashion. While input from members of target groups to a decision may be of value, the decision needs to be made by someone who has ultimate accountability for its impact. Another consideration in limiting involvement is time. When there is a deadline for a union contract, the fiscal year, or some organizational changes, a design team process may not be appropriate. Design teams may take from 3 to 6 months to complete their tasks, depending on the complexity of the assignment. If they are not included in the process, the target-group participants will have to be persuaded by how the plan is communicated, implemented, and managed over time.

6. *If others are involved, give them the freedom to design the right plan.* Executives who are excited and impatient about designing changes to reward systems often want to prescribe numerous dimensions of the new plan. For example, they may stipulate who will be eligible and who will not be, the level of payout or additional compensation, the types of measures, the frequency of payouts, and so on. If a design team is used, team members must be given the freedom to consider all the facts and develop the best plan possible. Otherwise, if the executives prescribe the plan provisions or ignore/deny the team's recommendations because of personal values, the chance of a successful plan will be severely limited. The executives may express their desires and wishes, and the design team should consider them. The design team needs to consider many perspectives, and the ultimate design plan needs to support a variety of constituencies. In this way, the use of a design team can be legitimate and sincere.

7. *Define what people need to do differently and how they will benefit.* Personalizing the measures and the reinforcement process will enable people to see how they will benefit from the proposed

change. Describing what people should continue to do as well as what needs to change will give individual performers a strong sense of direction. These measures and goals need to be supported by the reward system and underlying management practices (i.e., performance management). One should clearly describe the opportunities for reward, recognition, and reinforcement in terms that will be meaningful to the receivers.

8. *Design the best possible plan and realize that it will need improvements over time.* A frequent concern of many design teams is that the plan they create needs to remain untouched for at least 5 years or that it must somehow be perfect. While in theory one does not want to change the basic features of a plan too frequently, plans do need to be improved as they are implemented. It is important for the target group and sponsors to realize that improvements should be made, consistent with the basic plan purpose and design principles. Each of the design teams in the preceding case studies stayed committed to do the very best job they could, and each plan has become better over time. In this way we realize that we truly do live in a world that requires "continuous improvements."

9. *Monitor and reinforce the process of change.* The measures inherent in the new reward system offer an opportunity for monitoring the progress of the change. However, they often need for be supported by more detailed and unit-specific measures. These measures indicate the true process of change. By monitoring them, one creates additional opportunities to reinforce progress. By using feedback and reinforcement, people can become excited by the small, everyday wins. When problems arise, the solutions can be developed on a real-time basis. This supports the process of continuous improvement discussed earlier.

10. *Get started!* The process of analysis, design, and testing can be very worthwhile. The key task, however, is to turn ideas into action. Take action as soon as possible. In some cases, it is often more appropriate to ask for forgiveness than to ask for permission. If one truly believes that the changes will produce the desired results, then the longer one waits, the greater will be the cost, the further market share will decline, and the more the workforce will be alienated from the company's strategic imperatives (Figure 14-1).

1. Focus on the vital few.
2. Tie changes in the reward systems to the needs of the business.
3. Clearly communicate what will be done and why
4. If you don't have the support you want, find the support you need.
5. If appropriate, involve the target group in the design process.
6. If others are involved, give them the freedom to design the right plan.
7. Define what people need to do differently and how they will benefit.
8. Design the best possible plan and realize that it will need improvements over time.
9. Monitor and reinforce the process of change.
10. Get started!

Figure 14-1 Ten key principles for successfully implementing change in reward systems.

An organizational culture that reflects compliance or entitlement characteristics impedes a company's ability to adapt to new environmental conditions. In a compliance environment, managers and employees wait for specific direction because they have learned that that is the way to ensure that they will be retained in the organization. In an entitlement environment, managers and employees do not need to be engaged because they feel that senior management will somehow protect them from the risks of the marketplace. They will continue to perform as they have in the past and let the process of change be handled by those in leadership positions. They never really needed to worry about their accountabilities in the past, and they know that the current situation isn't any different.

In an achievement environment, people are not only highly interested in what is going on that will have an impact on the organization, but they also seek ways to contribute or become more engaged. They realize that the organization's future is their responsibility and that they personally have something more at stake than the risk to their job. In this environment, the reward system directly influences the relationship between the organization and its people. This is an organization that appreciates leadership, measurement, and feedback and shares in the value they create.

Ideas You Can Use and Those You Should Avoid

*People who are only good with hammers see
every problem as a nail.*

Abraham Maslow

ORGANIZATIONS FACE many common issues in encouraging
and rewarding desired performance. The art in the design of reward
systems lies in how well people develop and use ideas to support the
organization's desired strategy, culture, key initiatives, and management
practices. Further, the resulting programs need to be effective, as defined
by the principles outlined in this book. They will require effective
administrative systems, as well as trained managers and well-informed
employees.

The purpose of this chapter is to examine a variety of ideas and cautions that readers may find helpful in upgrading or developing new
reward programs. These idea and cautions are intended to prevent the
bureaucratic syndrome from emerging within the firm as it grows and

develops and to keep people focused on the strategy of the organization. These suggestions are keyed to the principles of effective total reward systems. Their use or adaptation will depend on the unique requirements of the organization. The most important thing to keep in mind as you reads this chapter is to look for things that may be different from past practices, bearing in mind that the principles and theories that underlie these new practices are what the organization requires.

Base Salary: Try These Ideas

The primary purpose of the base salary program is to attract and retain the talent the business needs to succeed. While external competitiveness is always a critical issue, the real message is in understanding how the firm should align its pay structure with the roles and contributions of people and the value-added nature of the work. This increases the capabilities of the organization, but it does not necessarily increase its performance. To this end, the following are preferred actions:

1. *Establish pay levels based on the importance of the tasks in creating value for the firm.* Providing what the customer wants with the optimal use of resources often creates the greatest value. Therefore, pay levels need to reflect the roles and/or talent individuals bring to the process of value creation, not what a particular job controls or manages.
2. *Calibrate your pay levels to the right market.* The right market is defined by the sources of talent the firm needs to do its business. It is often defined by the companies from which people are hired and to which they move on—and such companies may not be competitors. This flow of talent often determines where the company needs to focus its attention to remain competitive.
3. Review your situation annually, but do not necessarily make pay adjustments annually. Adjustments in pay should be based on several related factors. These include
   - The continual value of the employee's role within the strategy of the firm
   - How the market is paying for similar talent
   - The ability of the firm to pay (i.e., affordability)
   - The performance and contributions of individuals within this role

When a role is assessed from these perspectives, the firm may or may not make adjustments to base salary.

4. *Stay flexible, and make adjustments to base salary contingent on the performance of the individual, the unit/team, and the company.* If the performance is comparable with marketplace performance, make marketplace adjustments with confidence. If the performance is above or below marketplace performance, alter the adjustments to reflect this. Avoid the trap of having to make salary adjustments just because this is what is done by competitors or because of cost-of-living factors. However, do not withhold pay increases that may exceed those of competitors if excellent performance has been demonstrated.

Base Salary: Avoid These Pitfalls

1. *Don't tie pay primarily to the level or resources a position controls, is responsible for, or directs.* Instead, link pay levels to positions making the greatest contribution to creating value for customers consistent with your core values as a company.

2. *Don't try to keep pace with inflation.* In the 1970s and 1980s, many organizations attempted to keep people's pay increases in step with inflation, only to see the costs of living escalate beyond their ability to pay. Pay levels almost always exceed increases in inflation except in periods of very high inflation or at times when the rates are increasing rapidly. Cost-of-living pay raises should be abandoned because they do little for the organization and create an entitlement mentality within the workforce. Instead, create opportunities for people to earn additional compensation through performance- and achievement-centered programs.

3. *Don't pay for seniority unless it is one of your core values* (and for some organizations, it is). While organizations need people who are loyal and committed, this does not mean that the organization needs to link pay to tenure. Instead, equate pay levels with contributions and impact. Let people earn the right to receive additional pay, and provide many opportunities for this to occur. Reinforce people's long-term service with personal, meaningful

rewards, jobs that challenge their abilities, and opportunities to make a real difference in the areas where they have the most to contribute.

4. *Avoid the zero-sum game.* Many organizations have used traditional merit guidelines as a means of controlling pay increases (see Chapter 6). If someone were to get more than the budgeted amount, someone else would have to get less. While accountability for performance is critical, is this the most effective way to communicate either positive or negative messages? This is the zero-sum game, and it is no wonder people think that pay does not reflect performance in such situations. Instead, relate pay to achievements or to the application of increased capabilities. Use the financial budgeting system to control compensation expenses and reward/punish managers for using the system well/not well. Consider making the merit budget flexible, based on team or company performance.

5. *Don't depend on the base pay system to motivate people.* While in theory the base pay system should reinforce performance, actual practices make it basically ineffective. The rewards are often too infrequent, and the amounts are of little real financial meaning; they often have more symbolic meaning than material value. It therefore should serve to support other reward systems that do have more meaningful, immediate impact on performance. Do not expect the base pay system to do all you want it to do. It can assist, but it cannot determine the outcome of the game. Think of the base pay system as your human capital balance sheet, not a dynamic income or cash-flow statement.

Performance Management: Try These Ideas

The primary purpose of the performance management process is to provide real-time feedback and encouragement to performers. The purpose of performance recognition is to reward individuals and teams for the contributions they make and the results they achieve. As a complete process, this includes day-to-day management discussions, team celebrations, formal and informal recognition, and performance reviews. This enables performance to be managed at a level where people can understand the efforts taken, results achieved, and importance of the work. Use as much data as possible, but summarize the information in terms that people can understand and find meaningful:

1. *Focus on the variables critical to the firm's success.* All directives should point in common directions, and people should see many opportunities where they can contribute individually and collectively to these ends. This is a fundamental role of the firm's leaders. This may include both strategic results—what was accomplished—and core values of the organization—how were the results achieved. Each can provide meaningful measures that can connect people to the company they serve.

2. *Create a real-time, data-oriented feedback system.* Using the priority measures, display charts that reflect how well the firm is doing. This visual display should create interest and excitement as achievements are recognized. A store that provides mail services displayed its daily performance in the stockroom. It also listed its key customers and placed gold stars by their names when they were being served well and often. They even took pictures and displayed their favorite customers so that the sales staff could recognize them and call them by name.

3. *Create celebrations that mean something to the performers.* Often celebrations are more fun when they are done on a shoestring budget. This requires creativity, ingenuity, and true resourcefulness. Large companies can support small-unit recognition events through budget allocations and sharing of ideas and resources with other areas. You will know if these events are meaningful if the talk on the morning after reflects a desire to "do it again" (i.e., achieve the desired performance).

4. *Use performance reviews as an opportunity to reflect on "how we won" and "how we lost and what we learned."* Rather than thinking of performance reviews as an annual evaluation event, make them as often as necessary to enhance learning and focus on contributions. Performance reviews that give employees perception-based feedback quickly undermine the relationship. The manager may have opinions, but they need to be treated as just one perspective in a process of learning. The focus should be on understanding how the employee was able to overcome obstacles and achieve

great results (i.e., positive reinforcement) and on examining what can be done differently next time to avoid or handle difficult situations (i.e., learning). In both cases, the individual seeks to get the message, and the manager should understand the facts, not reinforce preconceived opinions about the situation.

5. *Anchor the memory of achievements.* An entitlement-oriented organization does not know when or how to celebrate. Their events are not tied to outcomes that people find meaningful or had a major role in achieving. People seldom turn down awards, and they may grow to expect them regardless of performance. Achievement-oriented firms measure a lot, accomplish milestones frequently, and do much celebrating. There is a lot of energy and excitement, surprises, and special events, and people enjoy working in such places. They see results from what they do, and they feel valued for their contributions. This process does not depend on the work or the nature of the business but rather on the leadership and the actions of managing performance. The greatest celebrations are those which firmly anchor the memory of an acknowledged accomplishment. Such occasions encourage people to believe that they can do it again and can achieve even more, and they will make every effort.

Performance Management: Avoid These Pitfalls

1. *Don't rely on annual performance appraisals.* For many reasons mentioned above, annual appraisals delay feedback and establish a confrontational situation between managers and employees. If there is little or no real-time feedback to performers, annual appraisals may make the company worse off than it was.

2. *Avoid recognition programs that honor only the individual—employee of the month, the top 10 percent, and so on.* These programs seldom yield desired performance and tend to reinforce the role of executives as all-knowing, all-powerful. We wish that executives could hear what people say about them after some awards ceremonies. If they did, they would never put on such a function again. There are simply better alternatives.

3. *Don't force-rank individuals for the purpose of awarding merit or incentive pay*. This process assumes that performance is based on individual actions alone or that individuals have the same performance opportunities. Neither is the case, and such actions give executives a misleading picture of their true stars. This does not make poor managers good, but it does make good managers do poor things.

4. *Avoid "doing what the Joneses do" and the "let's make a form" game*. While organizations can learn a great deal from benchmarking others and learning the practices of successful companies, this information needs to be interpreted in light of the firm's own history, business circumstances, and management practices. As a client executive of ours once said: "Our competitive advantage is achieved by not doing what others do; we don't follow our competitors. We know what we're going to do, and each person has a critically important job to do. When we get results, we want to know why." He meant that there are principles that need to be understood and practiced within a firm for it to be successful. Further, although intensity, impatience, and speed are characteristics of today's organizations, they also can lead a firm to approach tasks in a wasteful and not-well-thought-out manner. Employees frequently say of their previous employer, "We never had time to plan and get it right, but we always made time and paid for making the fixes." A new performance management form does not provide any answers. Rather, it gives the impression that progress is being made or problems are being solved. In reality, the key to success lies in the process. Forms should support the process and keep the criteria simple, clear, and well understood. Learning what one does by learning what others do can be of some value. But the best learning process is the one where gains are created in the workplace.

Variable Compensation: Try These Ideas

The purpose of the variable pay system should be to create a stake in the short-term results of the business. If the firm or unit/team does well, the rewards should be forthcoming. If the firm or unit/team does not do well, the financial rewards will not be there. It is essential that variable pay programs be truly contingent on performance. Otherwise, they reflect entitlement management:

1. *Focus the measures on what defines the success or progress of the firm.* Variable pay should be linked to a few high-priority measures of performance. Therefore, it needs to be linked to the results that enable the firm to be competitive in the present and in the future. This is perhaps the most important function of effective variable pay programs.

2. *Support the program with regular, meaningful feedback and frequent, valuable informal rewards.* When variable pay programs fail, it is often because people cannot see what they should do to change the numbers or because they don't pay attention to the metrics. Thus variable pay programs need to be translated into personalized measures that provide guidance to action. Then feedback and reinforcement of achievements encourage people to try harder, do better, and be successful.

3. *Make the payouts as frequently as possible, as long as they support the cycles of the business.* When variable pay programs have a long time horizon, they are basically nonfunctional for two-thirds to three-fourths of the performance period. Frequency can be an important element of the reward system. However, programs that have very frequent payouts can lead to an oversimplification of measures or excessive administrative burdens. In these cases, complement the payout cycle with more frequent and more creative recognition practices.

4. Consider using corporate measures to modify unit/team performance incentives to reflect the desired level integration across units. In small companies, a profit-sharing program can provide an important means to create the sense of a shared fate. As the firm grows and roles become more differentiated, the line of sight to profit sharing may diminish. It may be valuable for the executives but have little impact on the performers. A transition strategy can use the profit-sharing plan to create a funding pool for incentives or as a modifier to payouts on team-based measures. This can be achieved by using the pool to modify the

planned payouts given for performance or a performance score-card that includes corporate measures.

5. *Link managers with the performance of their units.* One fatal flaw in some incentive plans occurs when managers are measured on different measures than their staff members. This can create a situation in which the performers receive small payouts while the manager receives a large payout. There are few devices that undermine the collaboration and common spirit of an organization more than this. Therefore, use some or most of the manager's measures for the performance unit. In this way, the incentive payouts will be dependent on those the manager is expected to support. This situation creates mutual consequences in direct and meaningful ways.

Variable Pay: Avoid These Pitfalls

1. *Eliminate or minimize discretionary incentive plans.* This type of program serves to undermine the leadership of an organization in subtle ways. First, everyone quickly figures out that the key to an award is looking good to the manager. Customer needs take a backseat to the boss's perceptions. Second, such programs reinforce the executives' need for power rather than growth in the value of the company. While executives clearly have and should retain accountability for determining results and rewards, discretionary incentives should support their strategy and serve as a quality assurance process. While flexibility may be necessary because of ongoing changes in business conditions, care must be taken to prevent discretionary perceptions from being the most important determinant of rewards.

2. *Don't wait until the game is over before giving workers the score.* Regular feedback on the progress of performance is essential to winning the game. Most people can understand good news/bad news if they hear it on a regular basis. The data become believable, credible. They should hear how they are doing at least three and maybe five or more times during a performance period. People begin to take important actions when the feedback points toward

the possibility of achieving desired goals. This creates a strong sense of urgency.

3. *If incentives work for some, they can work for others. Be cautious, but don't be too restrictive.* The problem for many companies is their fear of including too many people in an incentive plan. They worry that additional money may be paid out when people have not earned it. They complain that a base salary is for an expected level of performance, so why should it be necessary to pay more? The reality is that people respond very effectively to incentive plans that they feel are fair—that meet the SMART criteria. Furthermore, the payouts should be justified by the performance of the organization and enable the company to reinforce several specific drivers of competitive strategy. However, if the performance of the organization is really determined by only a few people, the company should look to other reward programs to reinforce performance and create a competitive advantage.

Performance Recognition: Try These Ideas

Recognition, whether informal oral or written comments or formal programs and events, has been shown to be perhaps the most cost-effective way to reinforce desired actions. However, acting in isolation of compensation and equity-type rewards, recognition frequently looses much of its appeal. Employees ultimately resent executives who receive substantial bonuses and equity wealth when they receive only wonderful comments, trophies, and inexpensive celebrations. Consider an environment where there is substantial sharing of rewards and recognition throughout an organization, tied to the performance of the organization and its units and reflective of the roles and impact of individuals on these results. Thus consider these ideas when using performance-recognition programs and processes:

1. *Define the criteria for recognition by "how" things are done and how well progress is being made in achieving key goals.* When the criteria are unclear, either before or after the fact, the value of the recognition diminishes rapidly. Then, if the rewards are provided a second time, people "connect the dots" and fill in their own reasons. This often leads to a culture of entitlement.

2. *Make the rewards personal.* This concept has been discussed several times throughout this book, and it is often the primary reason why many recognition programs become a waste of time, money, and effort. One idea is to have employees/managers create a personal file of the things they value, like to do, or wish they had. The list should be open to other members of the group, and it should be used as a source for ideas. Although some will consider this like a "holiday wish list," simply ignore their concerns or put-downs to the process, and use the ideas shared on this list to be creative and resourceful.

3. *Recognize teams/groups in public, but consider whether or not individuals should be recognized in public.* Public recognition can be a very valuable or significantly embarrassing event. When teams are recognized in public and people see who is on the teams, the individuals who are concerned about recognition can hide behind the banner of the team. Work to encourage people to be part of successful teams as well as to make their teams more successful.

4. *Budget the resources (time and money) for recognition, and realize that more can be gained from these dollars in difficult times than in high-growth times.* Organizations often face challenging economic or performance times. This is not the time to reduce the amount of recognition but rather to refocus it on what actions are necessary for the organization to sustain its survival or return to its high-growth period. People will remember these events more often and perhaps more deeply than the recognition given in times of general economic growth.

Performance Recognition: Avoid These Situations

Recognition can backfire in more dramatic ways than many formal compensation systems. Much of the criticism of reward systems has to do with failures at effective recognition. Therefore, consider these cautions in your practices of recognition:

1. *Don't recognize a specific action every time it occurs.* This process creates a "transaction economy" within the organization—people stop doing things you want until you define what reward they

will receive. Behavioral research clearly shows that the most effective reinforcement occurs on a variable basis. The focus is still on the desired actions or results, but people do not know exactly when they will achieve the desired impact (i.e., receive the desired reward).

2. *Don't set up recognition systems that are defined by who is "not" included.* These are the typical "employee of the month" type clubs. Competition, on the other hand, used periodically, can energize those who enjoy the excitement of winner-type games. However, companies often come to believe that these programs are what make recognition meaningful. In fact, they only work for a short period. People would rather be appreciated by what they accomplished than by whom they defeated (unless it is the external competition) to win.

3. *Don't generalize about a positive experience.* A major dilemma with any system of rewards and recognition is that when it is successful, executives come to believe that the system should be applied universally and forever. People change, conditions change, and change is good—especially when it comes to recognition programs. One company changed the focus of its corporatewide recognition program (called the Service Star Program) each year. The focus became the theme for the year, and the theme was used as the basis for selecting individual and team awards. For example, the themes included service to our customers, capturing more of the customer's business, building our savings by increasing revenues and reducing costs, and so on.

Equity-Based Programs: Try These Ideas

Equity participation, whether actual stock or stock options in a publicly traded company, phantom-share or equity-simulator plans in a private company or subsidiary, or long-term project incentives, has a special value all its own. Equity-based programs can provide a reward system that is very different from those related to cash or appreciation. However, care has to be taken here as well.

1. *Set and reinforce the expectations appropriately about the opportunities associated with an equity stake in the enterprise.* For many, these pro-

grams have developed an expectation of wealth creation that may never be realized (although for many executives and individuals in successful startup companies, they have). The dynamics of the marketplace have disillusioned many people and have made this reward of questionable value. Thus, as individuals receive equity awards, the purpose and meaning of the award, as well as a realistic assessment of its future value, need to be communicated.

2. *Balance the value of the awards to the target performers with the potential dilution or cost impact on shareholders.* There is a great deal of legislation pending that will change the economic value of stock options and related programs. For some organizations, it is far better to expand the use of high-impact, cash-based incentive compensation plans than to provide stock options to the majority of the population. Then the stock awards are focused on those who are most critical to the long-term value creation of the business. This does not mean just the top executives. For other companies, equity participation is a critical element in the package to attract or retain their most important talent.

3. *Even though you are a private company, you can still create opportunities for long-term incentives.* There is a presumption that only firms that are publicly traded or going for an initial public offering are candidates for long-term incentives. The argument is one of cost, liquidity, or control—it will simply be too expensive for an organization to provide ownership participation, individuals will not have access to the value that is generated, or the current owners resist sharing the value of the wealth that they have invested in or created over time. Many of these concerns are both significant and valid. However, if one examines the many alternatives outlined in preceding chapters, there are mechanisms to use earned profitability and participation to create both tax-efficient and meaningful wealth-creating opportunities.

4. *Use stock options as a method of communicating "You are highly valued here."* Stock options and other forms of equity participation have come to symbolize a certain level of importance or affirmation of the individual within the organization. Use the process to reinforce the message of importance and commitment to the recipients. This involves considering how much, for what, and the manner in which the awards are made. If stock options are used

in a trivial manner, then it will take many more options or awards to achieve the same level of emotional and motivational impact. If the plan is based on a deliberate and careful assessment process, then those who receive the awards may see them in a different light. This process can be a highly effective opportunity for appraising key talent and identifying who will have the most impact on the firm's future. These programs can be important in their symbolic value, as long as one realizes that the value is created over the long term and not within fiscal quarters.

Equity-Based Programs: Avoid These Issues

1. *Set an appropriate level of expectations for executives about the impact equity awards will have on recipients.* Companies that have awarded stock options with the hope that someone people will act differently are likely to be very disappointed, although many people do feel differently about their employers once they become a shareholder. However, if people are not actively engaged in efforts that make an important difference to the company, then this feeling likely will fade. The program will rapidly become another entitlement program. Some companies consider broad-based stock options as a benefit program. We applaud their efforts at taking this action and not expecting a major impact on the performance of their people.

2. *Plan for the amount of equity you are willing to award and the potential value.* When executives or their advisers become enthusiastic about awarding equity to all employees, they sometimes fail to account for two factors: new people or the need to make additional awards in the future and the financial impact the plan may have on the financial reserves, tax liability, and attractiveness of the firm to potential buyers. Attorneys often advise their clients to be cautious, perhaps often exercising too much caution. Yet, if the owners do not consider the program over a 3- to 5- to 10-year period, they may soon find themselves without an ability to make additional awards without major dilution of existing shareholder value.

3. *Wait for changes in the tax laws.* The U.S. Congress, the Securities and Exchange Commission, and other government bodies con-

tinually threaten to overhaul the system of equity participation. They are responding both to excessive levels of executive compensation that many would argue are not justified by the performance and to philosophical and confidence factors about executive compensation. Also, creative tax, accounting, and legal advisers frequently develop new mechanisms to build up wealth on a tax-deferred basis. Proceed with caution because, as the old saying goes, "If it sounds too good to be true, it probably is." Watch for Congress or the government to take actions that have serious and costly implications.

4. *Don't rely on stock options as your main source for attracting and retaining people.* When the technology market grew rapidly and new companies were easily capturing new people from established companies, one of the primary tools was stock participation. Then, when the "bubble burst," there was little value left, and people felt that they had lost a major source of value—employers and employees alike. The answer is to find the right balance of rewards from a broad portfolio that will be meaningful and important to the talent the organization needs in order to grow. The rebalancing can be both painful and costly.

Building a Bridge from Here to There

This chapter has addressed the need to develop a game plan for implementing changes to reward systems. While the fundamental reason for these changes is to support a redirection in the business, one needs to develop a strategy for implementing change in specific programs. While we need to realize that the strategy will not be perfect, it should be the very best possible strategy that can be drawn up at the time. Then, as successes are realized or problems are encountered, adjustments can be made from a foundation of understanding and commitment.

The process of organizational change, especially in changing reward systems, is never easy. However, not to take action is also a form of taking action—not to decide is to decide. Change is not always bad. Resistance exists not because people do not support change but because they have a history of a process with which they are familiar. Not everyone will benefit from the change or at least be able to retain their current role or rewards.

The primary task involves increasing the rate of change that is focused on areas of success that are critical to the business. People will adapt to change when they realize that it is more meaningful to engage in the new behaviors than to retain the old ones. Further, not everything is going to change. We have to pinpoint what needs to change and how everyone can benefit from the process. If individuals do not choose to participate, at least they will have been given the opportunity to do so. As one executive stated, "I need to either change the people or change the people."

Reward systems create the opportunity for reinforcement; people take the actions necessary to take advantage of the opportunities. When reward systems are developed, planned, and executed in ways that build collaboration, we enhance our probability of success. There is no certainty of reward when people have a stake in the business. They operate in a partnership of common fate. With this kind of relationship, the firm has a unique competitive advantage. With this relationship in place, the possibilities are almost endless. The firm just needs a great strategy that employs its great organization.

Take Your Workplace to the Next Level

*The winds and the waves are always on the
side of the ablest navigators.*

Edward Gibbons

T HROUGHOUT THIS BOOK we have explored various drivers of organizational performance. Much has been written about the pressures of the global marketplace and the strategies for gaining competitive advantage. Many writers have presented compelling advice about what one should do and what other firms have done. Further, writers indicate that in order to fully realize or sustain its recommended approach, an organization needs to change its reward systems—compensation, recognition, and career paths. However, they do not indicate *how*, and one is left wondering what to do. A primary goal of this book is to provide readers with both tools and guiding principles to develop reward systems that support their firms' unique strategies.

A fundamental element to successful implementation of one's strategy is engaging people to use their skills and initiatives consistent with the firm's strategy. This commitment is strengthened when the reward systems are aligned with the strategy, success measures, and desired values of the organization. This provides a clear process to encourage and reinforce desired behaviors. Therefore, creating value is rooted in human behavior, and behavior is clearly linked to the consequences that shape and encourage it.

The Pressures for Change

In the 1960s, Bob Dylan wrote a song in which he said, "And the times, they are a changin.'" Little did he know that these words would continue to be a prophecy beyond those times. The political barriers that once divided people are coming down, and people are becoming more aware of different cultures and traditions. Cultures are changing throughout the world because of the increase in travel and media communications. While this has opened great opportunities, it is also posing a threat to the traditions and values of many cultures. These cultures are feeling a stronger need to protect their way of life while taking advantage of certain aspects of the global community. Wars and acts of terrorism are no longer just experienced by distant people; they are involving an increasing number of people either directly or through the media. These acts are a reflection of the inherent forces of global change. At times they will create great conflicts, and business organizations often will find themselves in the middle of this struggle for identity.

Information is becoming almost instantaneous around the planet. Telecommunications technology is enabling people to gain access to information, communicate with others, and provide services well beyond their traditional markets. Capital can be acquired from many sources and is flowing to support the greatest opportunities. These dynamics are reshaping our global community in ways that are difficult to predict. Buckminister Fuller captured the concept when the said, "We are realizing that we all live on Spaceship Earth."

Organizations are facing increasing challenges of competition and technology transformation. As organizations grow and expand globally, they are addressing issues of cultural diversity and values conflicts within themselves as well. As companies acquire other firms and operate in multiple countries, the efforts to effectively implement strategic plans will be made more complex. The leadership challenge will require thoughtful consideration of the balance among an organization's mission, its customers and the markets it serves, and the people it employs.

The Chinese symbol for crisis has two figures. The first means *danger*. When the forces of change are threatening survival—of a culture, a company, or a person—the first response is to deny them or fight them. When an organization resists change, its ability to survive decreases. Stiffening against the forces of change may work for a period of time, but such action can create a false sense of confidence. Other organizations then exploit this resistance and capture customers, markets, and suppliers. In the end, the lack of flexibility and adaptability actually may render the organization incapable of addressing the dangers effectively.

The second Chinese figure for crisis means *opportunity*. The drive for survival is very strong. This can be witnessed in a forest a few months after a fire has apparently destroyed it. New shoots emerge from the ashes, and the life that returns is stronger and more resilient. Similarly, opportunities emerge in every crisis in which an organization can use its talents to reshape the marketplace and its role in it. The organization may use downturns in the economy to shed unprofitable units or individuals who are not meeting minimum performance requirements. Companies use these times to renegotiate unfavorable contracts, refocus on their core missions and core competencies, and strengthen relationships with key customers. This requires identifying new ways to create value and serve customers, employing different perspectives, and taking bold action. In the end, the organization emerges from adverse times stronger and more capable of growing and serving its markets.

All change is not necessarily good. The challenge for leaders will be to identify which types of change need to be resisted and eliminated and which need to be adapted, integrated, or used to strengthen the ability of the organization to better serve its markets and customers. The answer depends on what the leaders of the organization see as the mission, values, and strategy of the enterprise they serve.

The pressures are different for every industry and every organization. The task of leadership is to see where the forces of change present danger and where they offer opportunity; both are always present. The purpose of strategic planning is to define and refine the value proposition, business model, and success measures to achieve competitive advantages for the organization. The objectives, goals, and plans can be established to provide members of the organization with the focus they need to make effective decisions and to take purposeful actions. When these strategies are communicated throughout the organization, they serve to provide clarity and encourage action. Whether or not they become reality depends on the level of capability and commitment within the organization. True engagement is achieved when individuals take ownership for and feel a personal stake in the activities of their organization.

Many executives are either not capable of or choose not to understand the leadership principles that influence human behavior in positive ways. The reason this weakness may exist is because people often use the concepts that have been reinforced in them in the past. Traditionally, negative consequences, such as embarrassing people in public, displaying outbursts of anger, and threatening to hold back rewards, have been highly effective in getting managers the fast response they wanted. Using these practices, managers achieved the desired results. Other managers have used inspirational techniques—vision, values, or broad, bold goals—to motivate their staff. Because they often received very positive, immediate responses, they come to believe that this is what works to motivate people. Finally, there are managers who "hold people accountable"—which in most cases means that if individuals do not do their part, they will suffer adverse consequences. Holding people accountable seldom means that people will be rewarded for doing their part. Therefore, when facing similar challenges, leaders, managers, and other people likely will use similar strategies again, never knowing why these actions worked.

We have learned through the many case studies presented in this book that negative consequences result in compliance, not commitment. In a compliance environment, people do as instructed and seldom seek to offer additional ideas or initiative. In high-achievement environments, people feel personally connected to the mission, strategy, goals, and values of the organization. They look for opportunities to make things more efficient, serve customers better, and grow the firm. They are proud of where they work and easily recommend others to join the firm. While new employees usually come with some degree of loyalty, commitment is built over time and is always a function of the rewards the individual experiences. Just because an individual does not take other job offers does not mean that he or she is committed to the organization. The interesting thing about commitment is that it needs to be earned by the organization in order to be given by the individual.

It is clear that organizations and leaders are adapting to the changing forces in the global environment. Inherent in these forces are both threats to survival and opportunities for great triumph. By using strategy, accountabilities, and goals, leaders provide the necessary *focus and direction*. By setting clear, compelling measures and tracking their progress, individuals receive the *feedback* necessary to manage performance. By using effective recruitment, selection, retention, promotion, training, and development initiatives, the organization enhances its *capabilities*. Then, by understanding, designing, and using total reward systems, the organization creates *the commitment and the engagement* it needs to succeed.

When organizations do not understand or use these core elements effectively, they create opportunities for others to gain a market advantage. The ability of the organization to implement its unique strategy clearly depends on the level to which it fully employs this framework for leadership and success. This is a fundamental characteristic of all high-performing organizations.

Creating the Achievement Workplace

In organizations that are winning the competitive struggle of the marketplace, there is a clear strategy that fits the opportunities of the marketplace. Further, there are usually wonderful developments taking place deep inside the organization. For example, a large electrical utility that has been undergoing re-creation-level change for several years celebrated the work of a supervisor and her team that was able to produce savings in excess of $50,000 per year. In the same company, a team in accounting was able to reduce account receivables exceeding 90 days by 90 percent. In a high-technology company, an accounts receivable clerk was conducting a routine phone call to a customer when he learned about a major problem in a recent delivery. He called the sales representative, and she was able to take immediate action. The customer was so impressed with the firm's responsiveness that it turned all competitors away.

In every organization, marvelous events occur every day. People cover for each other when one is overwhelmed with work. Products are sometimes hand-delivered to a customer (internal or external), even though it is not part of someone's job but is desperately needed. The talent within a firm is sometimes just incredible, and this presents a potential reserve that few executives truly understand, believe, or know how to engage.

In this book we have presented tools for implementing the strategy of an enterprise. These tools work because they are based on the science and concepts of understanding human behavior. As we have stated, human behavior is a function of four forces:

- *Focus*—the antecedents of communication that defines what needs to be done
- *Feedback*—the measures, information, and data used to track how one is doing
- *Competencies*—the know-how and capabilities to do what needs to be done
- *Rewards*—the consequences, usually positive, that one receives or believes will be received for doing what needs to be done, based on a desired action or result

Strategies, goals, and accountabilities come before the behaviors and, if effective, get them started. Measures are the systems to track how well performance is progressing; measures are the information life force of an organization. The competencies are the skills and abilities that people need to perform the desired functions and that are acquired or developed within the organization. The most powerful force, how- ever, is the consequences of actions, which determine whether or not people will continue or increase the desired behaviors or discontinue or decrease them. Will people find value in their efforts, or will they find them unfulfilling or frustrating? Are they doing the desired actions because they have to or because they want to? The primary challenge of leaders is to use rewards and consequences in a sincere and strategic manner to create win-win outcomes.

There are those who believe that consequences just reflect a "carrot and stick" relationship between managers and employees. Taken to an extreme, this reflects a tyrannical approach to leadership; this produces a culture of compliance. Further, there are those who seek to protect their employees from the threats and forces of the organization, with the hope that loyalty will provide the spirit for high performance. These companies then create entitlement and dependency-oriented organizations. This reflects a paternalistic approach to leadership.

An achievement-oriented environment results when the goals and roles are clear, measurement and feedback are frequent, and contributions and results are recognized often. Achievement comes from doing something of which one can be proud. It often requires concentrated or extra effort. The reinforcement, whether it comes from inside oneself or from someone noticing the value that is created, is positive. The feeling is that one *wants* to do it again. In the achievement-oriented organization, this relationship between action and consequences occurs thousands of times every day. The daily practices of executives, managers, and employees reinforce the desired actions of others as a regular habit. The beauty of this process is that it is simple to understand and clearly valuable to all. The opportunity for the organization is that few companies do this on a regular basis. Here is a unique way to establish competitive advantage.

The Primary Purpose of Reward Systems

Organizations can create conditions in which people find a wide variety of rewards in the work they do. Some of these rewards come from the work itself, some from peers, some from customers, and some from managers or supervisors. There are conditions within the workplace that encourage and reinforce people for serving their customers in a manner that achieves a win for the customers and a win for themselves.

Reward systems should be designed with the central purpose of providing people with an opportunity to share in the achievements of their contributions. The process does not imply that people are not already performing at a fully competent level. Rather, it is aimed at continually improving performance at a rate that is faster than that of competitors. Sincerity is key to the effective use of consequences. If reward systems are established as a way to manipulate people, they are likely to fail. If, on the other hand, they are established to reinforce progress, achievements, and service to the customers, they are very likely to succeed.

In making the transition to a more achievement- or performance-based organization, there are those who will seriously resist the change. They will complain about it, criticize it, or encourage others not to respond. If the leaders yield to this resistance, the more the "resisters" will be rewarded for their efforts and the less that will go to those who support the change. The best strategy is to ignore the resisters and focus attention and rewards on those who do respond, adapt, and become energized. If executives yield to those who resist desired change, they will create an environment where change can be ignored or resisted, and the innovators will feel defeated. The ability to adapt to a changing market will be diminished by the very people who are responsible for the organization's leadership.

What Makes Rewards Work

Throughout this book we have discussed a wide variety of reward systems—from salaries to variable pay, from equity participation to special recognition, from informal, immediate comments to formalized systems. There are different requirements for each of these different types of plans. However, they have several common themes that determine their effectiveness. These are

- *Strategy.* The measures, actions, and results should support the competitive strategy of the organization in a way that creates value and gives it an advantage in the marketplace.
- *Translation.* People know what needs to be accomplished and what actions they can and should take to maximize their contribution with sufficient scope that they can use their own natural creativity, ingenuity, and passion.
- *Relationships.* Results are achieved by people working together toward common goals, and reward systems need to encourage the desired relationships among shareholders, executives, leaders, managers, individuals, customers, and suppliers in a manner that maximizes the creation of value for what one contributes.
- *Integrity.* The process or system functions according to its design principles, fulfills its commitments, and retains the flexibility to adjust to changing conditions; the process simply needs to be trusted.

- *Value.* People see the rewards as personally meaningful within their frame of reference and culture.
- *Engagement.* The feedback and variety of rewards an individual receives should provide a sense of urgency, importance of the tasks, and value of the desired results so that the person wants to take desired actions.

In this way, performers can feel truly valued for what they accomplish, and this spirit is multiplied to all members of the organization. This enables the firm to be more competitive and successful.

Integrating Reward Systems into the Organization

So far we have discussed the challenges to leadership and the need to find a new pathway to success. We have examined the characteristics of an organization that is oriented toward achievement and success. We have explored many ideas, concepts, and examples of reward systems that are directed toward supporting the strategy of the organization. From the five factors above (i.e., STRIVE), we have determined what makes reward systems effective. However, the key task will be in integrating the reward systems into the organization's systems, structure, and practices.

To bring these concepts into reality, let's review the key messages for each of the key components of an organization's reward systems:

Reward Strategy

Traditional thinking about reward strategies focuses on the external marketplace and what is necessary to be competitive in attracting and retaining people. The guidelines presented in this book focus the reward strategy on the actions needed by people to implement a firm's competitive strategy. This means that one needs to understand the strategy in terms of the organization's key success factors and translate these factors into the types of behaviors or actions required of people within the firm. The resulting description may define what the firm currently does well and what needs to be increased or introduced. The basic premise is that people should be performing actions that are in accord with the strategy of the firm because it is in their self-interest as well. This strategy provides the foundation for the organization to succeed in an increasingly complex and competitive marketplace. Based on this context information, the purpose and desired requirements of the each of the various reward systems should be clearly defined. This will enable the organization to transform a portfolio of reward programs into an integrated system.

Base Salary

The fundamental purpose of the base pay system is to enable the company to acquire and retain the human capabilities it needs to perform its business. By its very nature, the salary program needs to support the values that are critical to the firm's long-term success. In human capital terms, base salaries reflect the balance sheet, or the assets, of the business that are either appreciating or depreciating. This includes understanding the needed competencies and either "buying" the talent (through competitive pay structures) or "developing" the capabilities [through pay-for-competencies-employed (PACE) programs or programs that support career development]. Base pay systems are oriented toward the individual and should be personalized to reflect the individual contributions and talents of the person. In this manner, we can create a system that is not zero-sum but reinforces collaboration, continual growth, and competitiveness in acquiring the talent the firm needs to succeed.

Variable Compensation—Cash and Equity Participation

The fundamental purpose of the variable pay system is to create a stake in the short-term success or progress toward the long-term success of the team, unit, or company. By its very nature, variable pay supports the economic factors of the organization. These include the ways it achieves its revenues, uses it resources, and performs its operations, satisfies customers, and builds greater capabilities. In human capital terms, variable compensation reflects the income statement, dynamic and continually changing based on the business. As performance is improved, individuals will have an opportunity to gain financially, and the firm will gain in financial and market leadership dimensions.

In this area we have explored the use of cash incentives as well as equity-related incentives. In all cases the measures are targeted at creating value for customers and the company. The performance dimensions include revenues, costs, profitability margins, resource yields, timeliness, accuracy, reliability, service, and customer satisfaction. Taken in combination, these measures enhance the competitiveness and value of the firm by strengthening relationships with customers and increasing marketplace leadership.

Recognition and Performance Management

While base salary can reflect *values* and variable pay can reflect *economics*, recognition and performance management reflect *the process*. The process includes how the work gets done between the points in time when other awards can be given. It also creates the environment in which people feel valued on a frequent basis for their achievements.

Recognition management is the ongoing process of encouraging and reinforcing the actions individuals and teams take to achieve results. The rewards may be verbal or social, tangible or symbolic, or work-related (such as special training, promotions, access to additional resources, etc.). Performance management is the "real time" process of managing people and the conditions in which they work. We have reviewed a wide variety of applications, including performance planning, coaching and feedback, periodic reviews, and rating and ranking activities. These are not single programs but rather are the processes engaged in by managers, teams, or individuals to monitor and reinforce desired actions. When desired actions are taken, desired results will be achieved. What could be more important to an organization?

Summary: Guiding Principles

Throughout this book we have attempted to offer alternatives, concepts, and guidelines from which readers can select to build a system of rewards that will work in their environments. Innovation is therefore defined as something that is new to the situation or organization; what is highly innovative for some is common practice for others. Therefore, one must develop the strategy that fits the organization's current and future needs in a way that provides it with a unique advantage in the marketplaces for talent, customers, and investors.

In building a total rewards system, it is necessary to understand some fundamental principles that have worked over time. These principles are based on solid research in both academic and industrial settings, as well as on personal experience gained through seeing results and analyzing the reasons for them. They were pulled from different sections in this book because they reflect the critical requirements for the success of any system of rewards. There are 10 guidelines that we would like to leave you with as you finish this book. They are not presented in any order of importance but do follow a logical flow.

I. Do It Now! Time Is Not on Your Side

If you believe that the practices of building total reward systems will support implementing strategic priorities in your organization, the longer you wait, the longer it will be before you realize any enduring improvement. One large financial institution discovered that it was wasting over $300,000 a day in excess costs that could be eliminated through the implementation of a few key reward programs. While one debates whether or not to change, the competitors are losing no time in approaching customers or gaining an advantage.

2. Keep Your Eye on What Creates Value for Customers and the Organization

Throughout this book, creating value for customers and the organization has been at the center. By building value for customers and strengthening relationships with them, a firm enhances its value proposition and its own market value. Suppliers should treat you as a customer, and you in turn can enhance their ability to serve you by treating them as customers. Customers need to be the primary focus because they provide a positive point for guidance to all activities.

3. Stay Focused, Take Action, and Become Engaged in New Ways

There is a commonly held belief that if an organization can establish the right reward system, it can replace the process of management. In fact, the opposite is true. Well-designed reward systems actually require more management, not less. However, the management required is different. The new model is more concentrated on providing people with meaningful measures, real-time feedback, and ongoing reinforcement. It demands that managers break down the walls, prompt actions to occur, and strengthen the relationships between the team and its customers. It is more positive, action-oriented, and results-focused than traditional management practice. Management is not a spectator sport, but it is an engaging experience.

4. Personalize Rewards to the Recipients

One of the advantages of having multiple reward systems is that everyone has an opportunity to receive the benefits of the systems. An essential tenet of effective reward systems is that what is received must be meaningful to the performer. The performer needs to see that the reward opportunities are linked directly to the effort and results achieved and that there is an appropriate return on investment. This occurs not only through the amount of awards but also through how the rewards are delivered. By personalizing the reward, you can anchor the meaning of the achievement more deeply than if you simply treat the reward as a mechanical administrative task.

In an earlier chapter we presented an example of a firm that took a creative approach to awarding incentive checks. It is appropriate to review it again because it is a good example of how to personalize rewards. When it came time to distribute incentive checks, the general manager brought everyone into the employee cafeteria; he spoke briefly about the value of the achievements; and then distributed the checks. Only instead of giving each person his or her own check, he gave them someone else's check. Each person's task was to find the recipient and tell him or her something special he or she had done to make this payout possible. If the check giver was not able to mention a specific achievement, he or she was just to thank the person for his or her efforts. This occasion was discussed for weeks and became an important symbol of the firm's efforts to build a more mutually supportive and competitive organization.

If you want to know how to make a reward meaningful, notice what people do when they have free time, go on vacation, or enjoy a weekend outing. People tend to do things that are meaningful and valuable to them when they have choices. Create rewards that are related to what employees do when they make the choice themselves. Never give a plaque to someone who does not have a wall to hang it on.

5. Make Sure Everyone Can Win

Reward systems built on principles of competition or compliance ultimately will be counterproductive, if not downright destructive. As we discussed earlier, collaboration can be achieved only when benefits are maximized and affect as many people possible. Many traditional systems seek to pit one team or employee against another, a technique that undermines the credibility of the organization as well as the commitment of its members. Unfortunately, managers who tend to rely on this method receive immediate gratification; it is no wonder that such practices are so hard to change. If done as a specific game, a short-term catalyst, such practices may have positive results. Do not define the top performers or the value of their rewards by those who were not selected. Instead, the rewards should go to those who meet or exceed their goals, but not just for being in the game. The challenge for management is both to get people over the goal line and to maximize the payouts—not by lowering the performance levels but by providing whatever assistance is appropriate for people to achieve. This creates a new role for management and leads to the creation of a true win-win situation.

6. Make Sure That Awards Are Contingent

Reward systems become entitlement systems when they lose their relationship to performance. A sense of entitlement is created when people are rewarded automatically and regularly for not doing anything special. They grow to expect their awards and often want even more. People appreciate surprises and benefits, but when they are noncontingent, people come to think of them as their right. This has become a major issue in the current struggle over rising employee health insurance premiums. Employees feel that something is being taken away when they are asked make higher copayments. They feel that it is their right to receive the present level of benefits, even though the market has changed radically. This is the central issue with entitlement.

While companies do and should provide programs and services based on membership, not performance, it is important to achieve the right balance between membership- and performance-based rewards. Employee benefit and services programs should distinguish the company in the market and address the primary needs of its workforce. Keep employees aware of their value. However, awards, merit pay, bonuses, special recognition, stock options, and so on should be fully earned, and people should understand exactly what they have done to receive them. If payouts cannot be made, the progress people have made should be reinforced.

7. Don't Expect It All at Once—Test, Learn, and Grow into It

The process of developing effective total rewards is one of change and continual improvement. While changing programs in the middle of the process is problematic, few plans are perfect the first time out. Create the expectation among participants that problems will be identified and improvements will be made. Present the design and management of the reward system as something that will be upgraded as the abilities and capabilities of the organization increase. Solicit employees' ideas about ways to improve or enhance the effectiveness of the reward system. This is the spirit of continuous improvement, collaboration, and engagement.

8. Remember That Your Rewards Are in Competition with Other Consequences

An organizational environment has thousands of consequences happening at every moment of every day. While management is a very powerful source of consequences, it is not the only source. People are influenced by their peers, their staff, and their customers. Behaviors are influenced by the outside interests, personal history, and work habits of the individual. Because reward systems are constantly in competition with other consequences for the hearts and minds of the workforce, they need to be effective and meaningful to the performer in order to have an impact. This is both the risk and opportunity whenever one introduces changes into the chemistry of consequences.

9. Do It from the Heart, Do It with Spirit, and Do It with Integrity

People will not respect or respond favorably to consequences that are intended to be manipulative or aversive. The fundamental purpose of reward systems is to build a powerful partnership between the individual and the organization. This is why collaboration is an essential theme of success. The general manager of a division that recently introduced a team incentive plan took personal responsibility to manage the actions that would maximize the payout. He knew that if the plan paid out to the maximum, everyone would be a winner, the firm would improve its financial performance and be a stronger competitor in the marketplace, and members would gain a great deal financially. This was not based on a "carrot and stick" philosophy but on a sincere interest in building a partnership relationship within the organization. The drive was to win, and everyone felt the same commitment. They became truly engaged, and it worked.

10. Have Fun While You Are Doing It

The process of developing new reward systems, whether they involve compensation systems, special-recognition programs, or new performance management practices, is always a difficult one. Do not underestimate the amount of work necessary or the resistance that will be encountered. If a job is worth doing, it is worth measuring progress and celebrating achievements. Therefore, examine every aspect of the process to see what can be done to make it more satisfying and exciting. Successful companies seek every avenue to bring purpose and meaning into the workplace because that is the spirit of reinforcement and achievement. Special-recognition occasions can range from an ice cream sundae party for a goal-sharing design team that has reached a major project milestone, to a special visit by an executive who is enthusiastic about the work of the managers in developing new measurement and feedback systems, to a surprise party by employees for their supervisors who are attempting new ways to reinforce performance. These all add to the excitement and fun of making change. One needs to reward those who reward others if one wants to see the effectiveness increase.

Thoughts about the Winds of Change

The quote at the beginning of this chapter is by nineteenth-century author Edward Gibbons. It offers a unique insight into a central message in this book. When one travels on a sailing ship, one cannot see the wind or the forces under the surface of the water, but the navigator can discern them. The winds and water have powerful influences on the speed, direction, and maneuvers needed to achieve the ultimate destination. The ablest navigator uses these "unseen" forces to take maximum advantage of the capabilities of his or her ship.

In this book we have looked at the forces that influence human behavior within organizations. We now know that those forces exist and affect behaviors in significant ways, and we have examined a variety of strategies to use them effectively. For many people, however, these forces are "unseen" and, for some, even "unreal."

Like a navigator, we can use our knowledge to steer our ship. Without this knowledge, we are left to the influences that we think cannot be controlled or to use tools that have little effect. With this knowledge, we can see what others cannot. We can create unique competitive advantages. However, knowledge without application is just unrealized potential. Your task is to use this knowledge to achieve your mission: a workplace that creates value for customers, shareholders, and members—a place where everyone wins. In this way, we can leave our world a little different and a little better than it was when we arrived.

Notes

Foreword

1. Kanter, R. M., *When Giants Learn to Dance: Mastering the Challenges of Strategy, Management, and Careers in the 1990s* (New York: Simon and Schuster, 1989).
2. Kanter, R. M., "The View from the 1990s: How the Global Economy Is Reshaping Corporate Power and Careers," in *Men and Women of the Corporation* (New York: Basic Books, 1993).

Chapter 2

1. Herrnstein, R. "Behavior, Reinforcement, and Utility," *Psychological Science* 1, no. 4 (1990): 18–26.
2. Hamel, G., and C. I. Parhalad, *Competing for the Future* (Boston: Harvard Business School Press, 1994).
3. Ulrich, D., and D. Lake, *Organizational Capability* (New York: Wiley, 1990).
4. Dickinson, A., and M. P. Rosow (eds.), *Industrial Behavioral Modification: A Management Handbook* (New York: Pergamon Press, 1982).
5. Maslow, A., *Motivation and Personality* (New York, Harper & Row, 1970).
6. Kotter, J., *Leading Change* (Boston: Harvard Business School Press, 1996).
7. Skinner, B. F., *Science and Human Behavior* (New York: Macmillan, 1953).
8. Dickinson, A. M., "The Detrimental Effects of Extrinsic Reinforcement on 'Intrinsic Motivation,'" *The Behavioral Analyst* 12, no. 1 (1989): 1–15.
9. Senge, P., *The Fifth Discipline: The Art and Practice of the Learning Organization* (New York: Doubleday/Currency, 1994).

Chapter 3

1. Taylor, F. W., *The Principles of Scientific Management* (New York: Harper and Brothers, 1911).
2. *Ibid.*

3. Bennis, W. *On Becoming a Leader* (Cambridge, MA: Perseus Publishing, 1994).
4. Kotter, J., and J. Heskett, *Corporate Culture and Performance* (New York: Free Press, 1992).
5. Boyatzis, R. E., *The Competent Manager* (New York: Wiley, 1982).
6. Champy, J., *Reengineering Management: The New Mandate for Leadership* (New York: Harper Business, 1995).
7. Wilson, T., *Rewards That Drive High Performance: Success Stories from Leading Organizations* (New York: AMACOM, 1999).
8. Kanter, R., *Evolve! Succeeding in the Digital Culture of Tomorrow* (Boston: Harvard Business School Press, 2001).
9. Tichy, N., *The Leadership Engine: How Winning Companies Build Leaders at Every Level* (New York: HarperCollins, 1997).
10. Watson Wyatt Surveys (www.watsonwyatt.com) and Aon Compensation Consulting (www.aon.com).
11. Wilson, *op. cit.*
12. Porter, M., *Competitive Strategy: Techniques for Analyzing Industries and Competitors* (New York: Simon & Schuster, 1998).
13. Norton, D., and R. Kaplan, *The Strategy-Focused Organization* (Boston: Harvard Business School Press, 2001).

Chapter 4

1. Parsons, H. M., "What Happened at Hawthorne?" *Science* 183, (1974): 922–933.
2. Herzberg, F., B. Mausner, and B. Snyderman, *The Motivation to Work* (New York: Wiley, 1959); Herzberg, F. "One More Time: How Do You Motivate Employees," *Harvard Business Review* 46, no. 1 (January–February 1968): 109–120.
3. Premack, D., "Toward Empirical Behavior Laws: I. Positive Reinforcement," *Psychological Review* 66 (1959): 219–233.

Chapter 5

1. Deming, W. E., *Out of the Crisis* (Cambridge, MA: MIT Press, 1986).
2. Kaplan, R., and D. Norton, *The Balanced Scorecard—Translating Strategy into Action* (Boston: Harvard Business School Press, 1996).
3. O'Byrne, S., and D. Young, *EVA and Value-Based Management: A Practical Guide to Implementation* (New York: McGraw-Hill, 2000).
4. Slater, R., *Jack Welch and the G.E. Way: Management Insights and Leadership Secrets of the Legendary CEO* (New York: McGraw-Hill, 1998).
5. Kirn, S., A. Rucci, and R. Quinn, "The Employee-Customer-Profit Chain at Sears," *Harvard Business Review* (January–February 1998): 82.

Chapter 6

1. Lawler, E., *Strategic Pay* (San Francisco: Jossey-Bass, 1990).

2. Hamel, G., and A. Heene, *Competence-Based Competition* (New York: Wiley, 1994).

Chapter 7

1. "ACA: Skill-Based Pay—Practices, Payoffs, Pitfalls, and Prescriptions," a study sponsored by WorldatWork (at the time, the American Compensation Association), Scottsdale, AZ, 1992.
2. *Ibid.*

Chapter 8

1. "Employee Evaluation Process Often Gets Mediocre Grades," *ACA News* 38, no. 5 (May 1995).
2. Longenecker, C., and S. Goff, "Why Performance Appraisals Still Fail," *Journal of Compensation and Benefits* (November–December 1990): 36.
3. Society for Human Resource Management, "2000 Performance Management Survey," Society for Human Resource Management, 800 444-5006.
4. Balcazar, F., B. Hopkins, and Y. Suarez, "A Critical, Objective Review of Performance Feedback," *Journal of Organizational Behavior Management* 7 (Fall 1985/Winter 1986): 65–89.
5. Longenecker, C., and L. Fink, "Keys to Designing and Running an Effective Performance Appraisal System: Lessons Learned," *Journal of Compensation and Benefits* (November–December 1997): 24–31.

Chapter 9

1. "2001–2002 Total Salary Increase Survey," published by WorldatWork, Scottsdale, AZ, 2002.
2. *Ibid.*
3. Wilson, T., "The Case of Continuous Improvement at Corning," in *Rewards That Drive High Performance: Success Stories from Leading Organizations* (New York: AMACOM, 1999).
4. Doyle, R., and P. Doyle, *Gain Management* (New York: AMACOM, 1992).

Chapter 10

1. McAdams, J., and E. Hawk, "Capitalizing on Human Assets," research report sponsored and published by WorldatWork (formerly American Compensation Association), Scottsdale, AZ, 1992.
2. McClellan, D., *The Achieving Society* (Princeton, NJ: Van Nostrand, 1961).
3. Daniels, A., *Bringing Out the Best in People* (New York: McGraw-Hill, 1994).
4. Lawler, E., *Strategic Pay* (San Francisco: Jossey-Bass, 1990).
5. Dickinson, A., "Exploring New Vistas," *Performance Management Magazine* 9, no. 1 (1991): 27–31.

6. Wilson, T., *Rewards That Drive High Performance: Success Stories from Leading Organizations* (New York: AMACOM, 1999).
7. McAdams and Hawk, *op. cit.*
8. National Labor Relations Board, Regulation No. 88, Washington, DC, 1986.
9. King, R., "New Guidelines from the NLRB on Participative Management Initiatives and Employee Committees," published by the Society for Human Resource Management, Washington, DC, November–December, 2001.

Chapter II

1. Nelson, B., *1001 Ways to Reward Employees* (New York: Workman Publishing, 1994).
2. Freiberg, K., J. Freiberg, and T. Peters, *Nuts: Southwest Airlines Crazy Recipe for Business and Personal Success* (New York: Bantam Doubleday Dell, 1998).
3. There are several references for these companies: Wilson, T., *Rewards That Drive High Performance: Success Stories from Leading Organization* (New York: AMACOM, 1999); Nelson, B., *1001 Ways to Reward Employees* (New York, Workman Publishing, 1994); and Martel, L., *High Performers: How the Best Companies Find and Keep Them* (San Francisco: Jossey-Bass, 2002).
4. Wilson, T., "Why Self-Managed Teams Work," *Industrial Management* (February 1993).
5. Modern Management, Ltd., "A Special Research Report on Employee Suggestion Systems," 1986.

Chapter 12

1. Kruse, D., and J. Blasi, "Employee Ownership and Corporate Performance," a research report conducted by Rutgers University, Camden, NJ, 2000.
2. "ESOPs: Are They Good for You?" *Business Week*, May 15, 1989, p. 116.
3. Drucker, P. F., *The Frontiers of Management* (New York: Harper & Row, 1986).

Chapter 13

1. Kanter, R. M., *When Giants Learn to Dance: Mastering the Challenges of Strategy, Management, and Careers in the 1990s* (New York: Simon & Schuster, 1983).
2. Kanter, R. M., *Evolve: Succeeding in the Digital Culture of Tomorrow* (Boston: Harvard Business School Press, 2001).
3. Beer, M., *The Critical Path to Organizational Renewal* (Boston: Harvard Business School Press, 1990).
4. Beckhard, R., *Changing the Essence: The Art of Creating and Leading Fundamental Change in Organizations* (San Francisco: Jossey-Bass, 1992).

Chapter 14

1. Wilson, T., *Rewards That Drive High Performance: Success Stories from Leading Organizations* (New York: AMACOM, 1999).
2. Bardwick, J. M., *Danger in the Comfort Zone* (New York: AMACOM, 1991).

Bibliography

"ACA: Skill-Based Pay: Practices, Payoffs, Pitfalls, and Prescriptions." Study sponsored by the American Compensation Association, Scottsdale, AZ, 1992.

Albrecht, K., and R. Zemke. *Service America: Doing Business in the New Economy.* Homewood, IL: Dow Jones-Irwin,1985.

Axelrod, B., H. Handfield-Jones, and E. Michaels. "A New Game Plan for C Players." *Harvard Business Review* (January 2002): 81.

Balcazar, F., B. Hopkins, and Y. Suarez. "A Critical, Objective Review of Performance Feedback." *Journal of Organizational Behavior Management* 7 (Fall 1985/Winter 1986).

Bandura, A. *Principles of Behavior Modification.* New York: Holt, Rinehart & Winston, 1969.

———. *Social Foundations of Thought and Action.* Englewood Cliffs, NJ: Prentice-Hall, 1987.

Bardwick, J. M. *Danger in the Comfort Zone.* New York: AMACOM, 1991.

Barrett, K., and R. Greene. *The Man behind the Magic: The Story of Walt Disney.* New York: Viking Press, 1991.

Becker, G. *Human Capital,* 3d ed. Chicago: University of Chicago Press, 1993.

Beckhard, R., and R. Harris. *Organizational Transition: Managing Complex Change.* Reading, MA: Addison-Wesley, 1987.

——— and W. Pritchard. *Changing the Essence: The Art of Creating and Leading Fundamental Change in Organizations.* San Francisco: Jossey-Bass, 1992.

Beer, M., R. Eisenstat, and B. Spector. *The Critical Path to Corporate Renewal.* Boston: Harvard Business School Press, 1990.

Belcher, J. G., Jr. *How to Design and Implement a Results-Oriented Variable Pay System.* New York: AMACOM, 1996.

Bennis, W. *On Becoming a Leader.* New York: Perseus Press, 1994.

——— and P. Biederman, *Organizing Genius: The Secrets of Creating Collaboration.* Reading, MA: Addison-Wesley, 1997.

Berger, L., and D. Berger, eds. *The Compensation Handbook.* New York: McGraw-Hill, 1999.

Bernardin, H. J., and P. C. Smith. "A Clarification of Some Issues Regarding Behaviorally Anchored Rating Scales." *Journal of Applied Psychology* 66 (1981): 458.

——— and R. W. Beatty. *Performance Appraisal: Assessing Human Behavior at Work.* Boston: Kent, 1984.

Bernthal, P., and R. Willins. "Leadership Forecast 2001: A Benchmarking Study." Research report by Development Dimensions International, Inc, Pittsburgh, PA, 2000.

Black, F., and M. Scholes. "The Pricing of Option and Corporate Liabilities." *Journal of Political Economy* 81 (May–June 1973): 637.

Blasi, J. R. *Employee Ownership*. Cambridge, MA: Ballinger Press, 1988.

Bok, D. *The Cost of Talent: How Executives and Professionals Are Paid and How It Affects America*. New York, Free Press, 1993.

Boyatzis, R. *The Competent Manager*. New York: Wiley, 1982.

Byham, W., A. Smith, and M. Paese. *Grow Your Own Leaders: How to Identify, Develop, and Retain Leadership Talent*. Englewood Cliffs, NJ: Prentice-Hall, 2002.

Caldwell, W. *Compensation Guide*. Boston: Warren, Gorham & Lamont, 1994.

Case, J. *Open-Book Management: The Coming Business Revolution*. New York: Harper Business Books, 1995.

Champy, J. *Re-engineering Management: The New Mandate for Leadership*. New York: Harper Business Press, 1995.

Churchill, N. C., and V. L. Lewis. "The Five Stages of Small Business Growth." *Harvard Business Review* (May–June 1983): 30.

Cohen, A., and D. Bradford. *Influence without Authority*. New York: Wiley, 1990.

"Compensation and Performance Management Practices in Companies with Total Quality Management." Study conducted by the Wyatt Company for the U.S. General Accounting Office, Washington, DC, 1991.

Collins, J. *Good to Great: Why Some Companies Take the Lead and Others Don't*. New York: Harper Business Press, 2001.

———— and J. Porras. *Built to Last: Successful Habits of Visionary Companies*. New York, Harper Business, 1995.

Conference Board. "Developing Business Leaders for 2010." Report No. 1315-02-RR, New York, 2002.

Cook, F. "An Interview with Motorola CEO George Fisher: Compensation Strategies and People Philosophies." *ACA Journal* (Autumn 1993): 14.

Cooper, W. H. "Conceptual Similarity as a Source of Illusory Halo in Job Performance Ratings." *Journal of Applied Psychology* 66 (1981): 302.

Covey, S. R. *The 7 Habits of Highly Effective People*. New York: Simon & Schuster, 1989.

CSRA (Civil Service Reform Act), Public Law 95-454, 1978, 92 Stat.

Daniels, A. "Parties—With a Purpose." *SKY* (December 1992).

————. *Bringing Out the Best in People: How to Apply the Astonishing Power of Positive Reinforcement*. New York: McGraw-Hill, 1993.

Davidow, W., and B. Uttal. *Total Customer Service: The Ultimate Weapon*. New York: Harper & Row, 1989.

Davis, S. *Future Perfect*. Reading, MA: Addison-Wesley, 1987.

Deci, E. L., and R. M. Ryan. *Intrinsic Motivation and Self-Determination in Human Behavior*. New York: Plenum Press, 1985.

Deming, W. E. *Out of the Crisis*. Cambridge, MA: MIT Press, 1986.

Dertouzos, M., R. Lester, and R. Solow. *Made in America: Regaining the Productive Edge*. Cambridge, MA: MIT Press, 1989.

Dickinson, A. M. "The Detrimental Effects of Extrinsic Reinforcement on 'Intrinsic Motivation'." *The Behavioral Analyst* 12, no. 1 (Spring 1989): 1–15.

——— and K. Gillette. "A Comparison of the Effects of Two Individual Monetary Incentive Systems on Productivity: Piece Rate Pay versus Base Pay Plus Incentives." *Journal of Organizational Behavior Management* 14, no. 1 (1993).

——— and M. P. Rosow, eds. *Industrial Behavioral Modification: A Management Handbook.* New York: Pergamon Press, 1982.

Doyle, R., and P. Doyle. *Gain Management.* New York: AMACOM, 1992.

Doz Y., and G. Hamel, *Alliance Advantage: The Art of Creating Value through Partnering.* Boston: Harvard Business School Press, 1998.

Drucker, *The Practice of Management.* New York: Harper & Row, 1954.

———. P. F. *The Frontiers of Management.* New York: Harper & Row, 1986.

Dumaine, B. "How Managers Can Succeed through Speed." *Fortune*, February 13, 1989.

———. "The Bureaucracy Busters." *Fortune*, June 17, 1991, pp. 37–50.

Eccles, R. G., R. Herz, E. Keegan, and D. Phillips. *The Value Reporting Revolution: Moving beyond the Earnings Game.* New York: Wiley, 2001.

Edwards, M., and A. Ewen. *360 Degree Feedback: The Powerful New Model for Employee Assessment and Performance Improvement.* New York: AMACOM, 1996.

"Executive Pay in 2000: Compensation in Turbulent Times." Research report published by Watson Wyatt Worldwide, Washington, DC, 2002.

Farrell, C., and J. Hoerr. "ESOPs: Are They Good for You?" *Business Week*, May 15,1989, p. 116.

Fein, M. *Improshare: An Alternative to Traditional Managing.* Norcross, GA: American Institute of Industrial Engineers, 1981.

Freiberg, K., J. Frieberg, and T. Peters. *Nuts: Southwest Airlines Crazy Recipe for Business and Personal Success.* New York: Bantam Doubleday Dell, 1998.

Fuller, R. B. *And It Came to Pass—Not to Stay.* New York: Macmillan, 1976.

Galbraith, J. *Designing Complex Organizations.* Reading, MA: Addison-Wesley, 1973.

Garbor, A. "Take This Job and Love It." *New York Times*, January 26,1992, p. 1.

Garfield, C., and H. Bennett. *Peak Performance: Mental Training Techniques of the World's Greatest Athletes.* New York: J. P. Tarcher, 1984.

Gilbert, T. F. *Human Competence—Engineering Worthy Performance.* New York: McGraw-Hill, 1978.

Goldratt, E., and J. Cox. *The Goal: A Process of Ongoing Improvement.* New York: North River Press, 1986.

Graham-More, B., and T. Ross. *Productivity Gainsharing.* Englewood Cliffs, NJ: Prentice-Hall, 1983.

Grate, R. "The Secrets of Performance Appraisal: Best Practices from the Masters." In *Across the Board.* New York: Conference Board, 2000.

Gray, R. "The Scanlon Plan: A Case Study." *British Journal of Industrial Relations* 9 (1971): 291–313.

Grayson, C., Jr., and C. O'Dell. *American Business: A Two-Minute Warning.* New York: Free Press, 1988.

Greiner, L. E. "Evolution and Revolution as Organizations Grow." *Harvard Business Review* (July–August 1972): 37.

Grove, A. *Only the Paranoid Survive: How to Exploit the Crisis Points That Challenge Every Company.* New York: Bantam Books, 1999.

Gupta, N., G. Ledford, Jr., G. Jenkins, and H. Doty. "Survey-Based Prescriptions for Skill-Based Pay." *ACA Journal* (Autumn 1992): 48.

Hamel, G., and A. Heene. *Competence-Based Competition.* New York: Wiley, 1994.

Hamel, G., and C. I. Parhalad. *Competing for the Future.* Boston: Harvard Business School Press, 1994.

Hamilton, R. H. "Scenarios in Corporate Planning." *Journal of Business Strategy* 2 (Summer 1981): 82.

Hammer, M., and J. Champy. *Reengineering the Corporation.* New York: Harper, 1993.

Hayes, R., and S. Wheelright. *Restoring Our Competitive Edge.* New York: Wiley, 1984.

Heller, R. *The Leadership Imperative.* New York: Penguin Books, 1995.

Herrnstein, R. "On the Law of Effect." *Journal of Experimental Analysis of Behavior* 13 (1970): 243–266.

———. "Behavior, Reinforcement, and Utility." *Psychological Science* 1, no. 4 (July 1990).

——— and D. Prelec. "Melioration: A Theory of Distributed Choice." *Journal of Economic Perspectives* 5, no. 3 (Summer 1991): 137–156.

Herzberg, F. "One More Time: How Do You Motivate Employees." *Harvard Business Review* (January–February 1968): 1.

——— B. Mausner, and B. Snyderman. *Motivation to Work.* New York: Wiley, 1959.

Heskett, J., E. Sasser, and L. Schlesinger. *The Service Profit Chain: How Leading Companies Link Profit and Growth to Loyalty, Satisfaction and Value.* New York: Free Press, 1997.

Hogarth, R. M. "Beyond Discrete Biases." *Psychological Bulletin* 90 (1981): 197.

Huey, J. "Nothing Is Impossible." *Fortune,* September 23, 1991, p. 134.

Imai, M. *Kaizen: The Key to Japan's Competitive Success.* New York: Random House, 1986.

Johnston, W. "Global Workforce 2000: The New World Labor Market." *Harvard Business Review* (March–April 1991): 115.

Judy, R., and C. DiAmico. *Workforce 2020.* New York: Hudson Institute, 1997.

Kanter, R. M. *The Change Masters.* New York: Simon & Schuster, 1983.

———. *When Giants Learn to Dance: Mastering the Challenges of Strategy, Management, and Careers in the 1990s.* New York: Simon & Schuster, 1983.

———. "The Attack on Pay." *Harvard Business Review* (March–April 1987): 60.

———. *Evolve! Succeeding in the Digital Culture of Tomorrow.* Boston: Harvard Business School Press, 2001.

———, B. Stein, and T. Jick. *The Challenge of Organizational Change.* New York: Free Press, 1992.

Kaplan, R., and D. Norton. "The Balanced Scorecard—Measures that Drive Performance." *Harvard Business Review* (January–February, 1992).

Kaplan, R., and D. Norton. *The Balanced Scorecard: Translating Strategy into Action.* Boston: Harvard Business School Press, 1996.

Katzenbach, J., and D. Smith. *The Wisdon of Teams: Creating the High-Performance Organization.* New York: McGraw-Hill, 1992.

Keillor, G. *In Search of Lake Wobegon.* New York: Viking Press, 2001.

King, R. "New Guidelines from the NLRB on Participative Management Initiatives and Employee Committees." *Journal of the Society for Human Resource Management* (November–December 2001).

Kinlaw, D. *Developing Superior Work Teams.* Lexington, MA: Lexington Books, 1991.

Kirn, S., A. Rucci, and R. Quinn. "The Employee-Customer-Profit Chain at Sears." *Harvard Business Review* (January–February 1998): 82.

Kotter, J. *Leading Change.* Boston: Harvard Business School Press, 1996.

———. and J. Haskett. *Corporate Culture and Performance.* New York: Free Press, 1992.

Kreitner, R., and F. Luthans. "A Social Learning Approach to Behavioral Management: Radical Behaviorists 'Mellowing Out.'" *Organizational Dynamics* (Winter 1993).

Kruse, D., and J. Blasi "Employee Ownership and Corporate Performance." Research report conducted by Rutgers University, Camden, NJ, 2000.

Kübler-Ross, E. *On Death and Dying.* New York: Macmillan, 1969.

Laabs, J. "Ben & Jerry's Caring Capitalism." *Personnel Journal* (November 1992): 50.

Land, G. *Grow or Die.* New York: Dell, 1973.

Latham, G., and K. Wexley. *Increasing Productivity through Performance Appraisal.* Reading, MA: Addison-Wesley, 1981.

Lawler, E. *Strategic Pay.* San Francisco: Jossey-Bass, 1990.

———. *Rewarding Excellence: Pay Strategies for the New Economy.* San Francisco: Jossey-Bass, 2000.

Lawrence, P., and J. Lorsch. *Organization and Environment: Managing Differentiation and Integration.* Cambridge, MA: Harvard University Press, 1967.

Levering, R. *A Great Place to Work.* New York. Random House, 1988.

Levitt, T. "Marketing Myopia." *Harvard Business Review* (July–August 1960): 26.

Likert, R. L. *New Patterns of Management.* New York: McGraw-Hill, 1961.

Longenecker, C., and S. Goff. "Why Performance Appraisals Still Fail." *Journal of Compensation and Benefits* (November–December 1990): 36.

——— and L. Fink, "Research on Performance Management in U.S. Manufacturing and Service Organizations." *Journal of Compensation and Benefits* (November–December 1997).

Loomis, C. "Dinosaurs?" *Fortune,* May 3, 1993, p. 36.

Luthans, F., and T. Davis. "Managers in Action: A New Look at Their Behavior and Operating Models." *Organizational Dynamics* (Summer 1980).

———. "Behavioral Self-Management—The Missing Link in Managerial Effectiveness." *Organizational Dynamics* (Summer 1979).

McAdams, J. *The Reward Plan Advantage.* San Francisco: Jossey-Bass, 1996.

——— and E. Hawk. "Capitalizing on Human Assets." Research project of the American Compensation Association, Scottsdale, AZ, 1992.

McClelland, D. *The Achieving Society.* Princeton, NJ: Van Nostrand, 1961.

———. "Achievement Motivation Can Be Developed." *Harvard Business Review* (November–December 1965): 6.

———, J. Atkinson, R. Clark, and E. Lowell. *The Achieving Motive*. New York: Appleton-Century-Croft, 1953.

McGregor, D. *Motivation and Personality*. New York: Harper & Row, 1970.

McGuire, J. W. *Factors Affecting the Growth of Manufacturing Firms*. Seattle: Bureau of Business Research, University of Washington, 1963.

McWhirter, D. *Sharing Ownership*. New York: Wiley, 1993.

Mager, R. F., and P. Pipe. *Analyzing Performance Problems, or "You Really Oughta-Wanna*. Belmont, CA: Fearon-Pitman, 1970.

Martel, L. *High Performers: How the Best Companies Find and Keep Them*. San Francisco: Jossey-Bass, 2002.

Maslow, A. H. *Motivation and Personality*. New York: Harper & Row, 1970.

Mawhinney, T. C., A. M. Dickinson, and L. A. Taylor. "The Use of Concurrent Schedules to Evalute the Effects of Extrinsic Rewards on Intrinsic Motivation." *Journal of Organizational Behavior Management* 10 (1989): 109–129.

——— and C. R. Gowen. "Gainsharing and the Law of Effect as the Matching Law: A Theoretical Framework." *Journal of Organizational Behavior Management* 2, no. 11 (1992).

Michel, W. *Introduction to Personality*. New York: Holt, Reinhart & Winston, 1976.

Milkovick, G., and C. Milkovick. "Strengthening the Pay-Performance Relationship: The Research." *Compensation and Benefits Review* (November–December 1992): 53.

Mintzberg, H. *The Structure of Organizations*. Englewood Cliffs, NJ: Prentice-Hall, 1979.

Nelson, B. *1000 Ways to Reward Employees*. New York: Workman Publishing, 1994.

———. *1001 Ways to Energize Employees*, New York: Workman Publishing, 2000.

O'Byrne, S. "EVA and Management Compensation." *ACA Journal* (Summer 1994): 60.

——— and D. Young, *EVA and Value-Based Management: A Practical Guide to Implementation*. New York: McGraw-Hill, 2000.

Odiorne, G. *Management by Objectives: A System of Managerial Leadership*. Belmont, CA: Fearon-Pitman, 1965.

O'Rourke, L. "Redesigning Performance Evaluation and Compensation Systems to Support Total Quality." *The Quality Letter for Healthcare Leaders* 5, no. 3 (April 1993).

Ott, E. "Team-Based Pay: New Wave Strategic Incentives." *Sloan Management Review* (Spring 1990): 19.

Pfeffer, J. *Competitive Advantage through People: Unleashing the Power of the Workforce*, Boston: Harvard Business School Press, 1994.

———. "Six Dangerous Myths about Pay," *Harvard Business Review* (May–June 1998): 109.

"People, Performance and Pay." Study by the American Productivity Center and the American Compensation Association on Non-Traditional Reward and Human Resource Practices, Scottsdale, AZ, 1986.

Porter, M. *Competitive Strategy*. New York: Free Press, 1980.

Prahalad, C., and G. Hamel. "The Core Competence of the Corporation." *Harvard Business Review* (May–June 1990): 79–91.

Premack, D. "Toward Empirical Behavior Laws: I. Positive Reinforcement." *Psychological Review* 66 (1990): 219–233.

Reich, T. B. *The Next American Frontier.* New York: Penguin Group, 1983.

Risher, H., ed. *Aligning Pay and Results.* New York: AMACOM, 1999.

Ross, T., and R. Ross. "Productivity Gainsharing: Resolving Some of the Measurement Issues." *National Productivity Review* (Autumn 1984): 382.

Rostow, W. W. *The Stages of Economic Growth.* Cambridge, England: Cambridge University Press, 1960.

Savage, C. *Fifth Generation Management.* Maynard, MA: Digital Press, 1990.

Schlender, B. "How Toshiba Makes Alliances Work." *Fortune,* October 4, 1993, pp. 116–120.

Scholtes, P. "An Elaboration on Deming's Teachings on Performance Appraisal." *Performance Appraisal,* 1987.

Schultz, H. *Pour Your Heart into It: How Starbucks Built a Company One Cup at a Time.* New York, Hyperion, 1997.

Schuster, J. R., and P. K. Zinghein. *Pay People Right.* New York: Jossey Books, 2000.

Senge, P. *The Fifth Discipline: The Art and Practice of the Learning Organization.* New York: Doubleday/Currency, 1994.

Skinner, B. F. *Science and Human Behavior.* New York: Macmillan, 1953.

———. *Contingencies of Reinforcement: A Theoretical Analysis.* Englewood Cliffs, NJ: Prentice-Hall, 1969.

Slater, R. *Jack Welch and the G.E. Way: Management Insights and Leadership Secrets of the Legendary CEO.* New York: McGraw-Hill, 1998.

Smart, B. *TopGrading: How Leading Companies Win by Hiring, Coaching and Keeping the Best People.* Englewood Cliffs, NJ: Prentice-Hall, 1999.

Smith, A. *The Wealth of Nations.* London, 1776.

Snyder, G. "Incentive Pay at St. Elizabeth's Hospital." *Performance Management Magazine* 9, no. 3 (1992): 18–24.

———. "Top Gun Performance at Allied Systems." *Performance Management Magazine* 8, no. 4 (1992): 32–34.

———. "May I Make A Suggestion?: Dow Chemical Canada Says 'Yes.'" *Performance Management Magazine* 8, no. 2 (1993): 10–15.

Spratt, M., and B. Steele. "Rewarding Key Contributors." *Compensation and Benefits Review* (July–August 1985).

Steward, T. "Re-Engineering: The Hot New Managing Tool." *Fortune,* August 23, 1993, pp. 41–48.

Taylor, A., III. "U.S. Cars Come Back." *Fortune,* November 16, 1992, pp. 52–85.

Taylor, F. W. *Principles of Scientific Management.* New York: Harper & Brothers, 1911.

Thomas, B., and M. Olson. "Gain Sharing: The Design Guarantees Success." *Personnel Journal* (May 1988).

Tichy, N. *Managing Strategic Change: Technical, Political, and Cultural Dynamics.* New York: Wiley, 1983.

——— and R. Charan. "Speed, Simplicity, Self-Confidence: An Interview with Jack Welch." *Harvard Business Review* (September–October 1989): 112.

Tulgan, B. *Winning the Talent Wars*, New York: Norton, 2001.

Ulrich, D., and D. Lake. *Organizational Capability*. New York: Wiley, 1990.

Ulrich, D., J. Zenger, and N. Smallwood. *Results-Based Leadership*. Boston: Harvard Business School Press, 1999.

Vroom, V. H. *Work and Motivation*. New York: Wiley, 1964.

Watson, D., and R. Tharp. *Self-Directed Behavior*. Pacific Grove, CA: Brooks/Cole, 1989.

Welch, J., and J. Byrne. *Jack: Straight from the Gut*. New York: Warner Books, 2001.

Whitcomb, J. "Rewards Get Results" *Workforce Magazine*, April 2002, p. 42.

White, J. K. "The Scanlon Plan: Causes and Correlates of Success." *Academy of Management Journal* 22 (1979): 292–312.

Wilson, T. "Group Incentives: Are You Ready?" *Journal of Compensation and Benefits* (November–December 1990): 25–29.

———. "Is It Time to Eliminate the Piece-Rate Incentive System?" *Compensation and Benefits Review* (March–April 1992): 43–49.

———. "Making Negative Feedback Work." *Personnel Journal* (December 1978): 680.

———. "Changing the Purpose of Pay Programs." *Performance Management Magazine* 9, no. 2 (1993): 29–32.

———. "Why Self-Managed Teams Work." *Industrial Management* (February 1993), special supplement.

———. "Establishing Reward Systems That Support Change." In J. Lowery (ed.), *Culture Shift: A Leader's Guide to Managing Change in Health Care*. Chicago: American Hospital Association, 1997.

———. "Re-Energizing the Performance Management Process." In W. Caldwell (ed.), *The Compensation Guide*. Boston: Warren, Gorham and Lamont, 1997.

———. "Reward Strategy: Time to Rethink the Models and the Methods" *ACA Journal* (Fall 1998): 62-70.

———. "Key Issues in Designing Group Incentive." In H. Risner (ed.), *Aligning Pay and Results*. New York: AMACOM, 1999.

———. *Rewards That Drive High Performance: Success Stories from Leading Organization*. New York: AMACOM, 1999.

——— and S. Malanowski. *Rewarding Group Performance: An Approach to Designing and Implementing Incentive Pay Program*. Scottsdale, AZ: WorldatWork, 2002.

Index

About the Author

THOMAS B. WILSON is an international authority in the field of reward systems and high-performance organizations. He has written more than 25 articles and book chapters and has been quoted in *Fortune* magazine, *The Financial Times, Time, Newsweek,* and *The Wall Street Journal.* Wilson is the founder and President of the Wilson Group, Inc., a consulting firm that specializes in developing customized reward systems to drive business strategies and create desired cultures. Wilson frequently presents at major national and regional conferences.